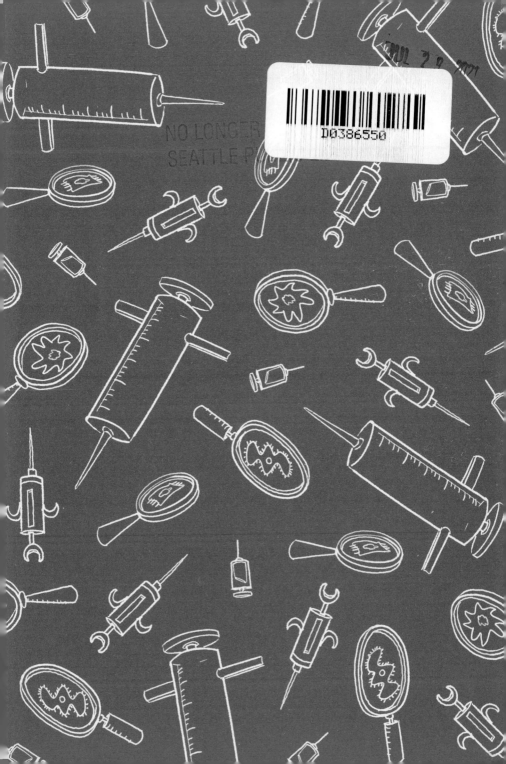

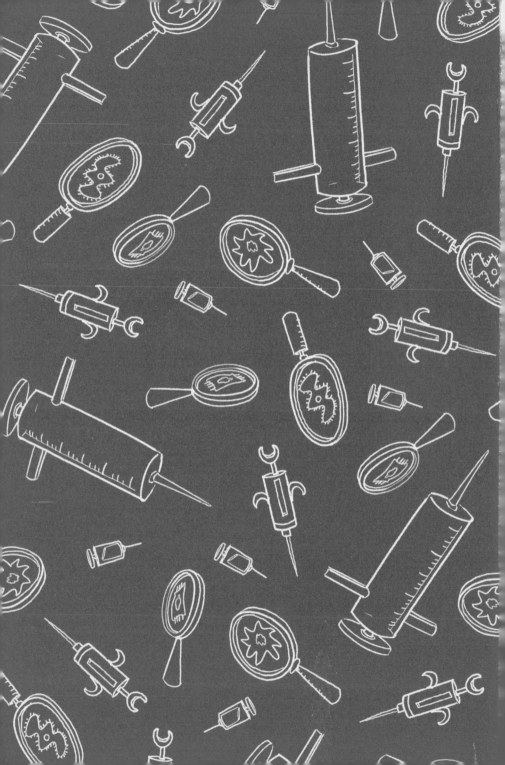

BIG IDEAS
THAT CHANGED THE WORLD

A SHOT IN THE ARM!

DON BROWN

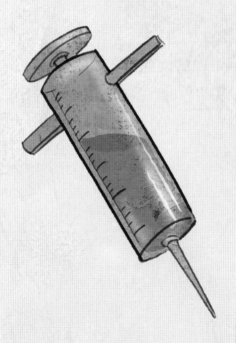

AMULET BOOKS • NEW YORK

The artwork in this book combines hand and digital drawing
with digital color collage and printing.

Cataloging-in-Publication Data has been applied for and may be obtained
from the Library of Congress.

ISBN 978-1-4197-5001-4

Text and illustrations copyright © 2021 Don Brown
Edited by Howard W. Reeves

Printed and bound in Thailand

10 9 8 7 6 5 4 3 2 1

Amulet Books are available at special discounts when
purchased in quantity for premiums and promotions as well as fundraising
or educational use. Special editions can also be created to specification.
For details, contact specialsales@abramsbooks.com or the address below.

Amulet Books® is a registered trademark of Harry N. Abrams, Inc.

ABRAMS The Art of Books
195 Broadway, New York, NY 10007
abramsbooks.com

To the essential workers who kept the
world turning during the COVID-19 pandemic

Note to reader: Unless otherwise noted by an asterisk,
quotation marks signal actual quotes.

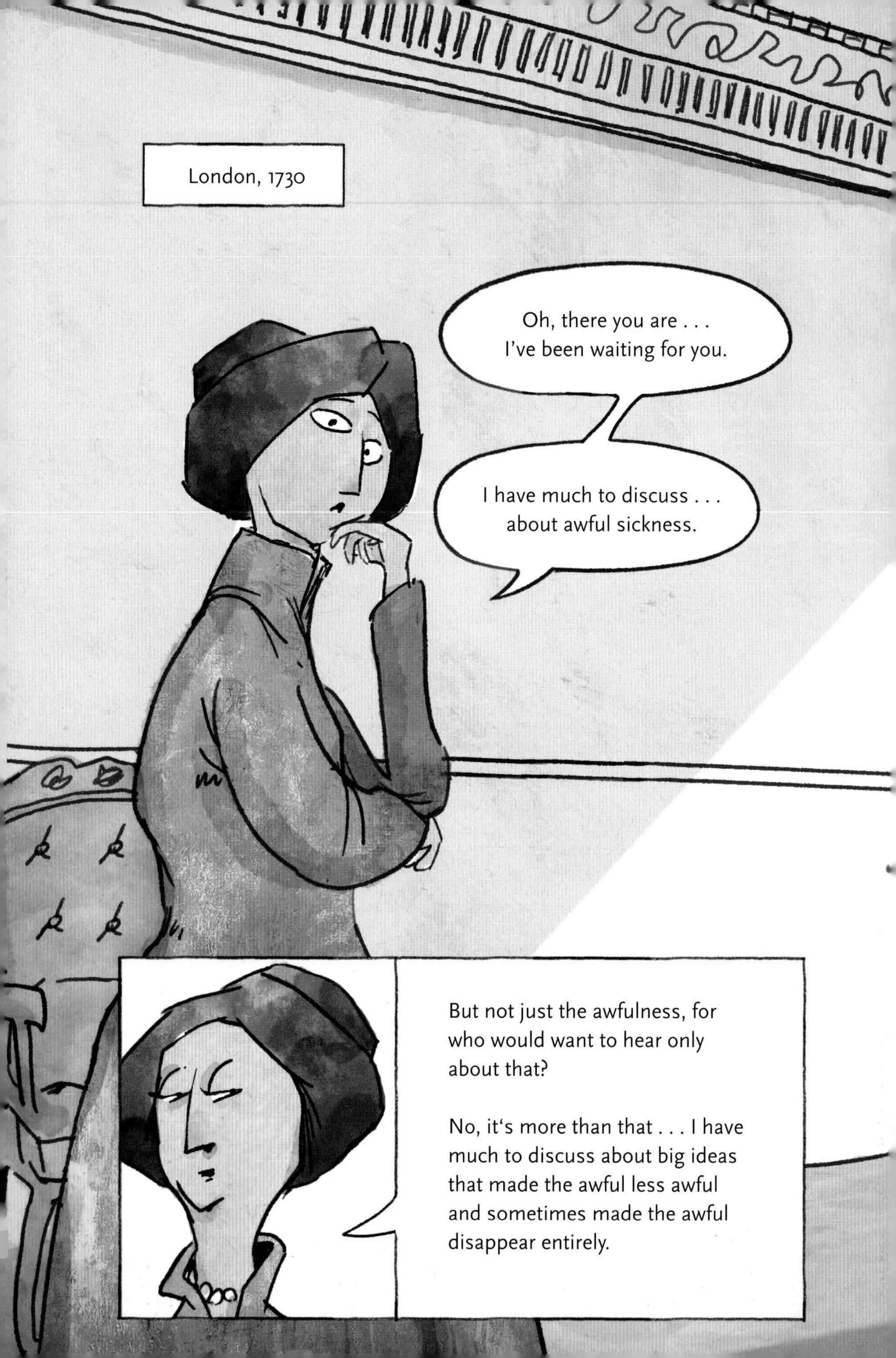
London, 1730
Oh, there you are . . . I've been waiting for you.
I have much to discuss . . . about awful sickness.
But not just the awfulness, for who would want to hear only about that?
No, it's more than that . . . I have much to discuss about big ideas that made the awful less awful and sometimes made the awful disappear entirely.

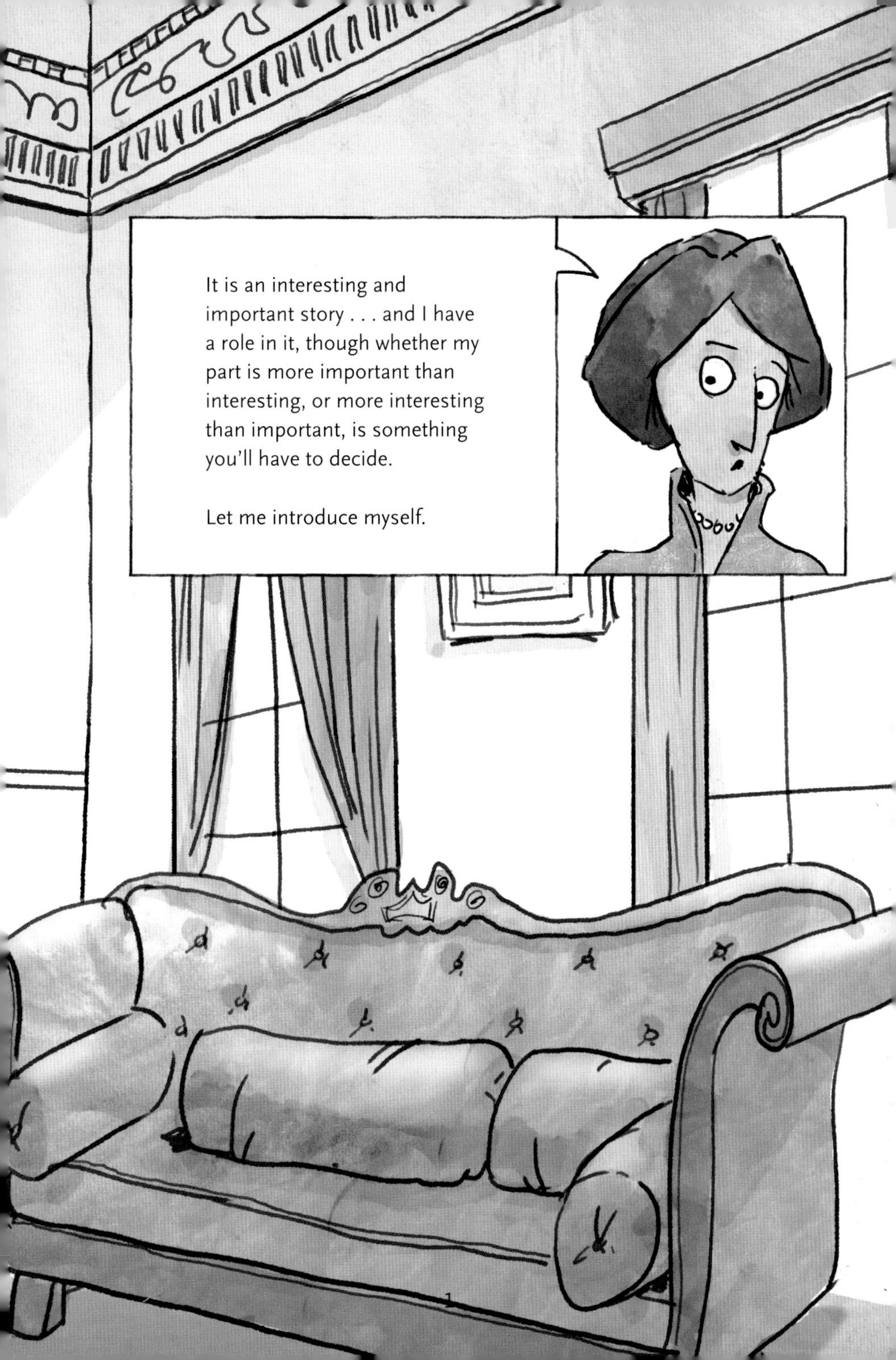
It is an interesting and important story . . . and I have a role in it, though whether my part is more important than interesting, or more interesting than important, is something you'll have to decide.
Let me introduce myself.

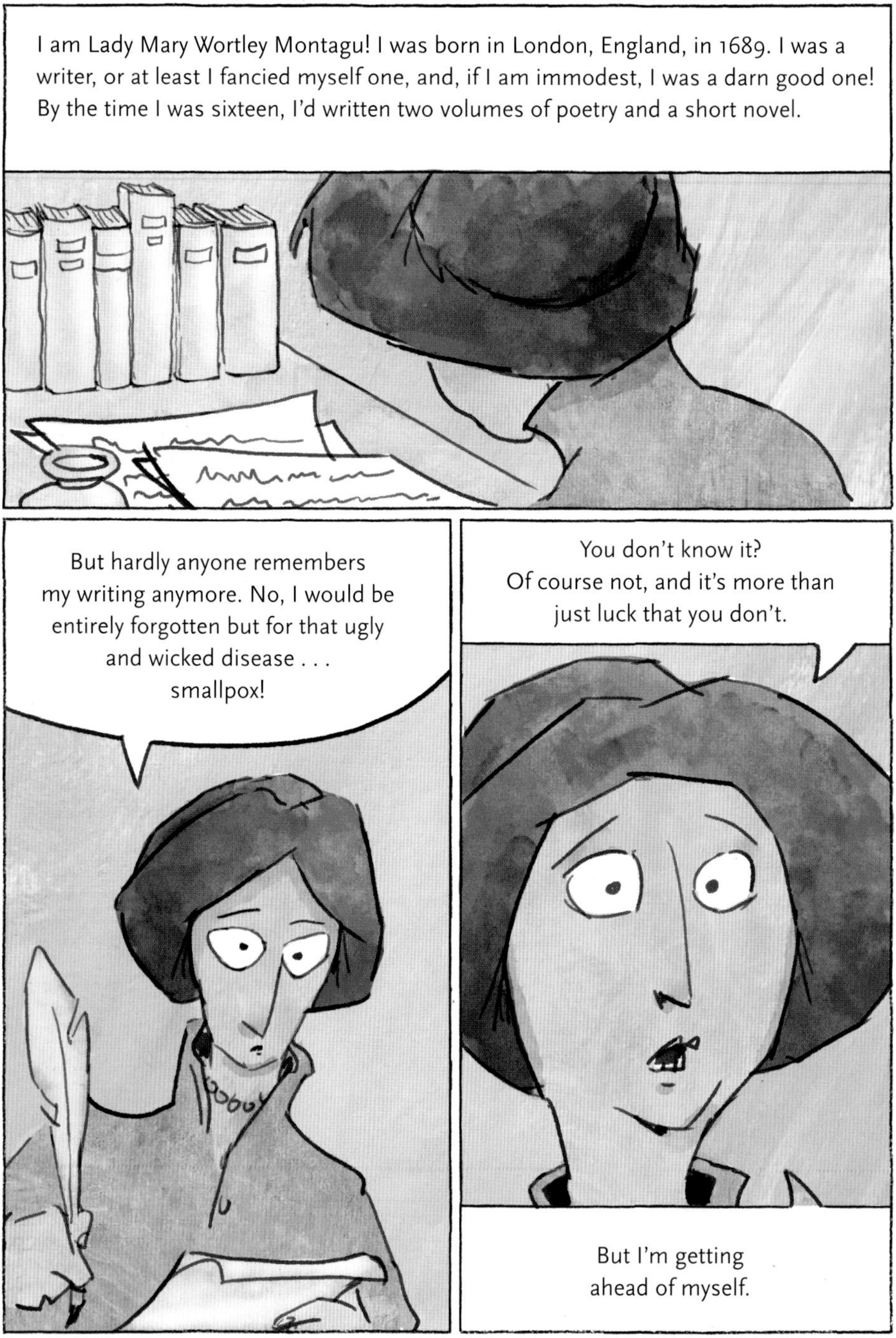
I am Lady Mary Wortley Montagu! I was born in London, England, in 1689. I was a writer, or at least I fancied myself one, and, if I am immodest, I was a darn good one! By the time I was sixteen, I'd written two volumes of poetry and a short novel.
But hardly anyone remembers my writing anymore. No, I would be entirely forgotten but for that ugly and wicked disease . . . smallpox!
You don't know it? Of course not, and it's more than just luck that you don't.
But I'm getting ahead of myself.

Smallpox is a disease that does its wickedness throughout the body, killing three out of every ten unfortunate sufferers. It blinds some. And its telltale rash can blanket the body in scarring blisters—pox—that can forever disfigure its victims.

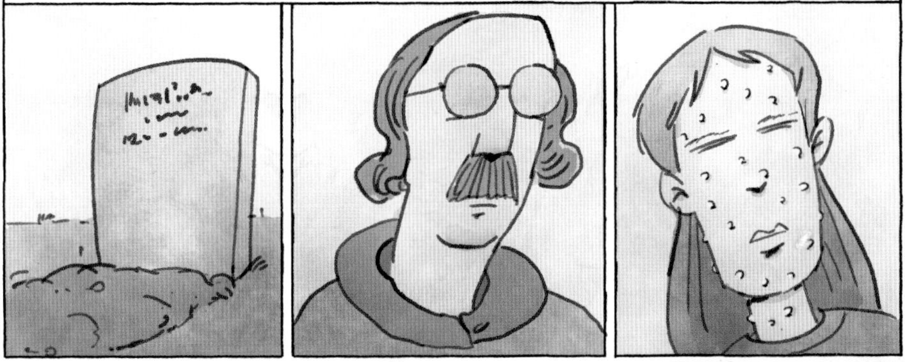

Appearances ruined by smallpox were a fact of everyday life in my time, and something I can speak to personally. But again, I'm getting ahead of myself.

Smallpox spreads through coughing and sneezing, and by contaminating things, such as bedding and clothing, with the fluid from its blisters.

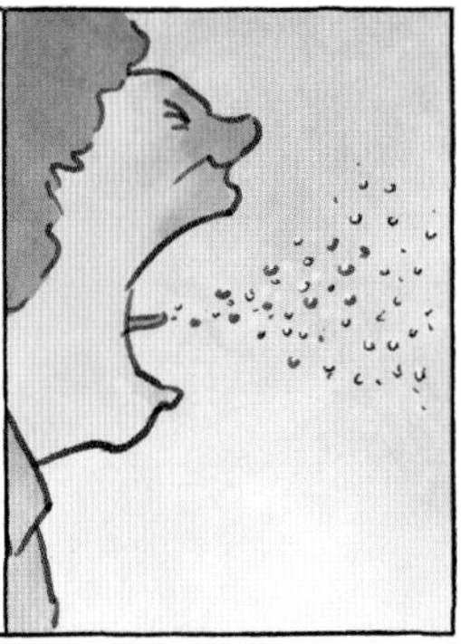

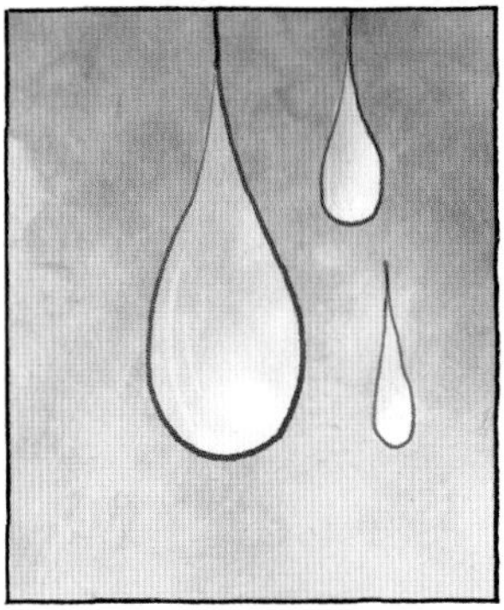

It's a mystery where smallpox came from. We know that it was doing its evil business three thousand years ago in ancient Egypt—we can spy smallpox scars on the mummy of Pharaoh Ramses V.

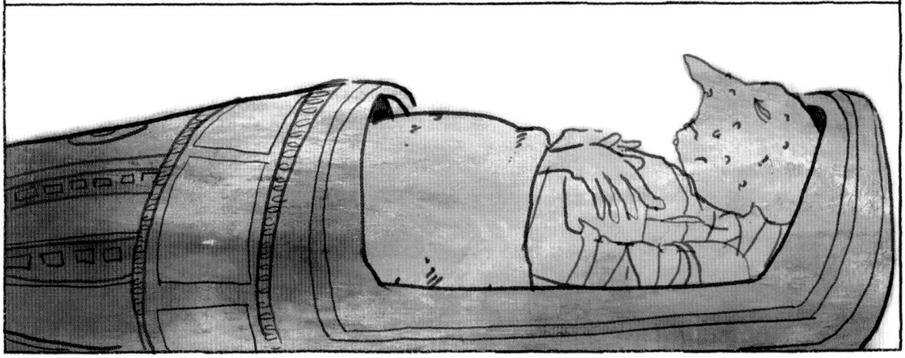

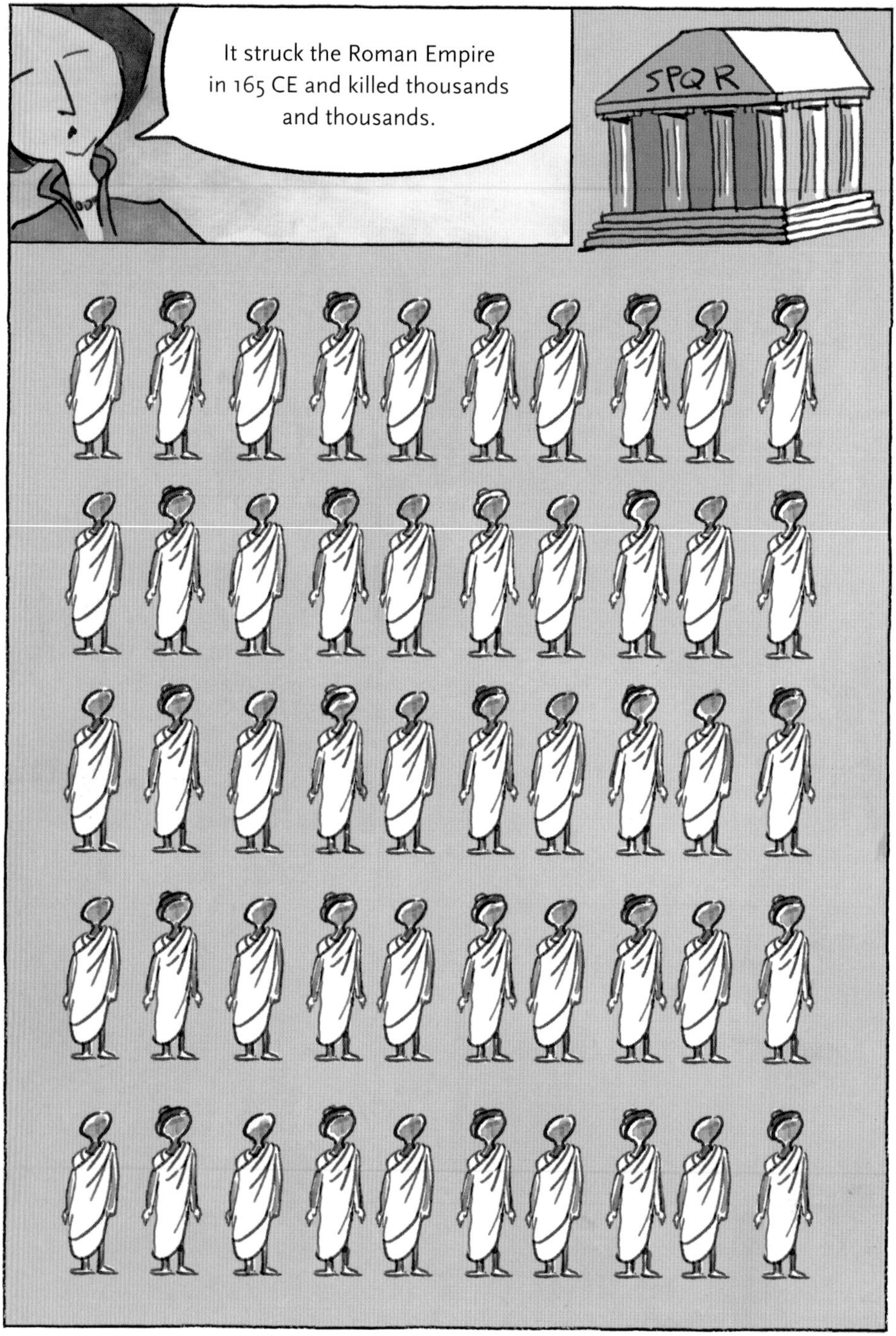
It struck the Roman Empire in 165 CE and killed thousands and thousands.
SPQR

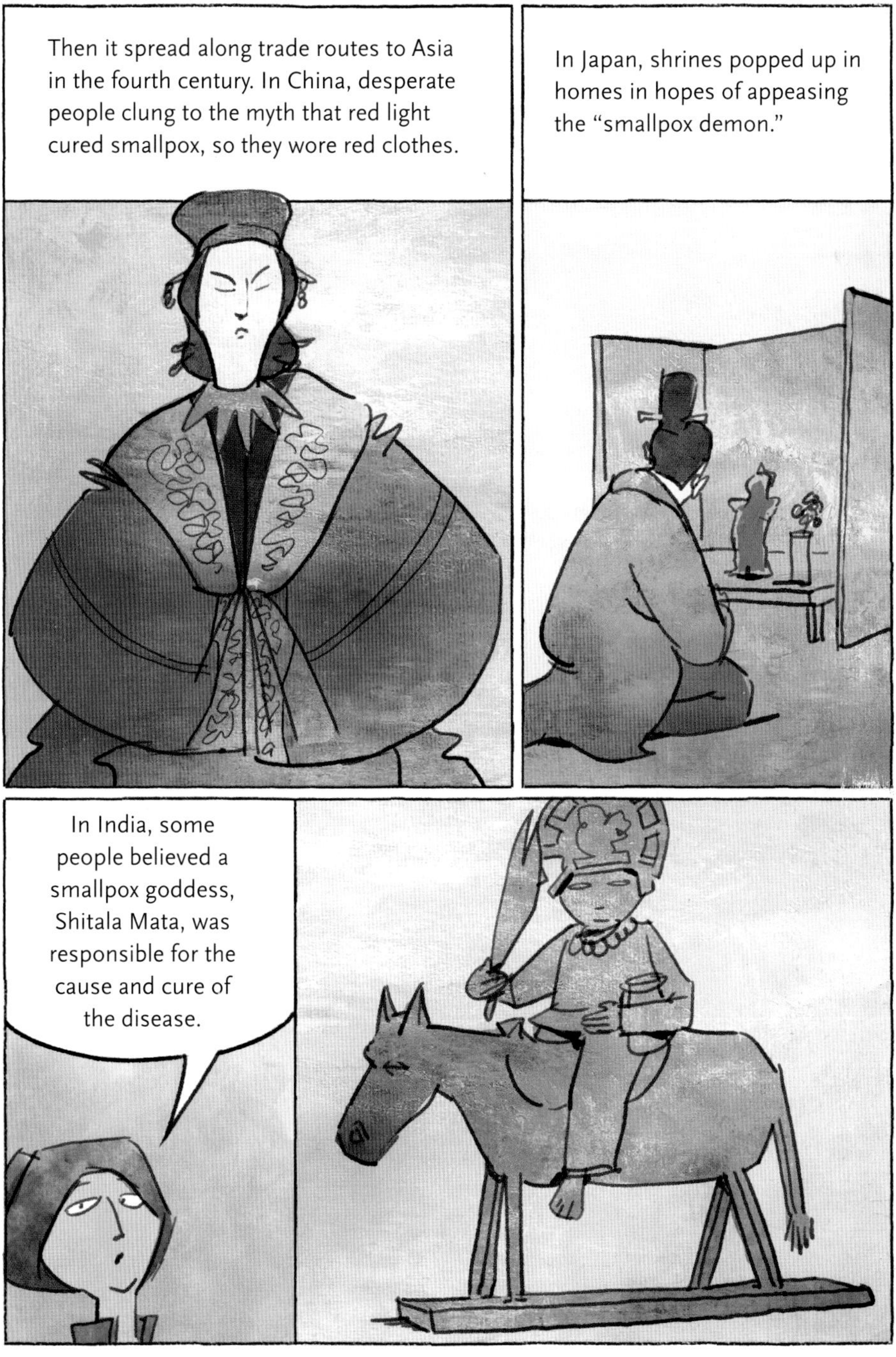
Then it spread along trade routes to Asia in the fourth century. In China, desperate people clung to the myth that red light cured smallpox, so they wore red clothes.
In Japan, shrines popped up in homes in hopes of appeasing the "smallpox demon."
In India, some people believed a smallpox goddess, Shitala Mata, was responsible for the cause and cure of the disease.

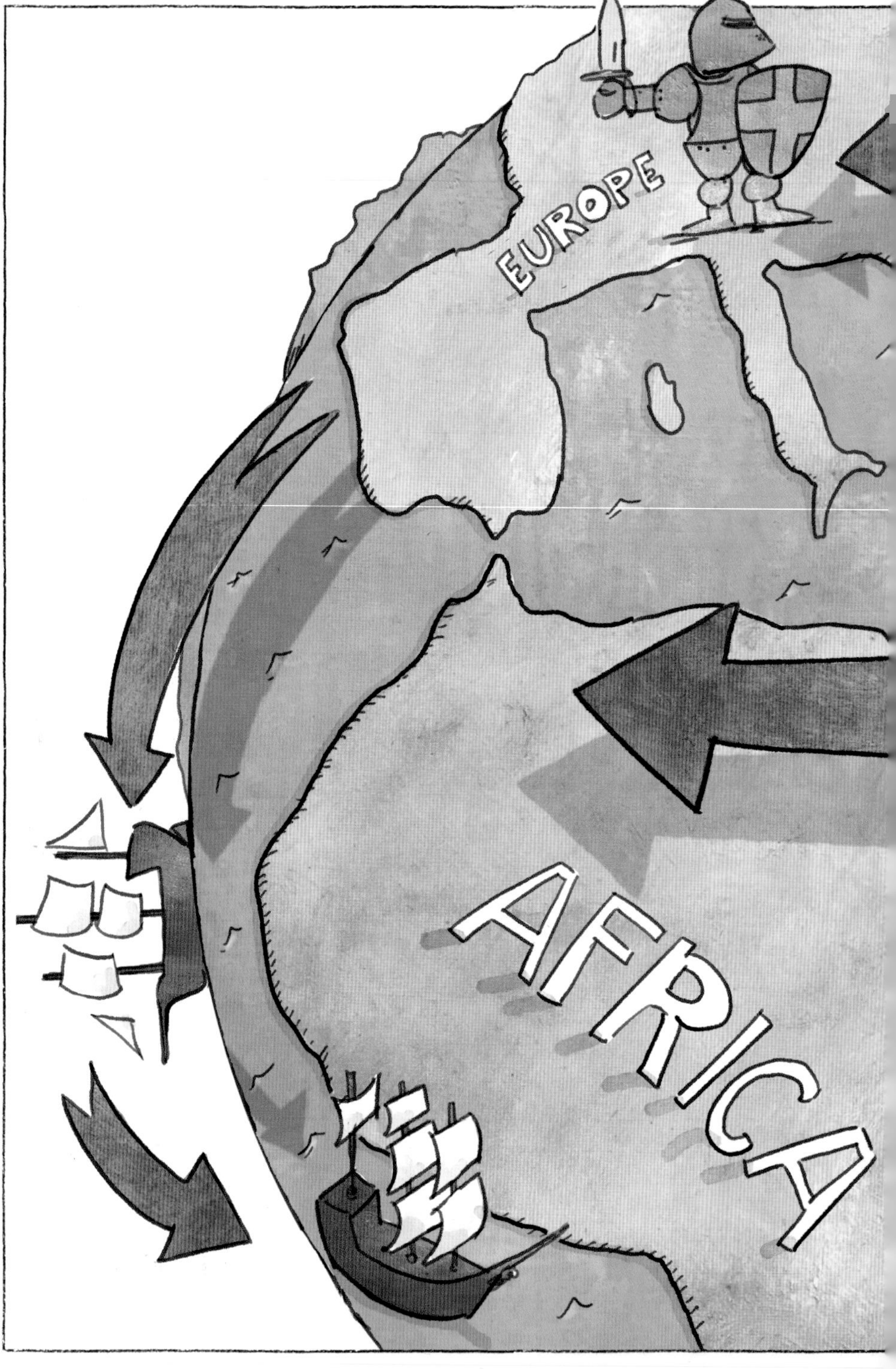
EUROPE
AFRICA

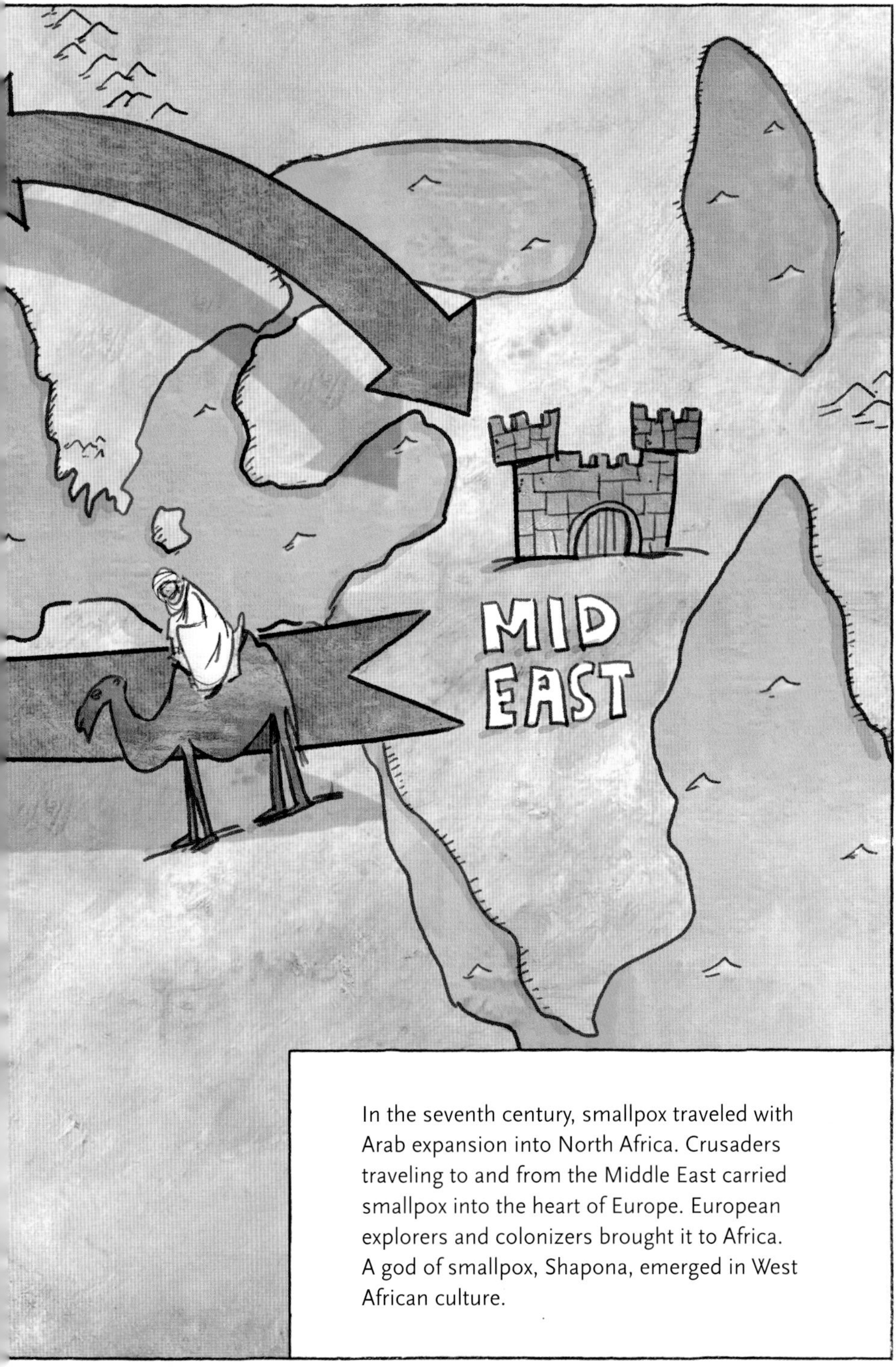
MID
EAST

In the seventh century, smallpox traveled with Arab expansion into North Africa. Crusaders traveling to and from the Middle East carried smallpox into the heart of Europe. European explorers and colonizers brought it to Africa. A god of smallpox, Shapona, emerged in West African culture.

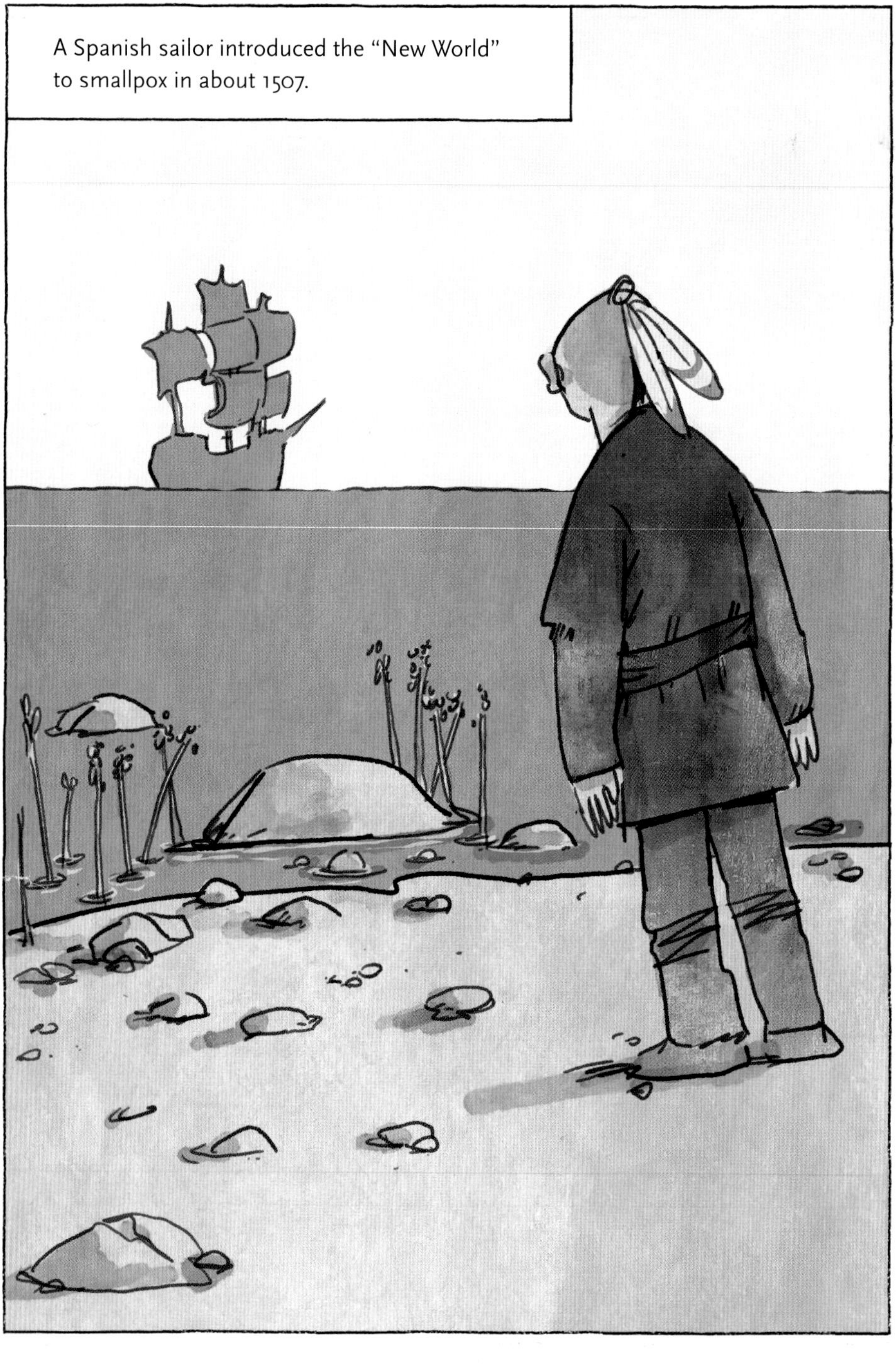
A Spanish sailor introduced the "New World" to smallpox in about 1507.

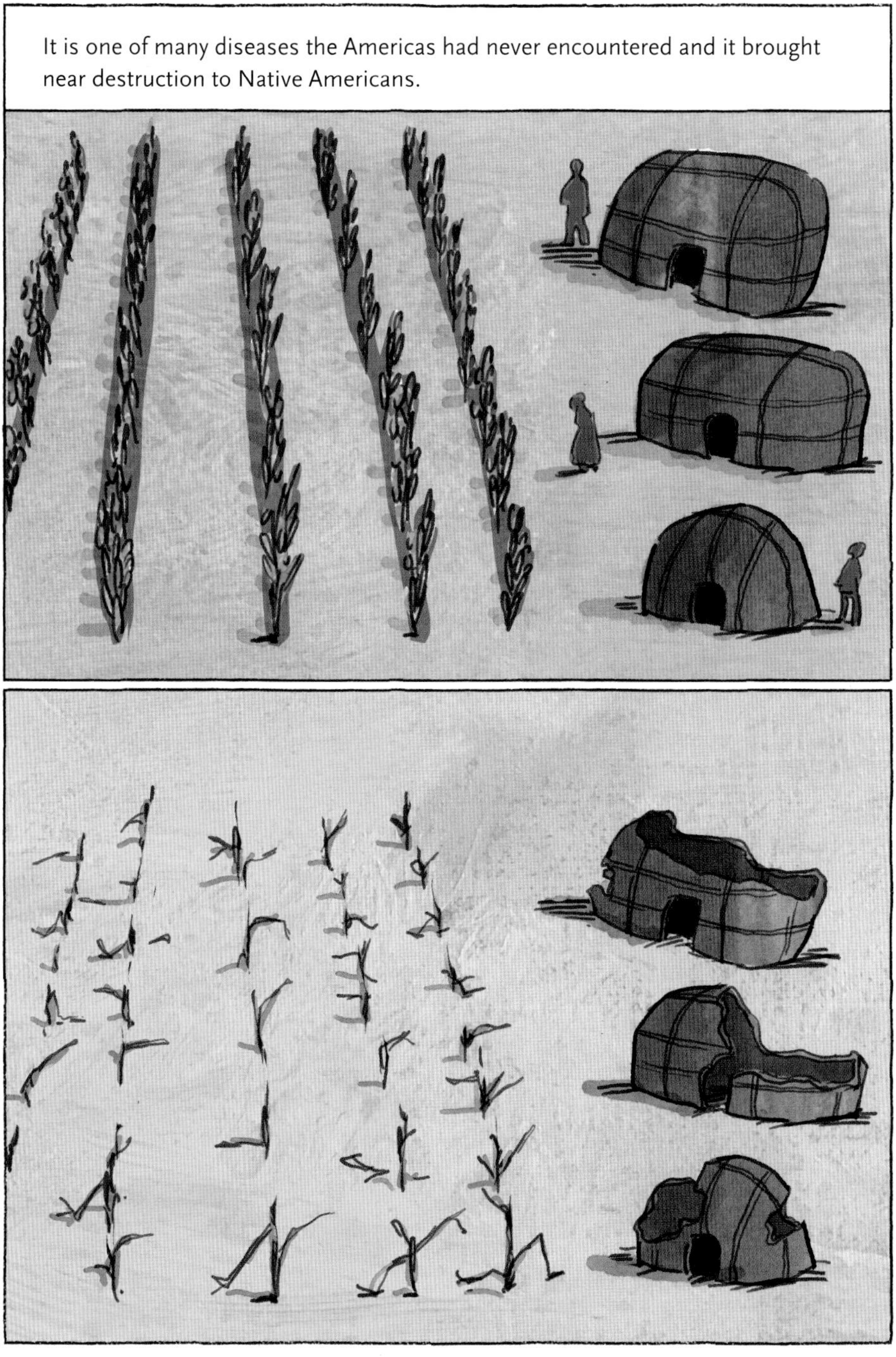
It is one of many diseases the Americas had never encountered and it brought near destruction to Native Americans.

In 1763, when British troops battled Native American leader Pontiac, the British, led by British General Jeffrey Amherst, had the idea to infect their opponents with smallpox-infected blankets.

"Could it not be contrived to Send the *Small Pox* among those Disaffected Tribes of Indians? We must, on this occasion, Use Every Stratagem in our power to Reduce them."

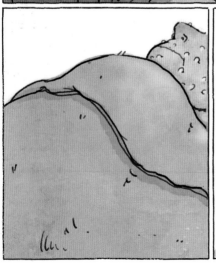

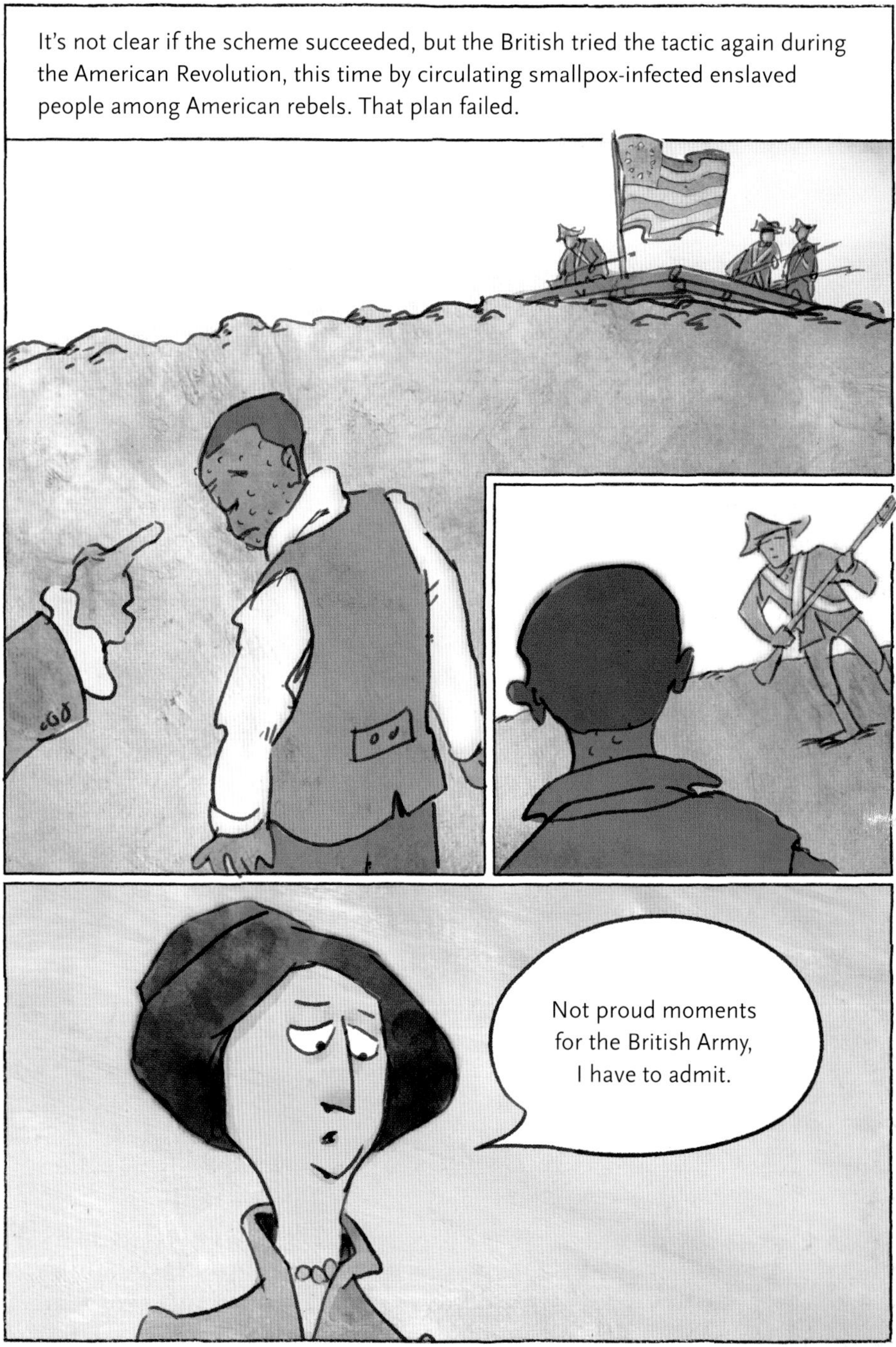
It's not clear if the scheme succeeded, but the British tried the tactic again during the American Revolution, this time by circulating smallpox-infected enslaved people among American rebels. That plan failed.
Not proud moments for the British Army, I have to admit.

In the eighteenth century, smallpox killed about four hundred thousand people a year in Europe. Everyone was at risk; it didn't discriminate between rich and poor, famous and anonymous, powerful and ordinary.

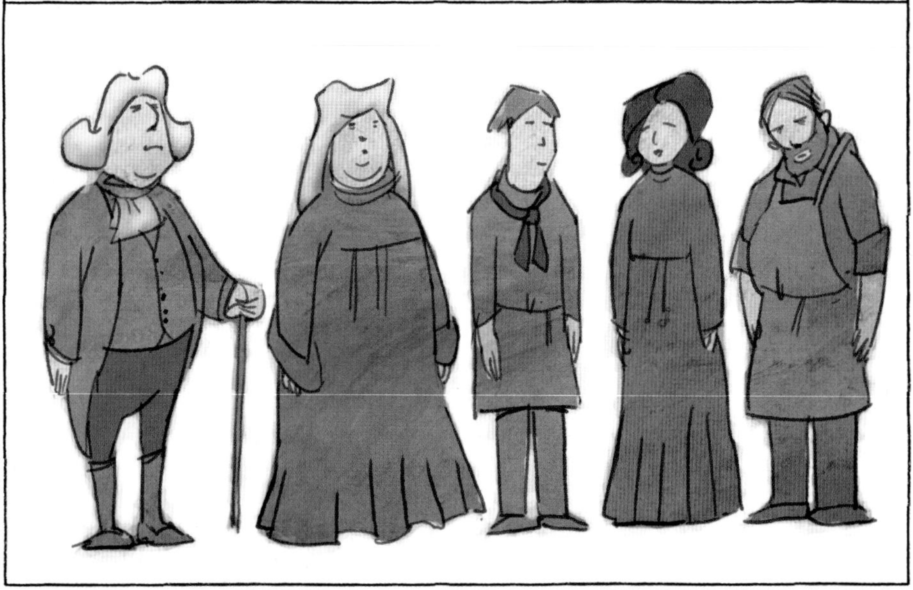

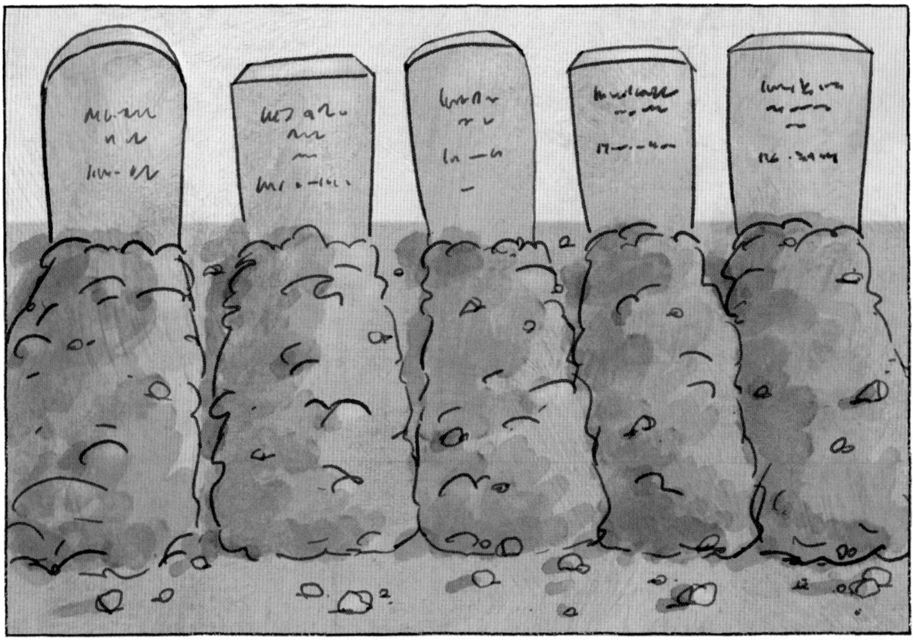

In the twentieth century, around three hundred million people worldwide died from smallpox. Even greater millions were blinded and disfigured. It is a misery too sad to calculate.

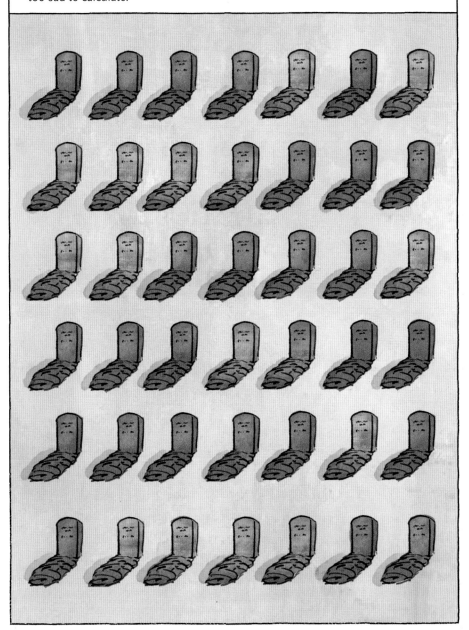

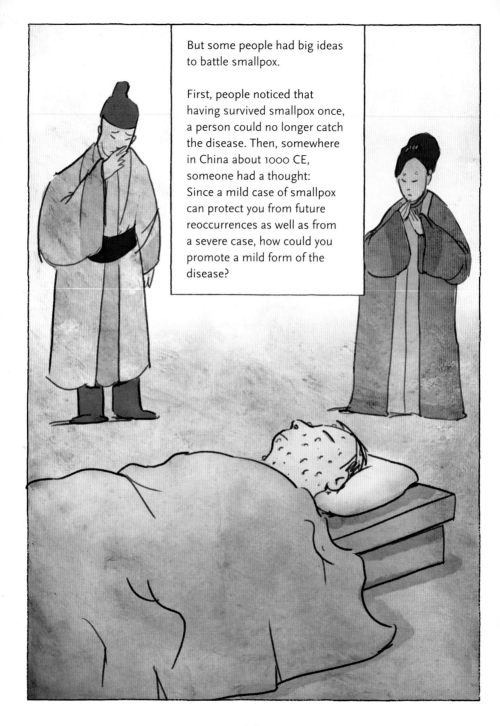

But some people had big ideas to battle smallpox.

First, people noticed that having survived smallpox once, a person could no longer catch the disease. Then, somewhere in China about 1000 CE, someone had a thought: Since a mild case of smallpox can protect you from future reoccurrences as well as from a severe case, how could you promote a mild form of the disease?

This ancient Chinese person had the big idea—hang on, it gets a little, well, *stomach-turning*—to harvest the dried smallpox scabs from a victim who had suffered a mild case of the sickness, grind the scabs into a dust, and then . . .

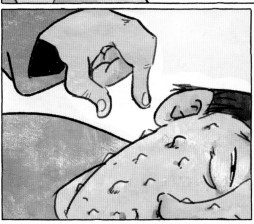

blow the dust up your nose!

Oh, there was an alternative to scab dust.

Gushy smallpox fluid from an active blister was placed on a cotton plug . . .

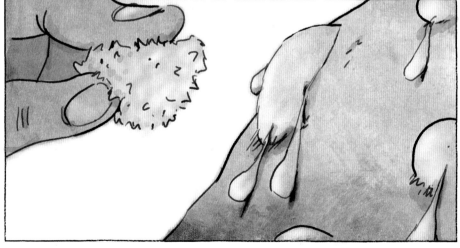

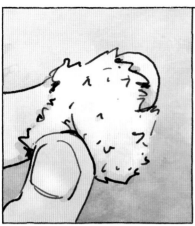

. . . and then pushed up your nose.

Yes, it is disgusting, but also, if you think about it, genius: The weakened smallpox is delivered deep into a person, who then suffers a mild form of the disease with a much lower risk of death, blinding, and disfigurement.

The idea worked, and insufflation—that's the big word that describes blowing stuff up your nose—eventually became an event that Chinese children would experience at five years of age, something of a ritual like a First Communion, bar mitzvah, quinceañera, or sweet sixteen.

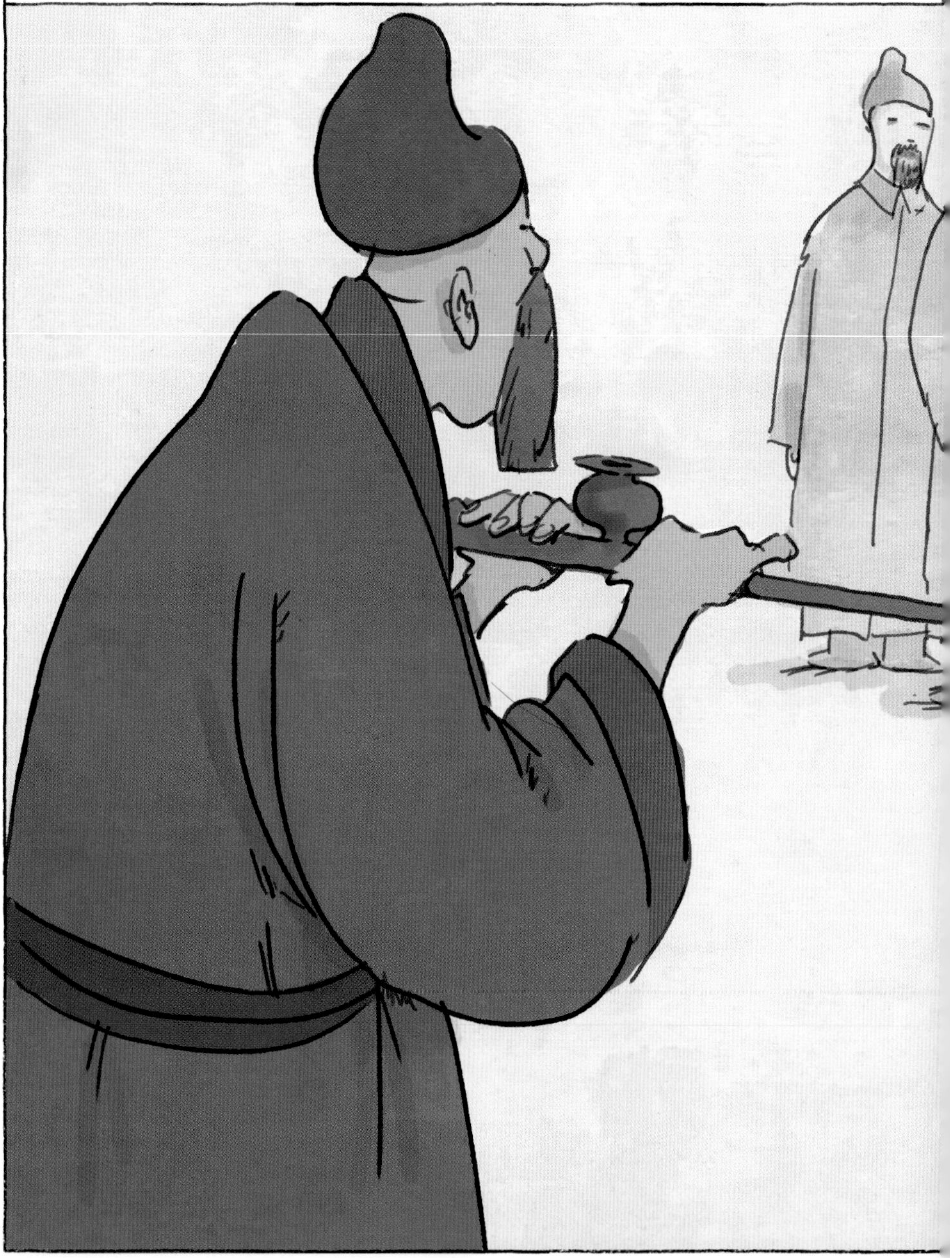

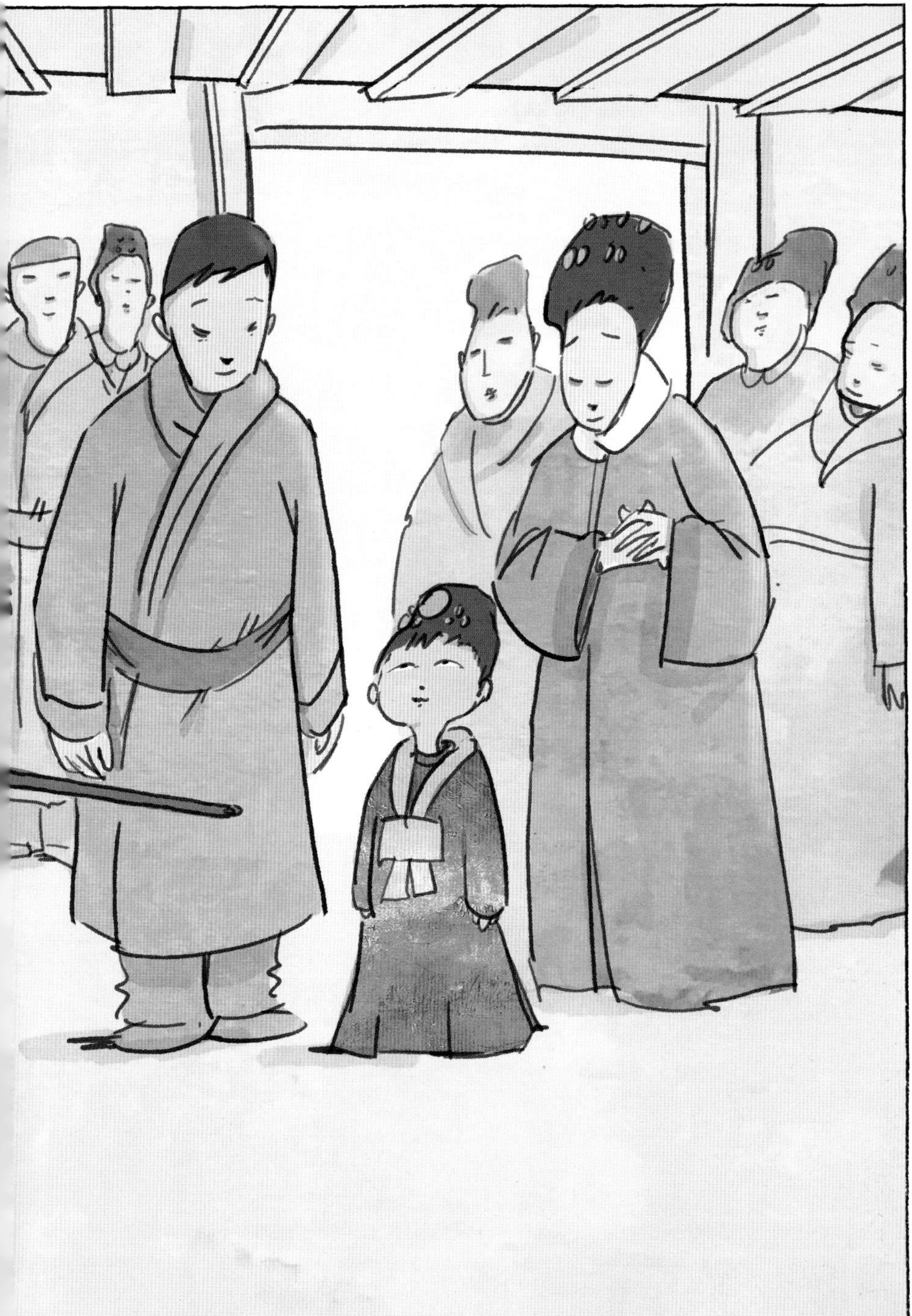

In India, instead of using smallpox dust to transfer the sickness, a sharp iron needle smeared with scab fluid was used to puncture a small circle on the upper arm. It was a bit less icky and also provided a measure of defense against the illness.

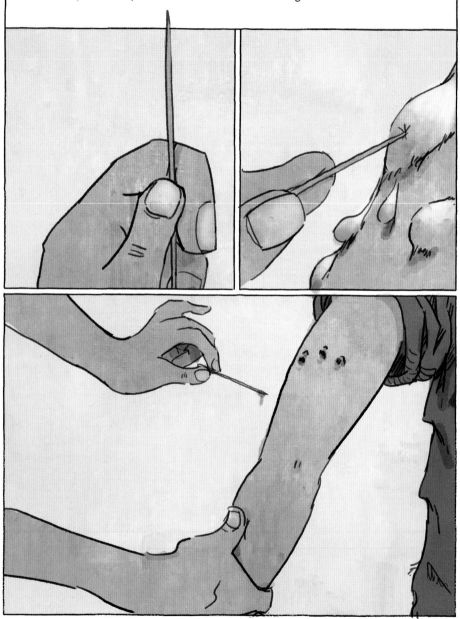

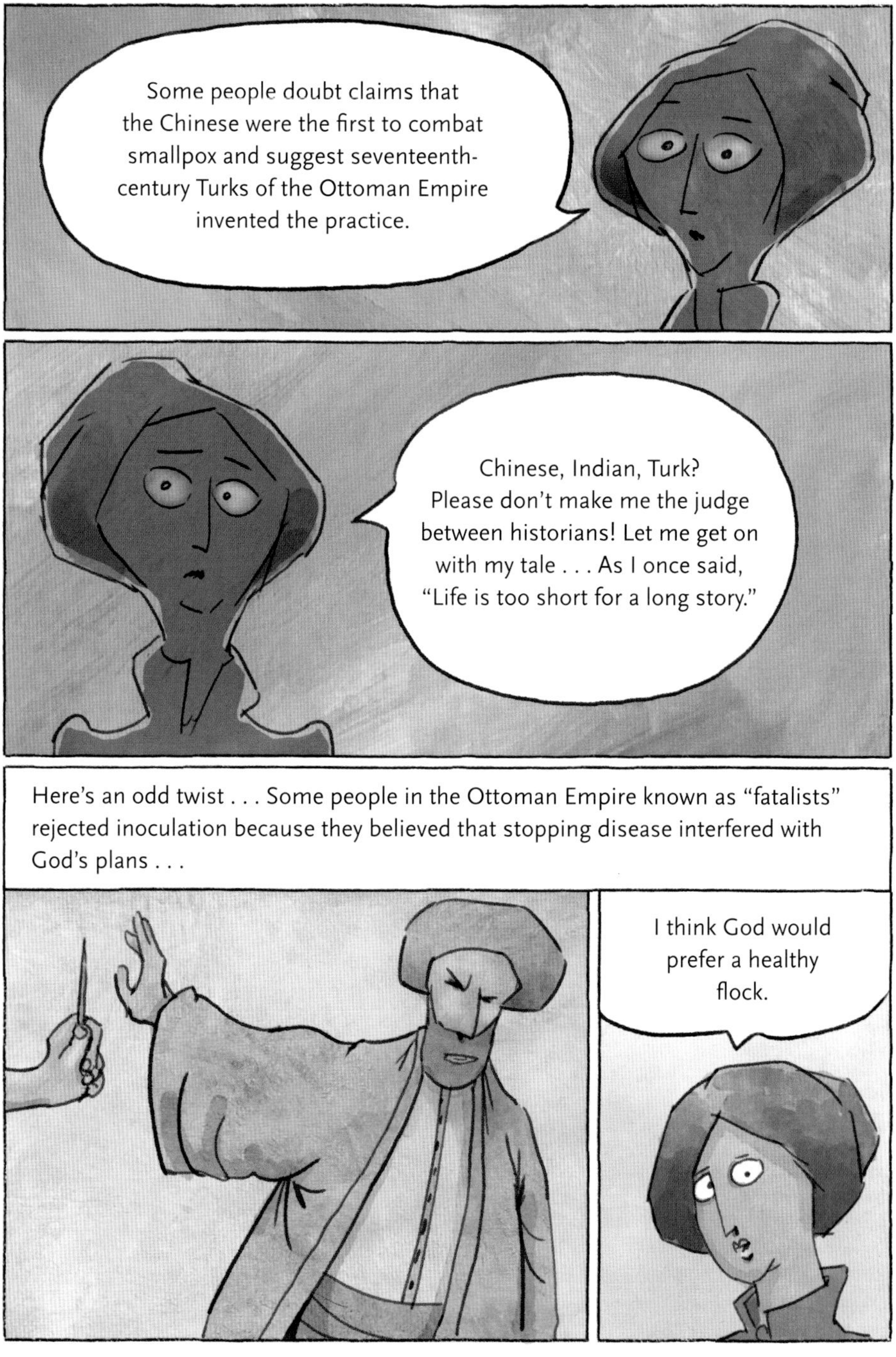
Some people doubt claims that the Chinese were the first to combat smallpox and suggest seventeenth-century Turks of the Ottoman Empire invented the practice.
Chinese, Indian, Turk? Please don't make me the judge between historians! Let me get on with my tale . . . As I once said, "Life is too short for a long story."
Here's an odd twist . . . Some people in the Ottoman Empire known as "fatalists" rejected inoculation because they believed that stopping disease interfered with God's plans . . .
I think God would prefer a healthy flock.

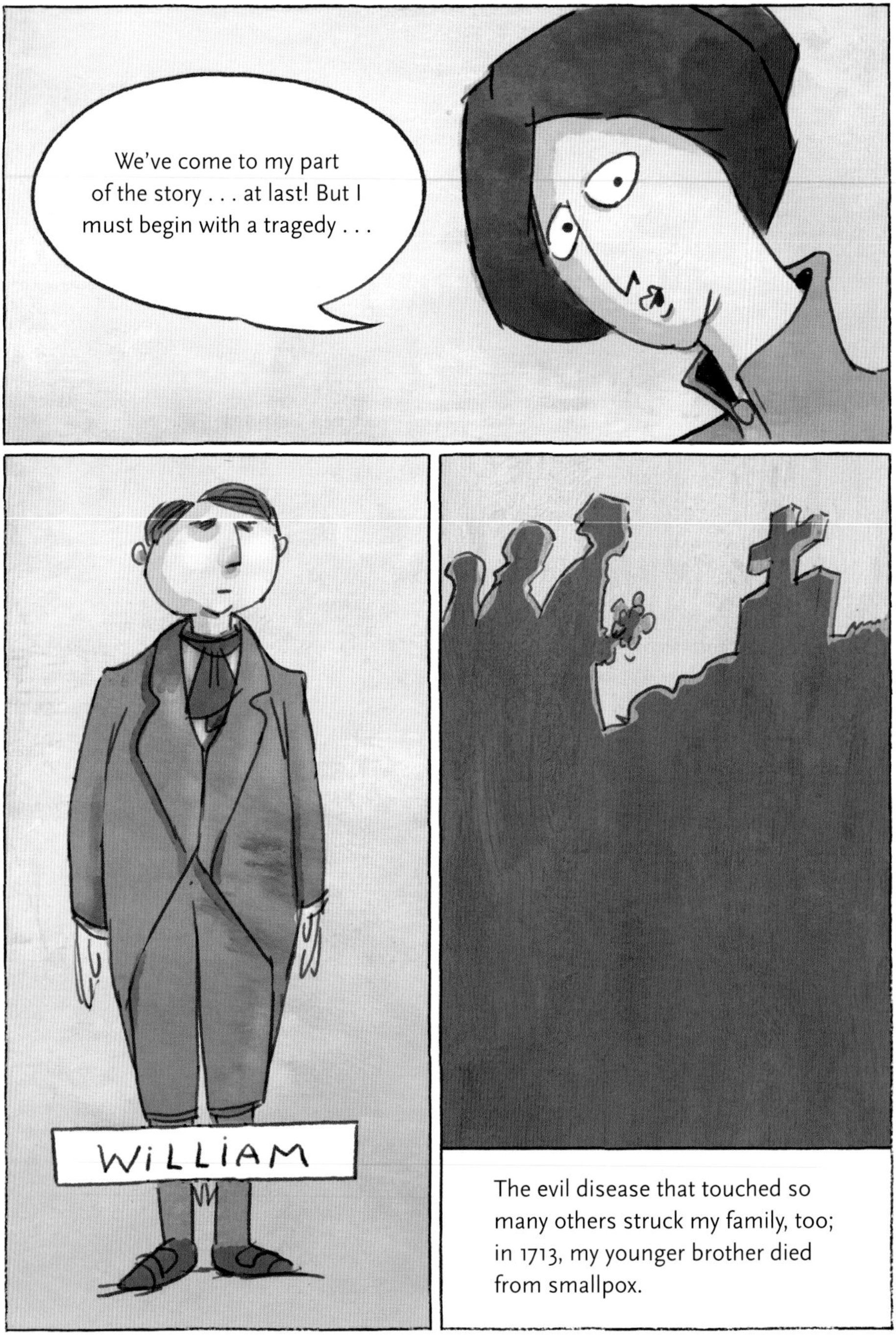
We've come to my part of the story . . . at last! But I must begin with a tragedy . . .
WILLIAM
The evil disease that touched so many others struck my family, too; in 1713, my younger brother died from smallpox.

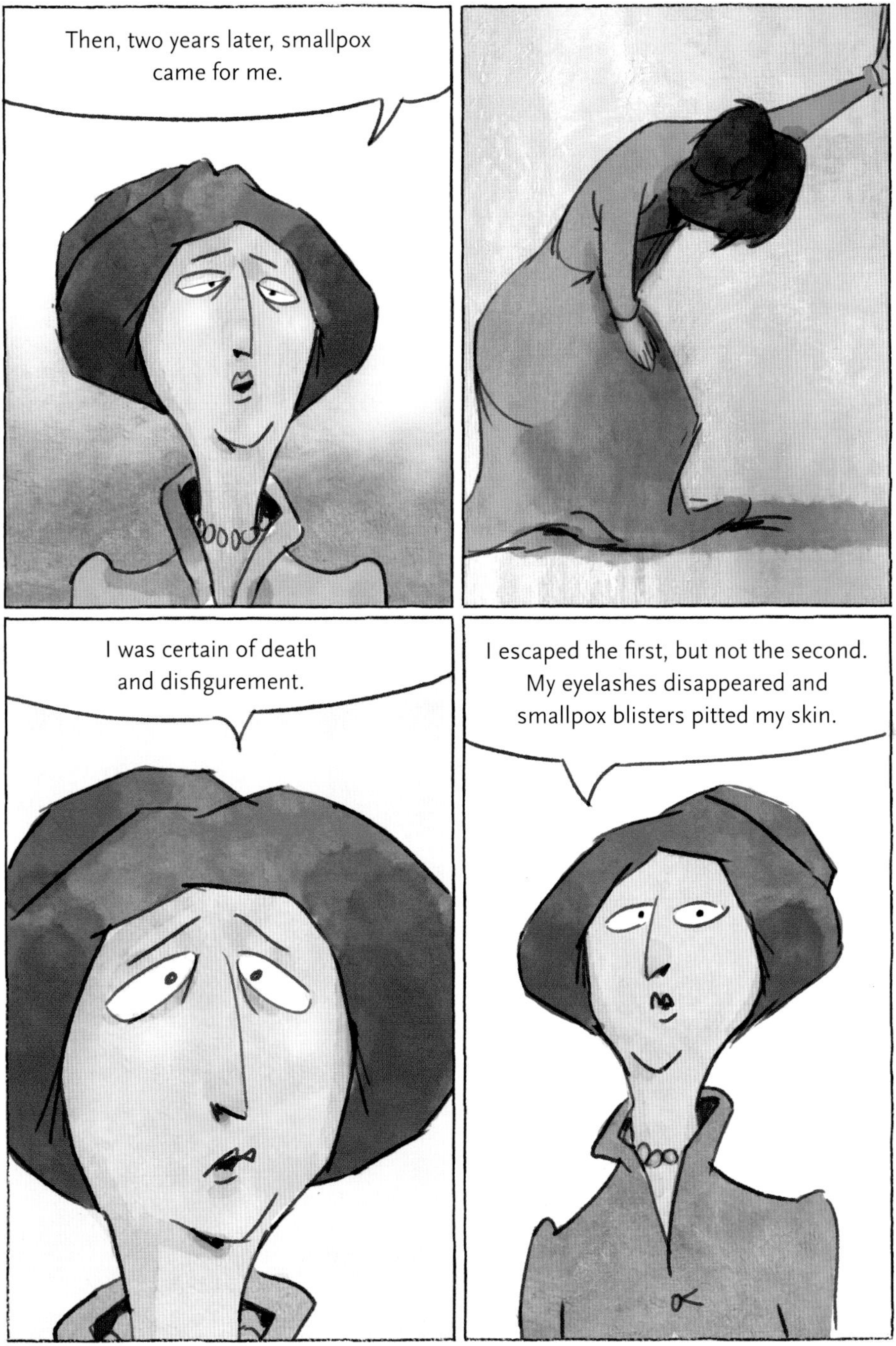
Then, two years later, smallpox came for me.
I was certain of death and disfigurement.
I escaped the first, but not the second. My eyelashes disappeared and smallpox blisters pitted my skin.

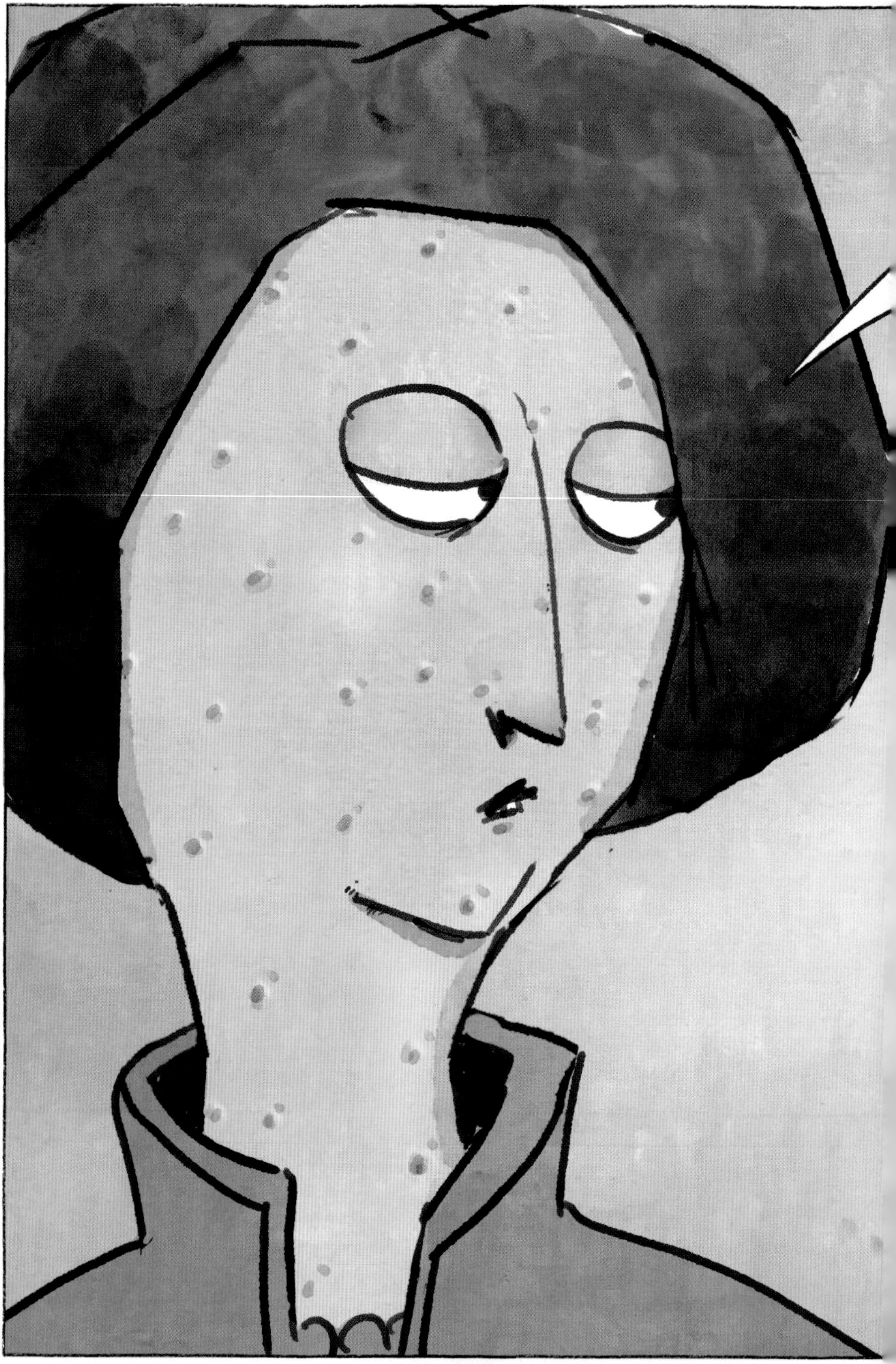

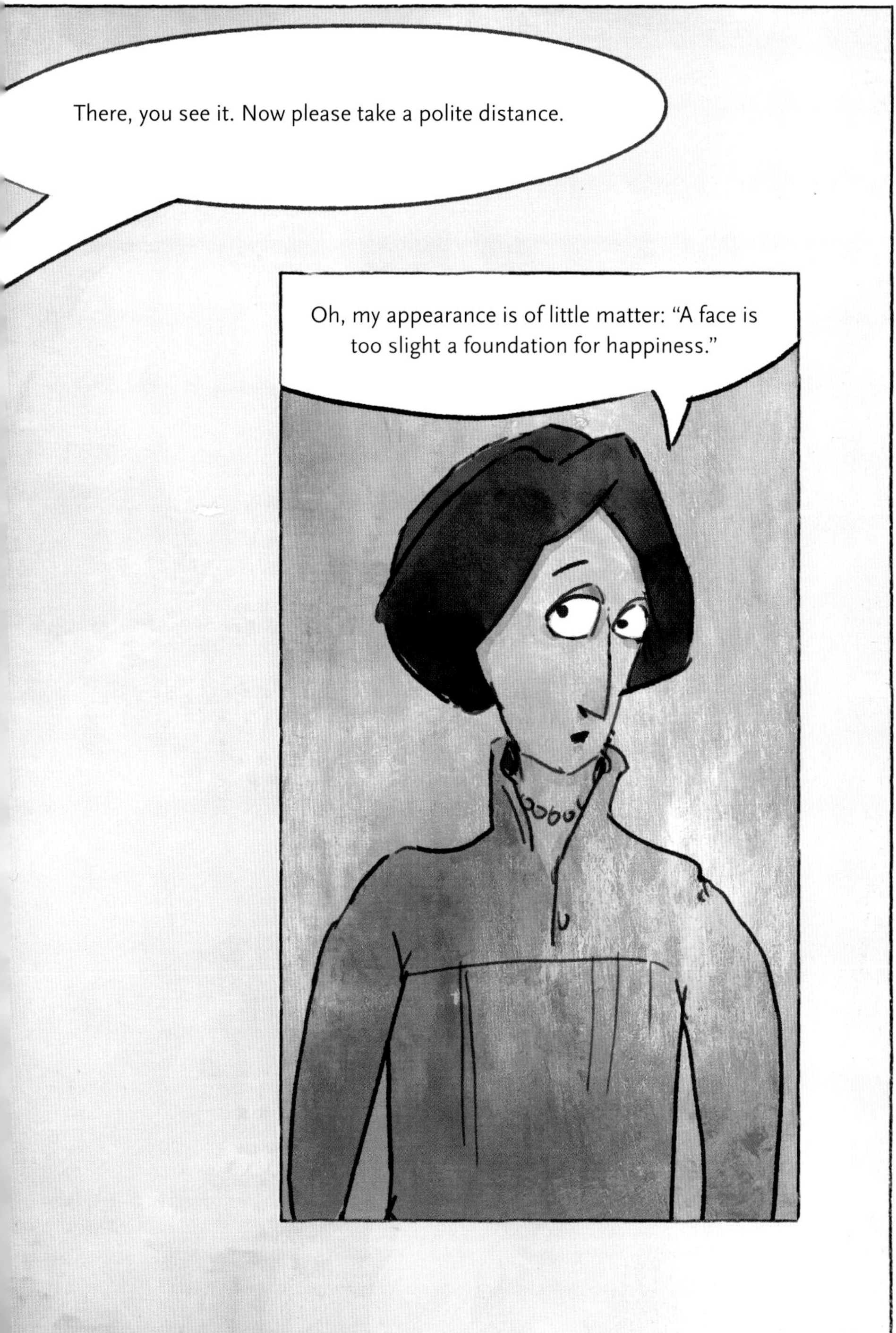
There, you see it. Now please take a polite distance.
Oh, my appearance is of little matter: "A face is too slight a foundation for happiness."

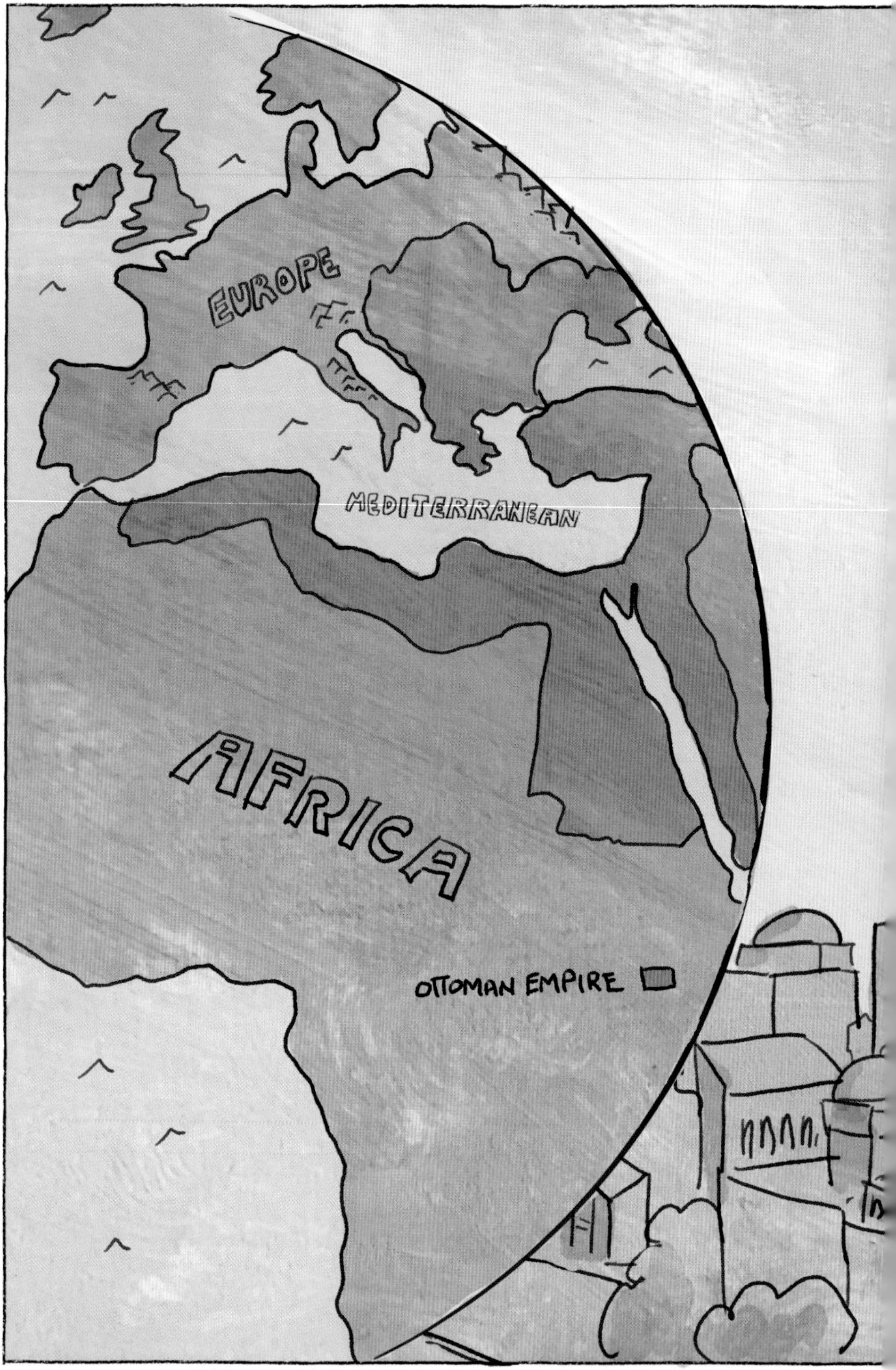
EUROPE
MEDITERRANEAN
AFRICA
OTTOMAN EMPIRE

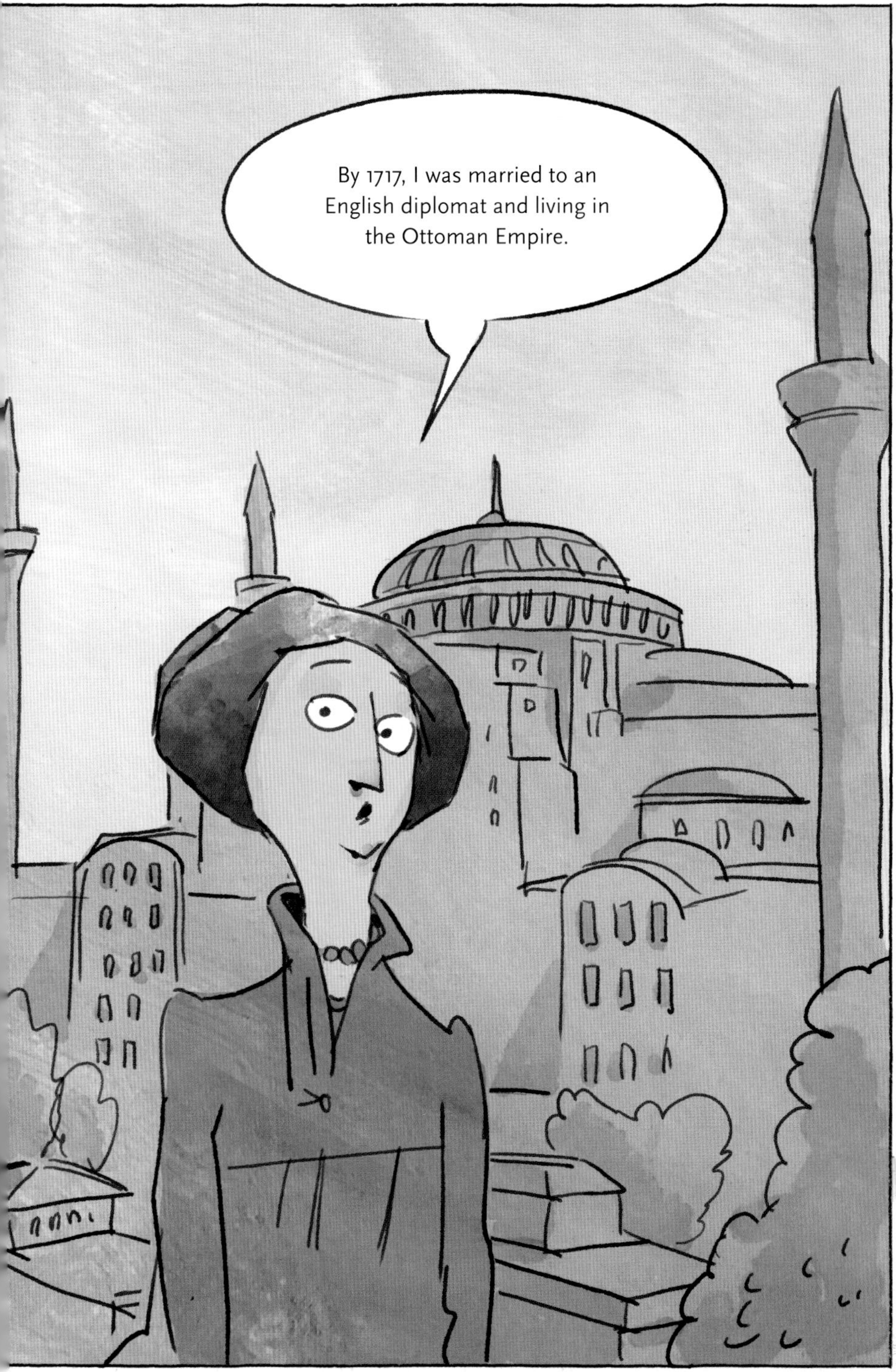
By 1717, I was married to an English diplomat and living in the Ottoman Empire.

It was there I learned of inoculation, the practice to ward off smallpox.

With my sad and tragic connection to disease in mind, I swore to use inoculation to keep its clutches off my four-year-old son, Edward.

Still, the practice was unheard of among the English diplomats in Turkey.

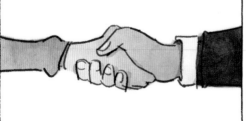

To avoid scandal and uproar, I asked Dr. Maitland of the British embassy to be my secret assistant.

I sent for an old Greek woman who knew the ways of the anti-smallpox scheme.

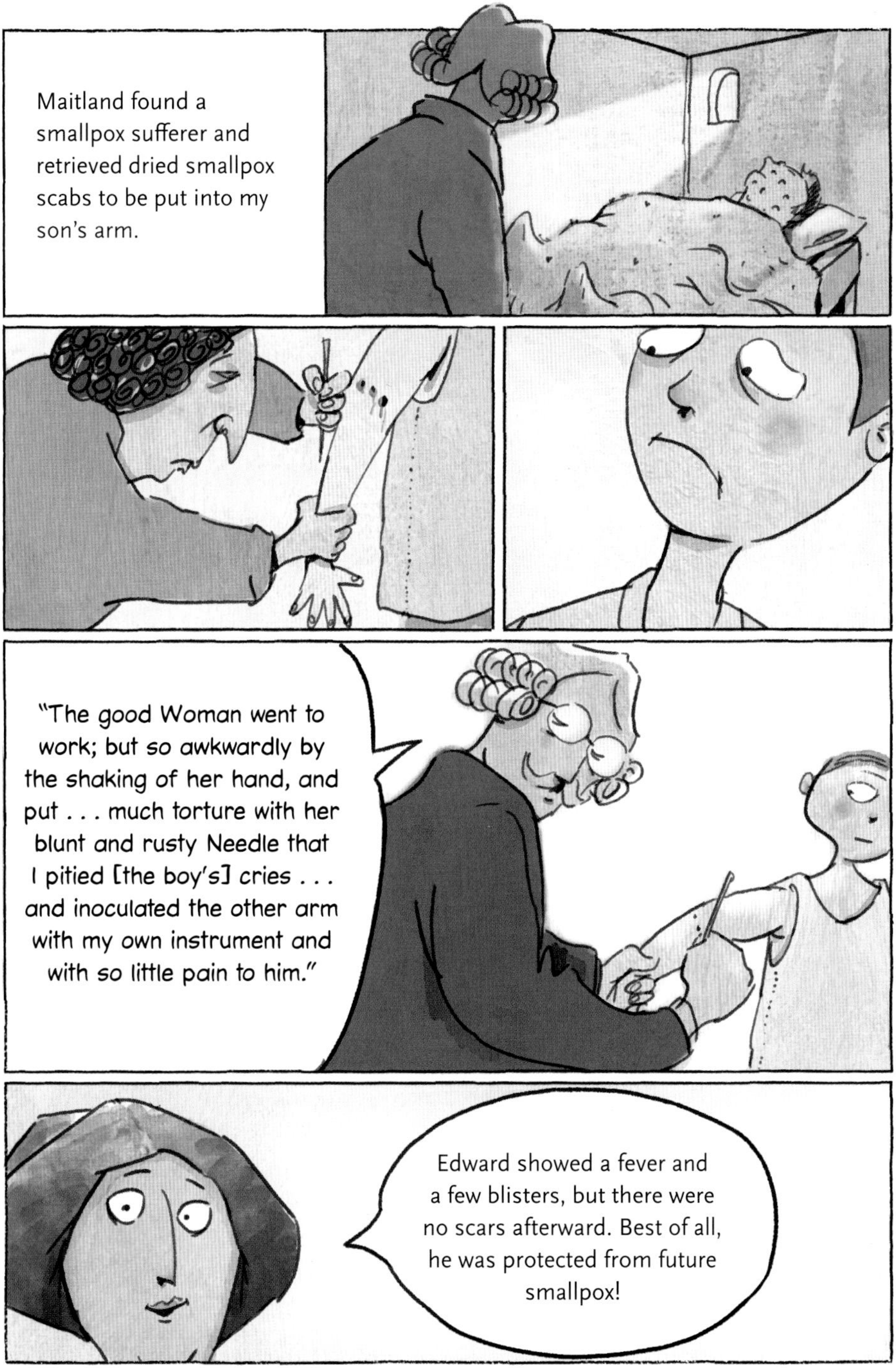
Maitland found a smallpox sufferer and retrieved dried smallpox scabs to be put into my son's arm.
"The good Woman went to work; but so awkwardly by the shaking of her hand, and put . . . much torture with her blunt and rusty Needle that I pitied [the boy's] cries . . . and inoculated the other arm with my own instrument and with so little pain to him."
Edward showed a fever and a few blisters, but there were no scars afterward. Best of all, he was protected from future smallpox!

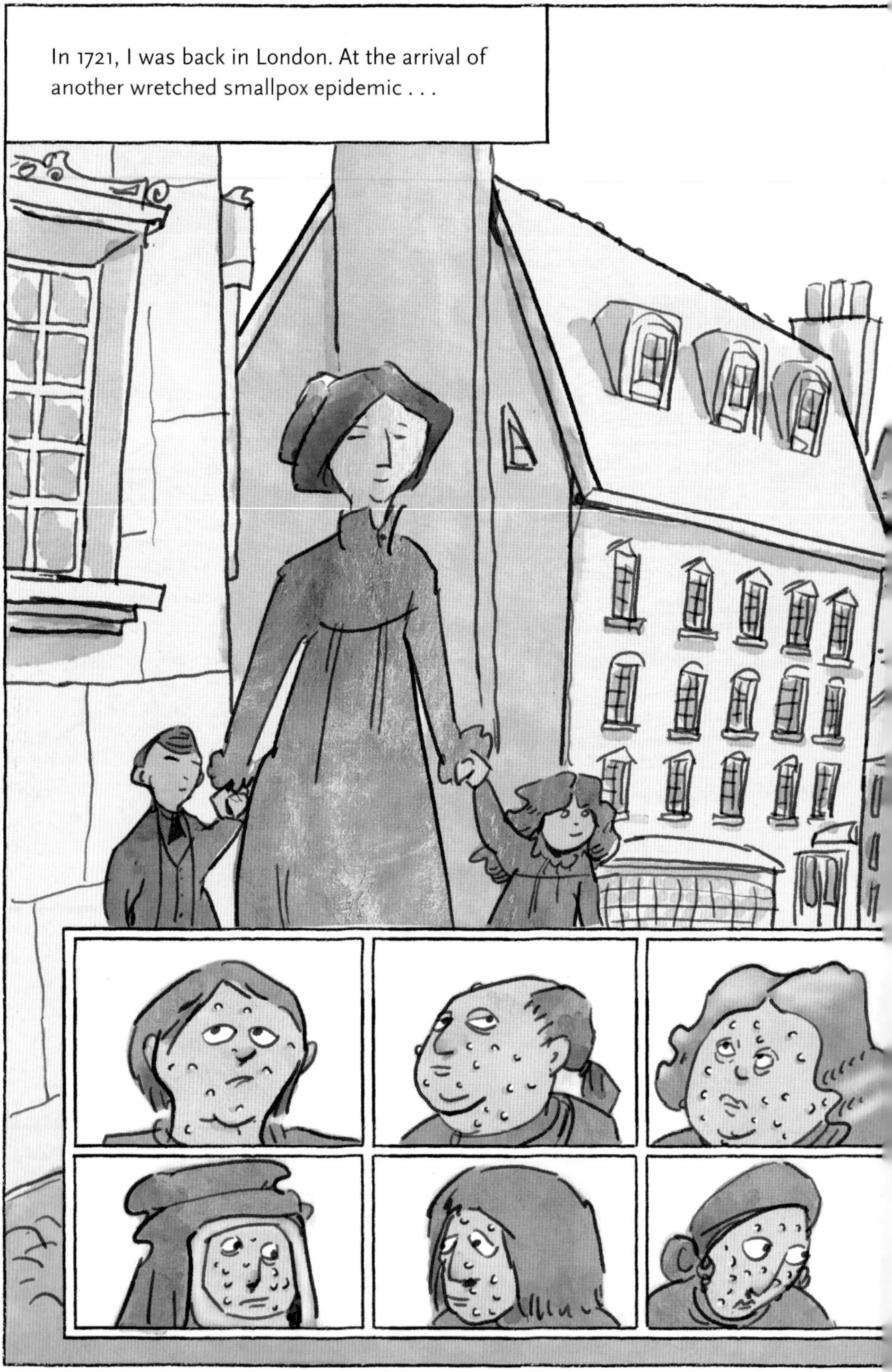
In 1721, I was back in London. At the arrival of another wretched smallpox epidemic . . .

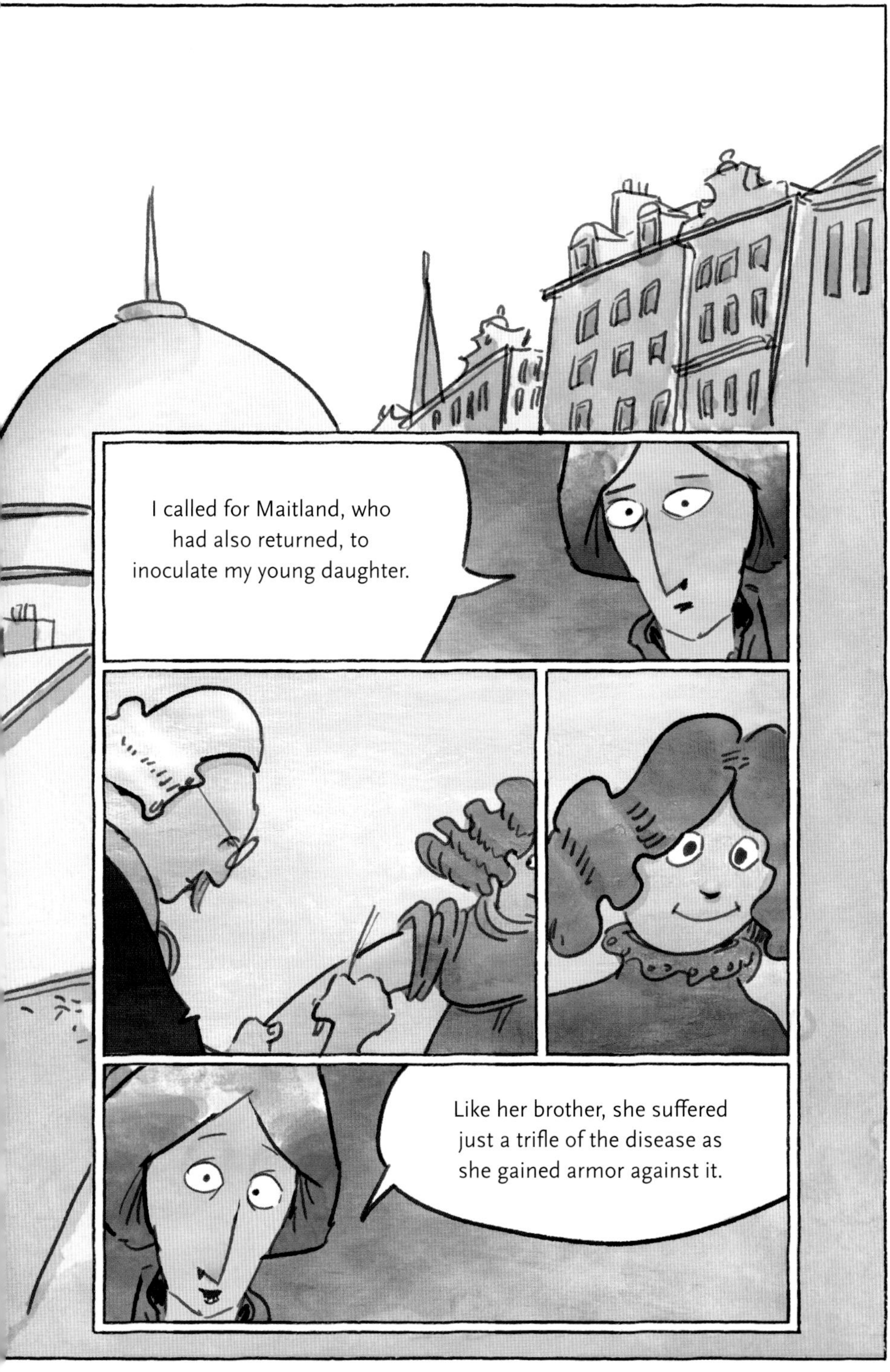
I called for Maitland, who had also returned, to inoculate my young daughter.
Like her brother, she suffered just a trifle of the disease as she gained armor against it.

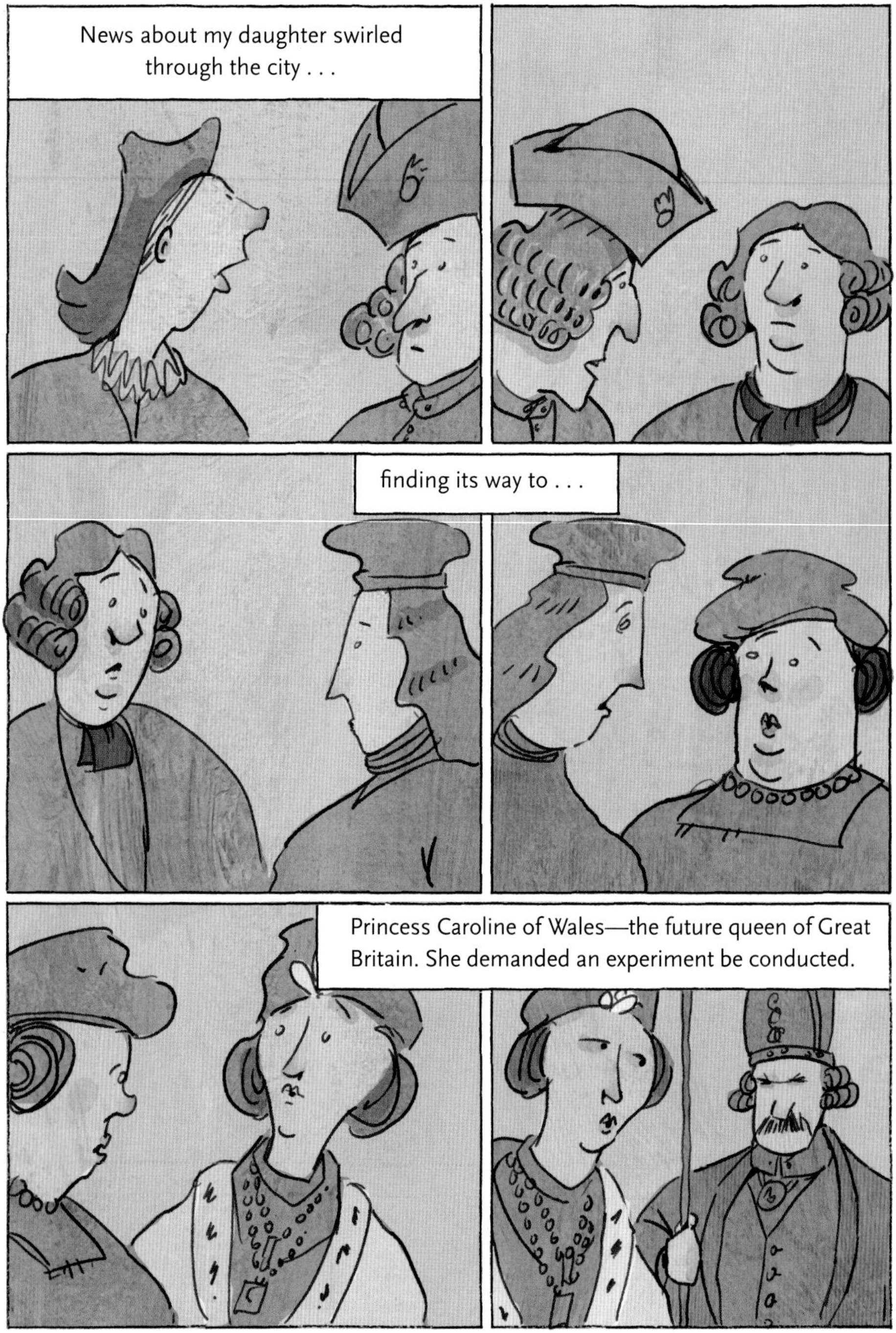
News about my daughter swirled through the city . . .
finding its way to . . .
Princess Caroline of Wales—the future queen of Great Britain. She demanded an experiment be conducted.

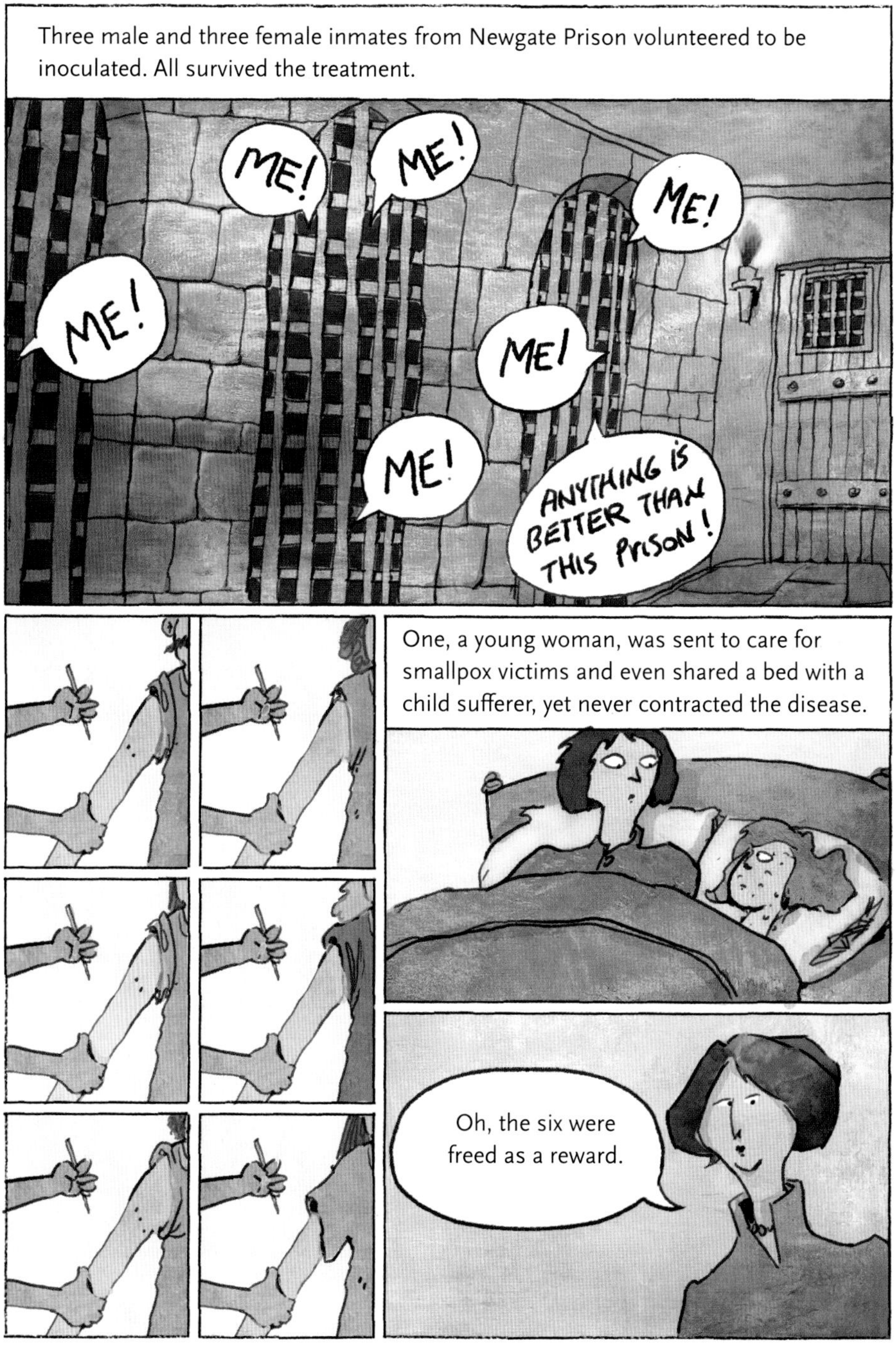
Three male and three female inmates from Newgate Prison volunteered to be inoculated. All survived the treatment.
ME!
ME!
ME!
ME!
ME!
ME!
ANYTHING IS BETTER THAN THIS PRISON!
One, a young woman, was sent to care for smallpox victims and even shared a bed with a child sufferer, yet never contracted the disease.
Oh, the six were freed as a reward.

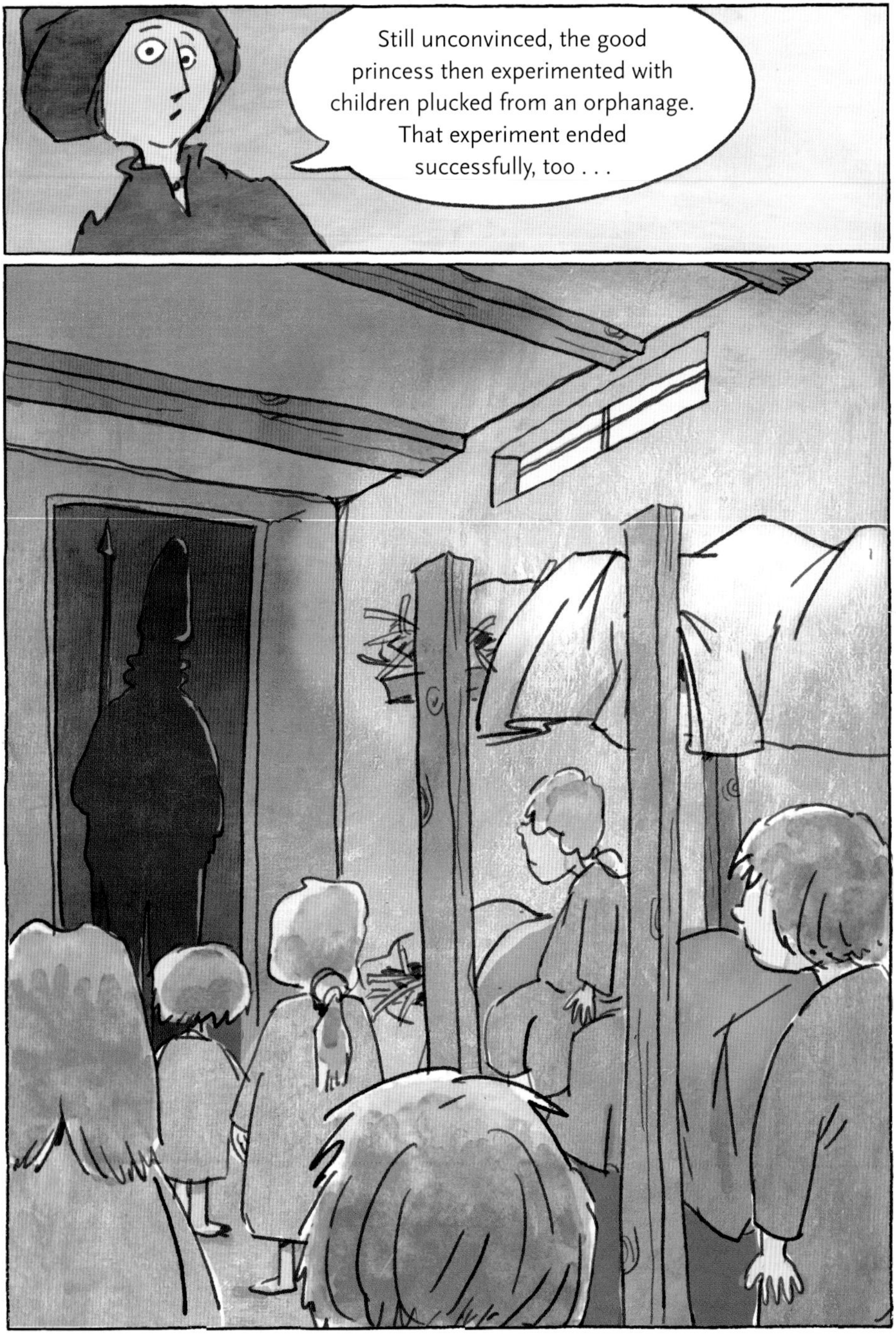
Still unconvinced, the good princess then experimented with children plucked from an orphanage. That experiment ended successfully, too . . .

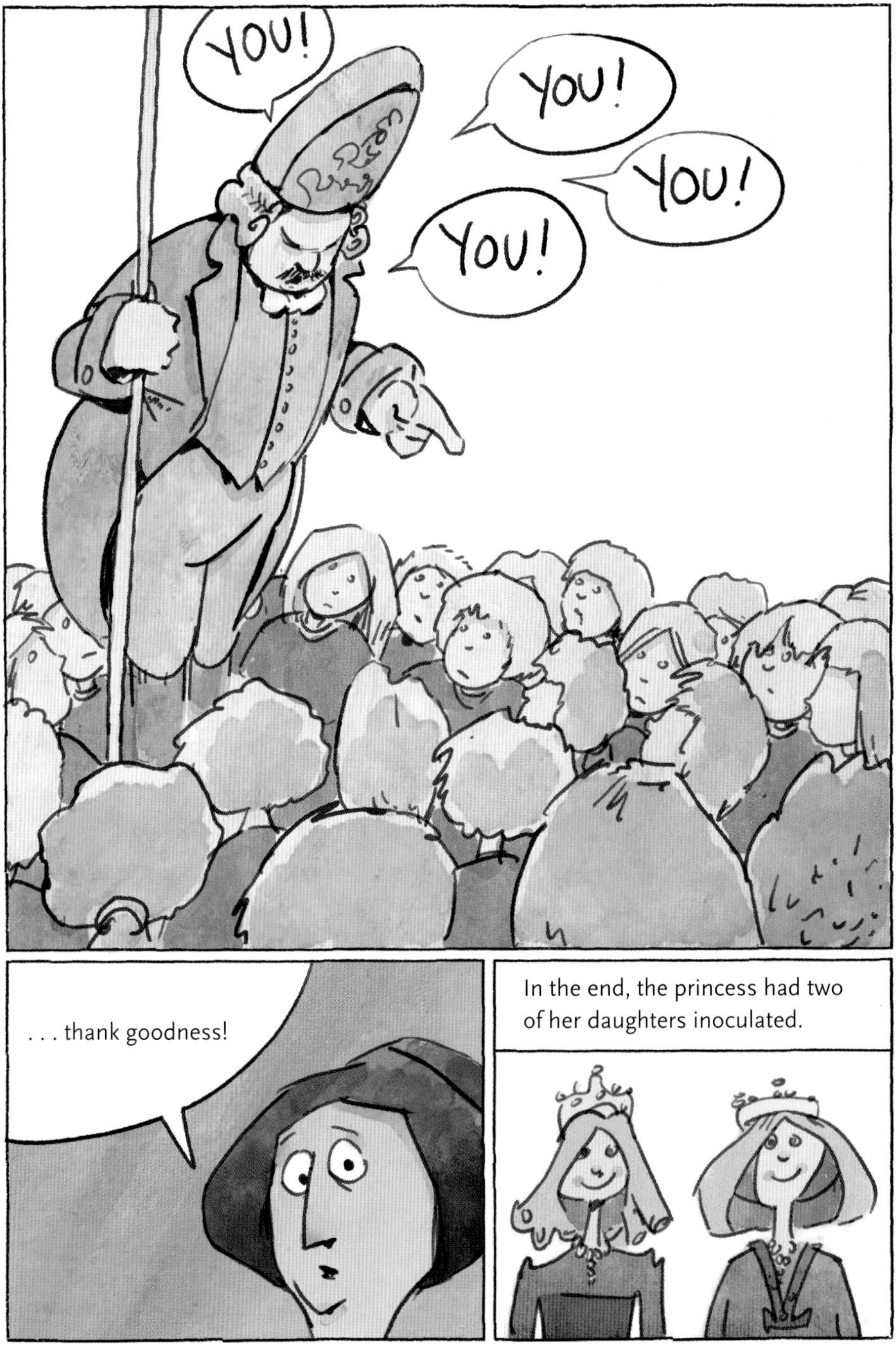
YOU!
YOU!
YOU!
YOU!
. . . thank goodness!
In the end, the princess had two of her daughters inoculated.

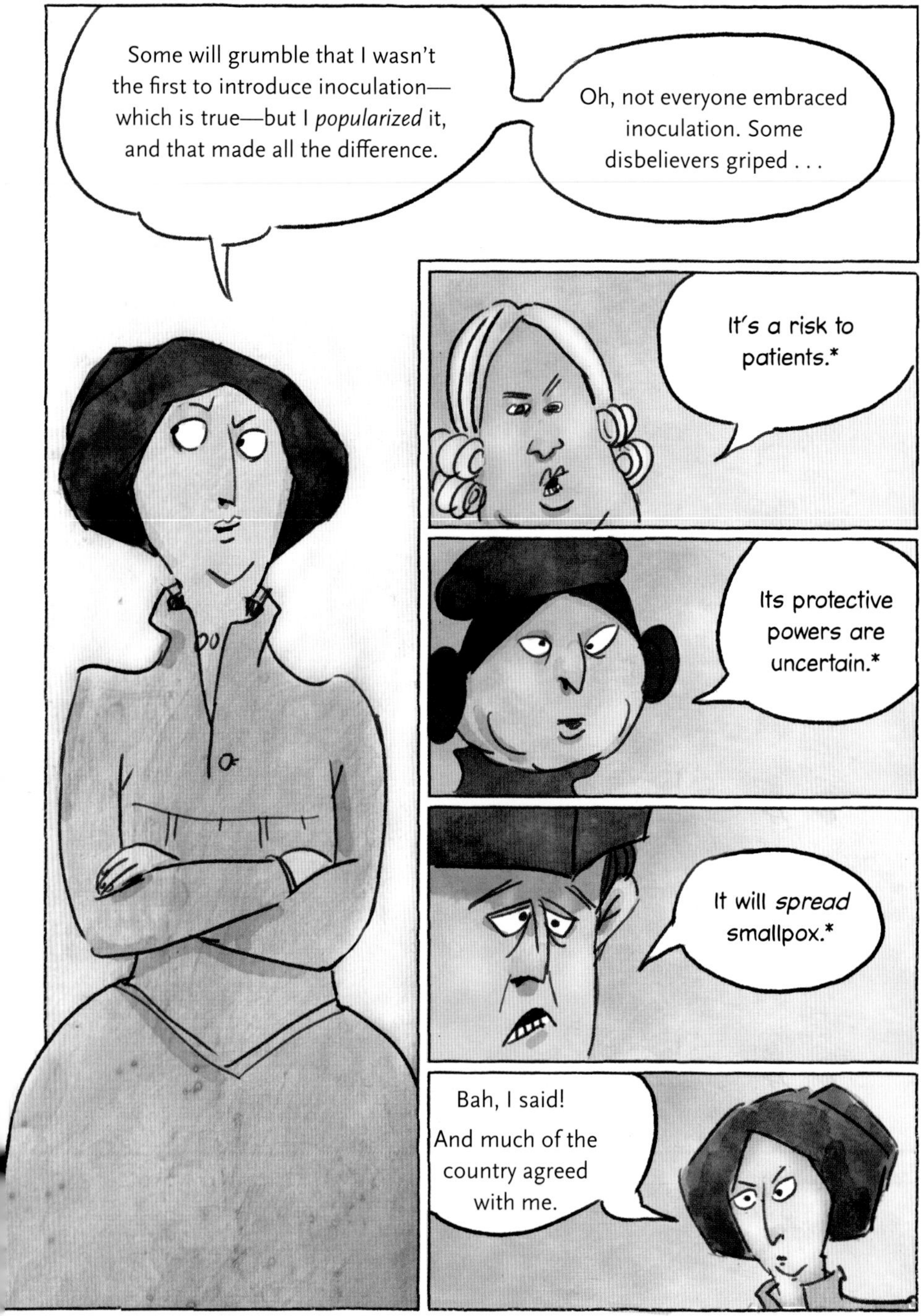
Some will grumble that I wasn't the first to introduce inoculation—which is true—but I *popularized* it, and that made all the difference.
Oh, not everyone embraced inoculation. Some disbelievers griped . . .
It's a risk to patients.*
Its protective powers are uncertain.*
It will *spread* smallpox.*
Bah, I said!
And much of the country agreed with me.

Inoculation spread and businesses grew up around providing it, including a comfortable quarantine for the treated person while he or she was contagious with the mild version of smallpox.

It was something like visiting a modern spa.

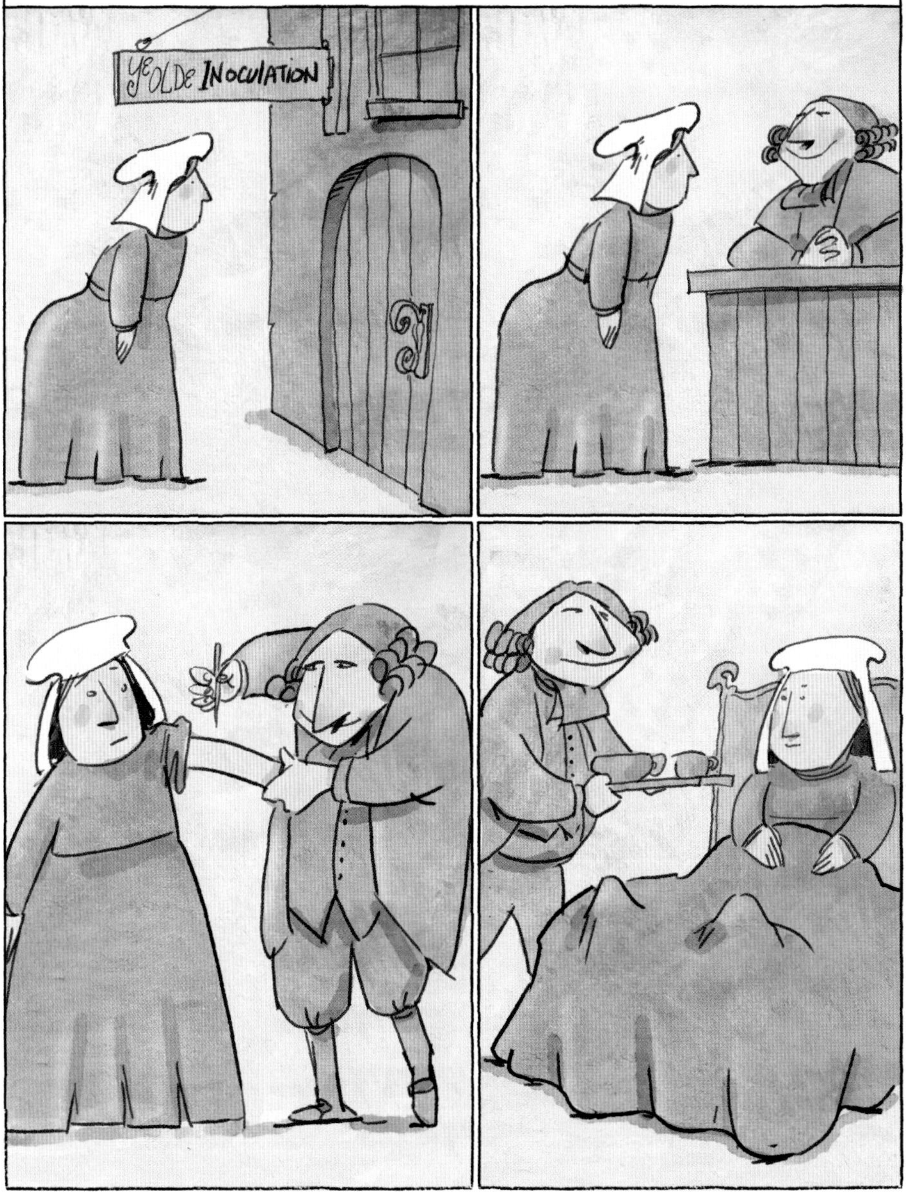
YE OLDE INOCULATION

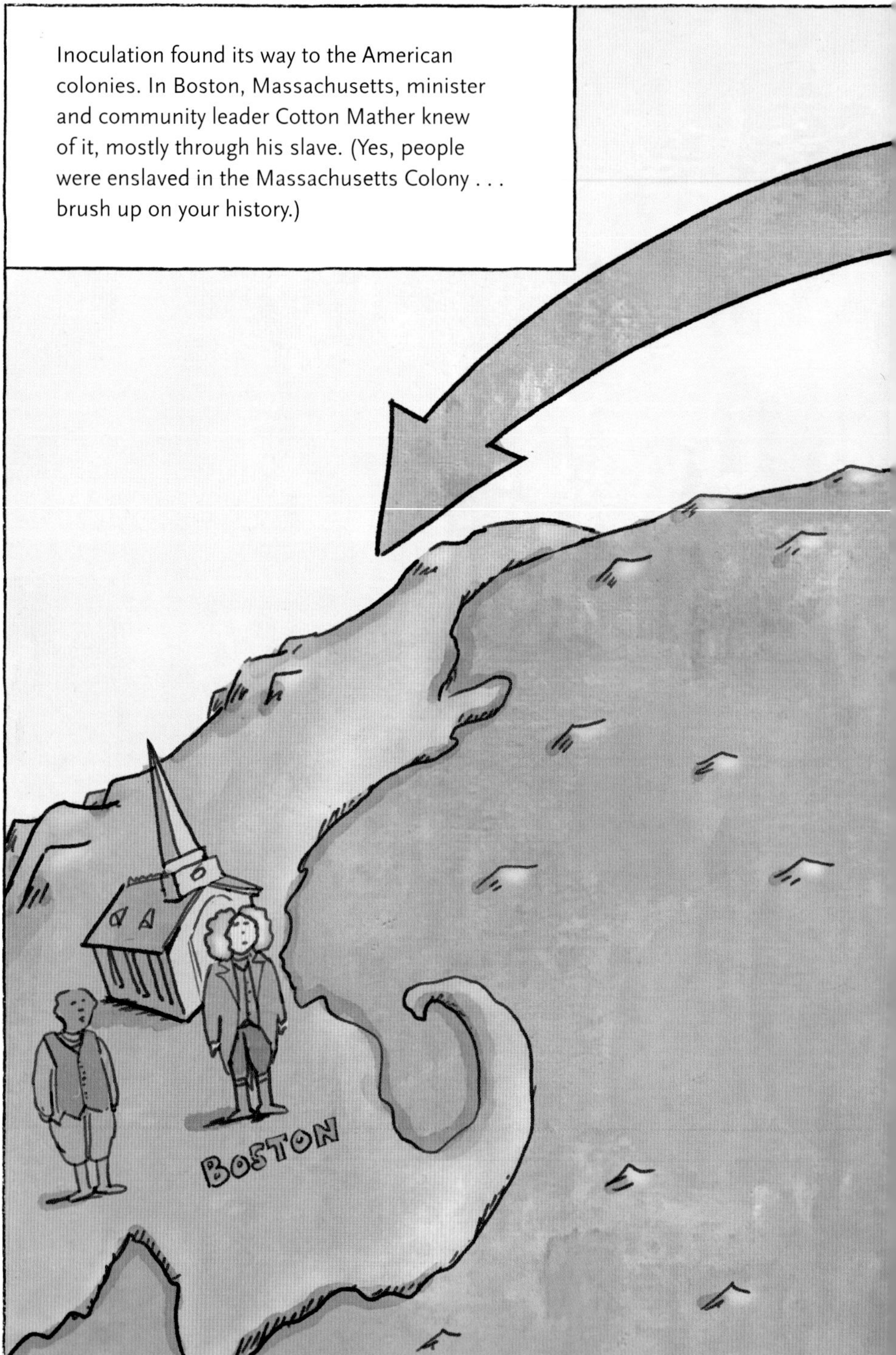
Inoculation found its way to the American colonies. In Boston, Massachusetts, minister and community leader Cotton Mather knew of it, mostly through his slave. (Yes, people were enslaved in the Massachusetts Colony . . . brush up on your history.)
BOSTON

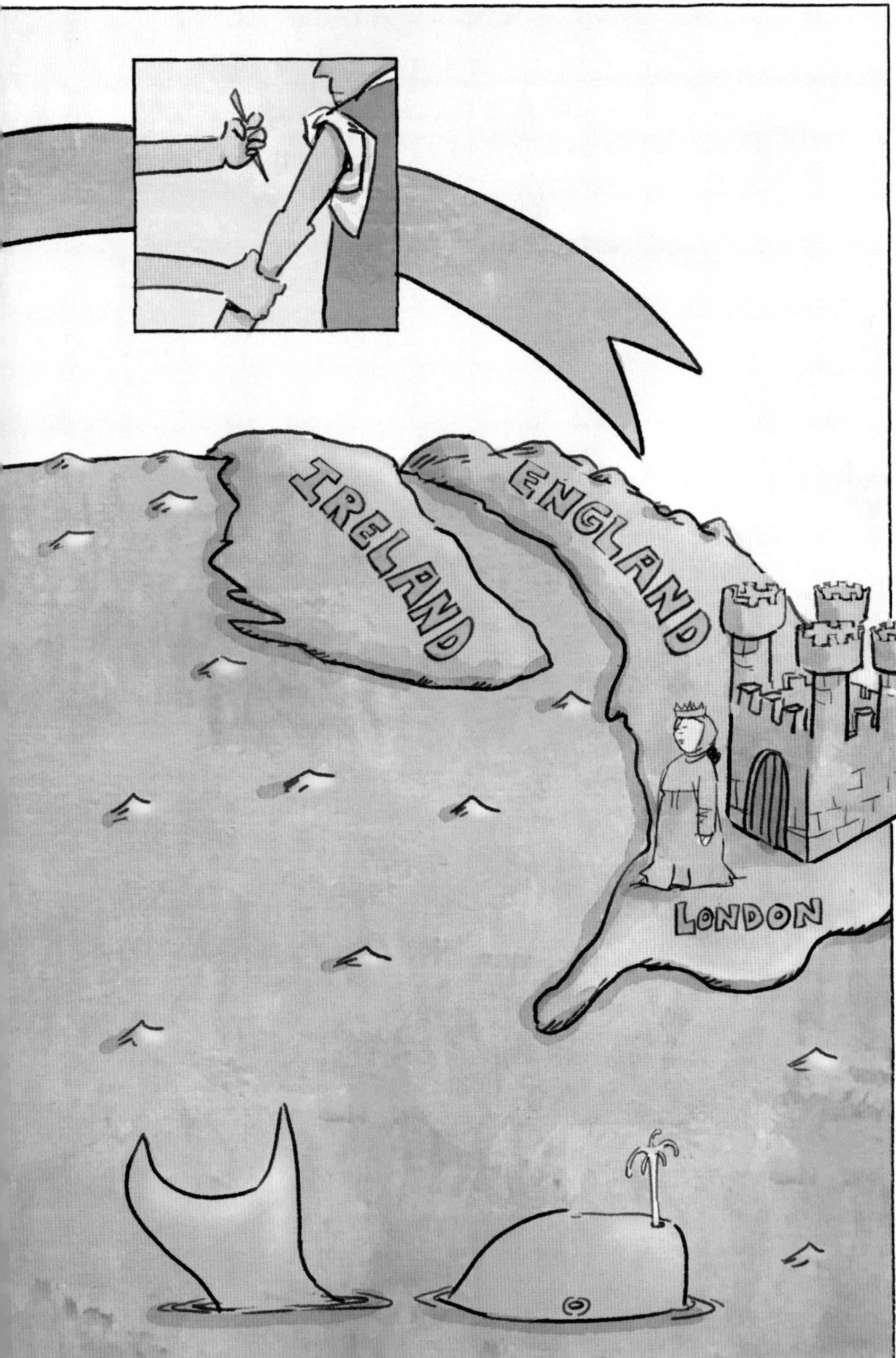
IRELAND
ENGLAND
LONDON

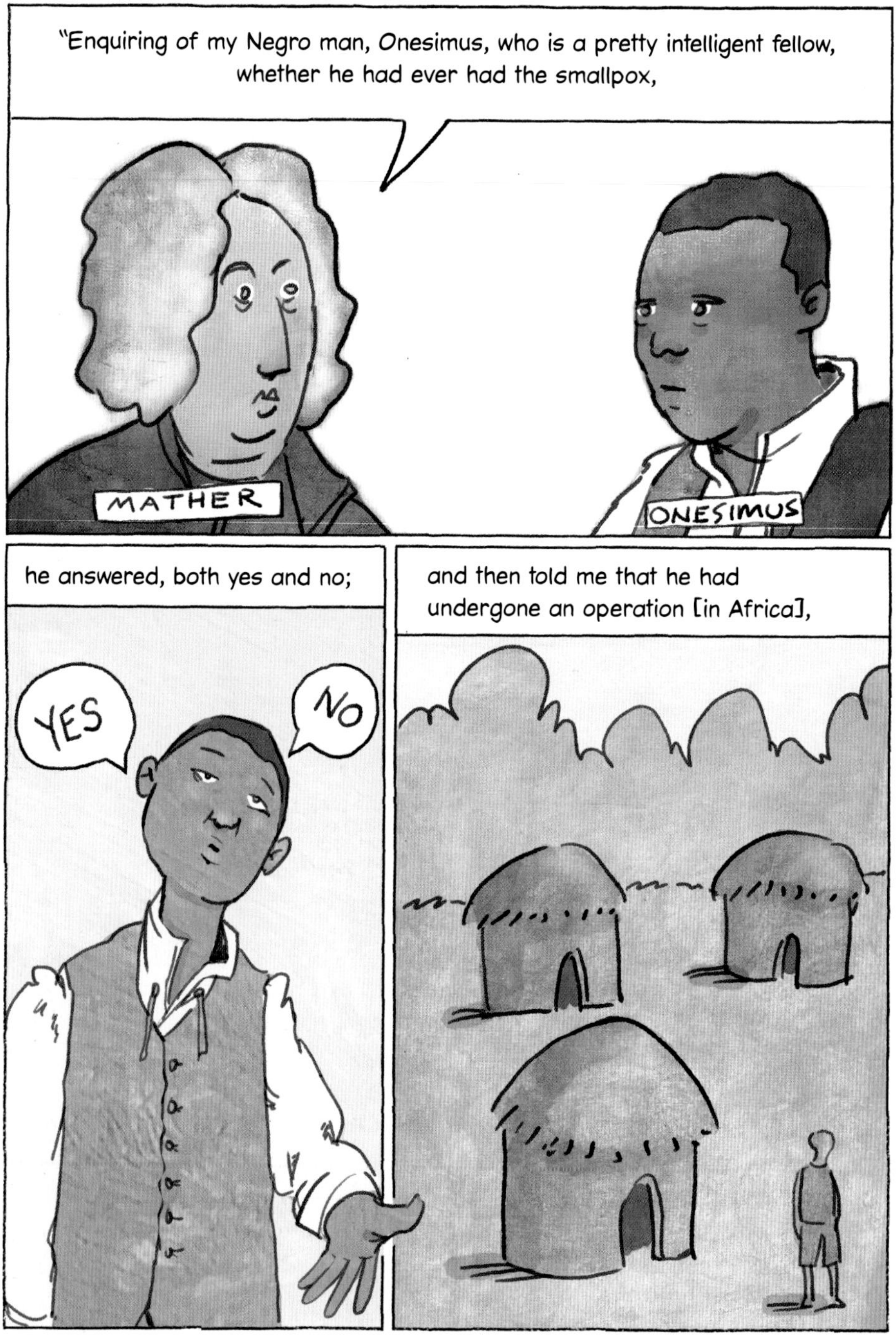
"Enquiring of my Negro man, Onesimus, who is a pretty intelligent fellow, whether he had ever had the smallpox,
MATHER
ONESIMUS
he answered, both yes and no;
YES
NO
and then told me that he had undergone an operation [in Africa],

which had given him something of the smallpox and would forever preserve him from it; adding . . .

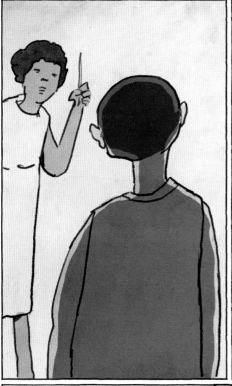

whoever had the courage to use it was forever free of the fear of contagion.

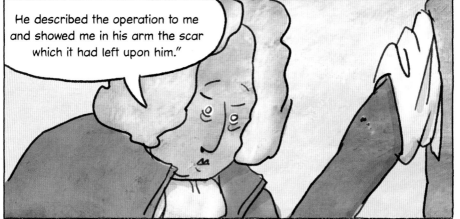

He described the operation to me and showed me in his arm the scar which it had left upon him."

When smallpox struck Boston in the spring of 1721, Mather became a champion of inoculation.

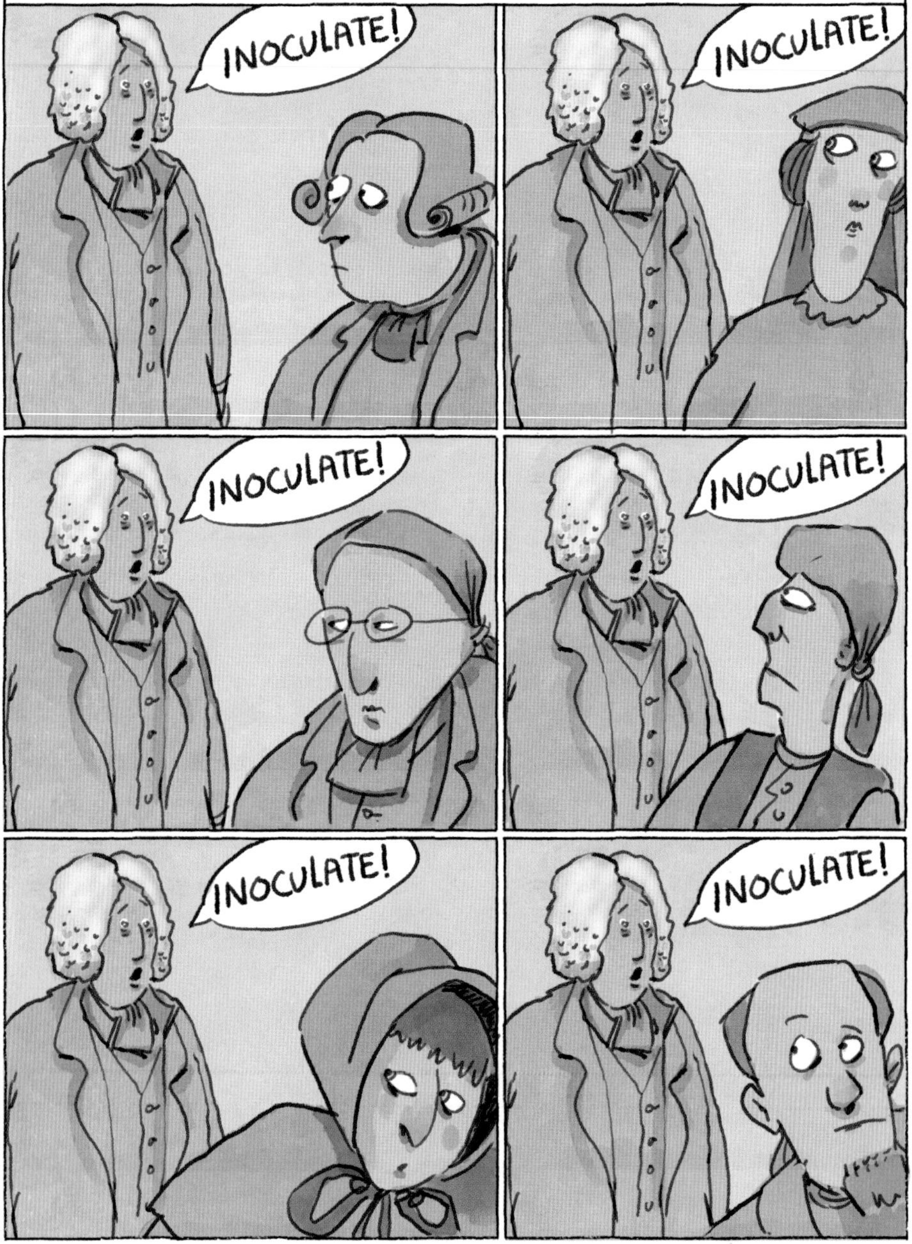
INOCULATE!
INOCULATE!
INOCULATE!
INOCULATE!
INOCULATE!
INOCULATE!

But a local doctor, William Douglass, opposed it, believing it was unproven and dangerous. Or perhaps he was just miffed because a tactless Mather had overstepped the bounds for someone not a doctor. In any case, a battle was joined.

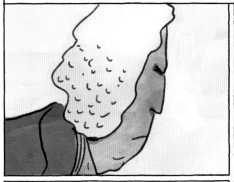 

Most doctors sided with Douglass.

Most Bostonians feared and condemned inoculation.

Town fathers sided with the doctors and ordered inoculations to halt.

Mather's allies ignored them and continued inoculating.

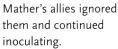

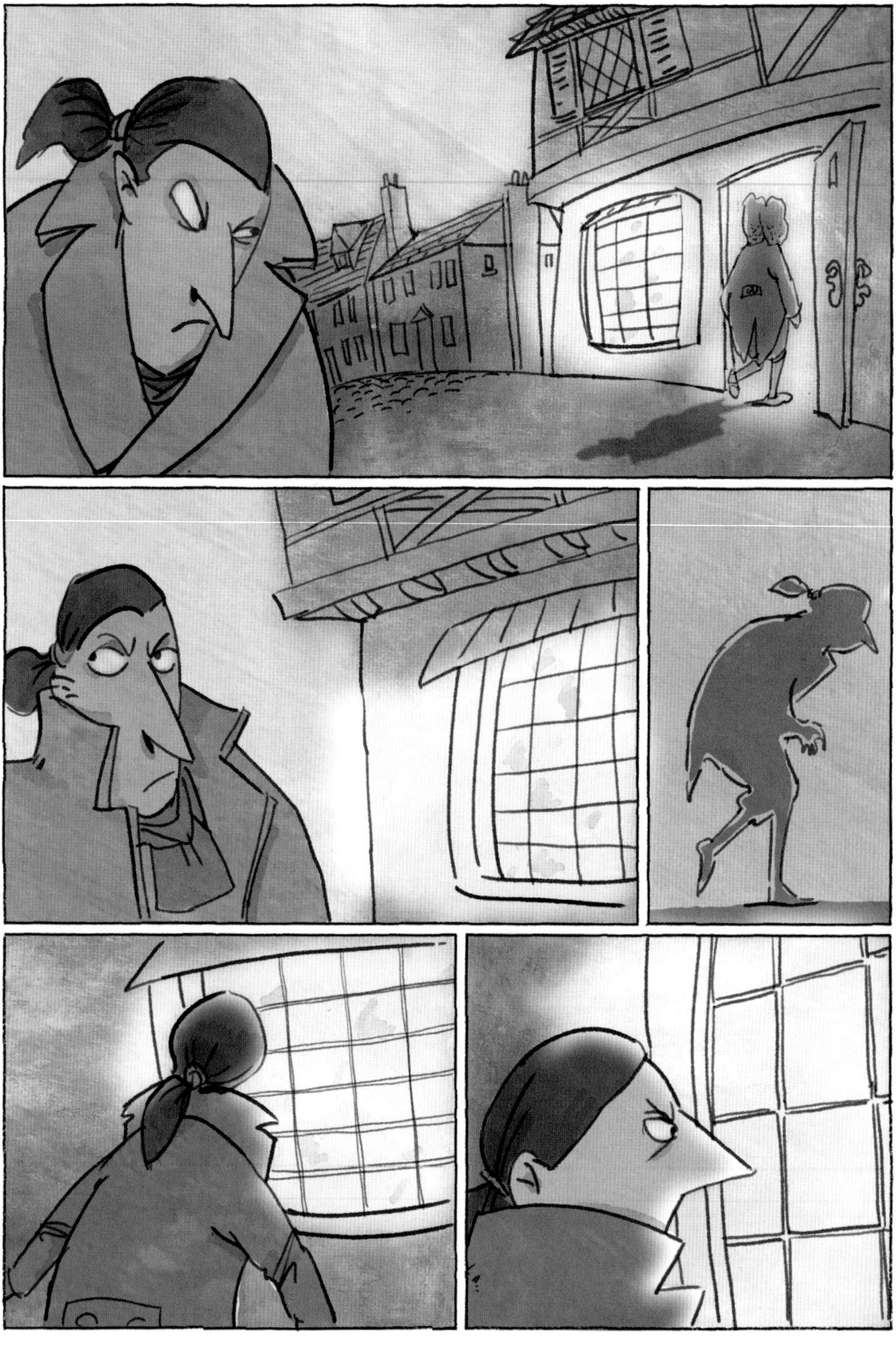

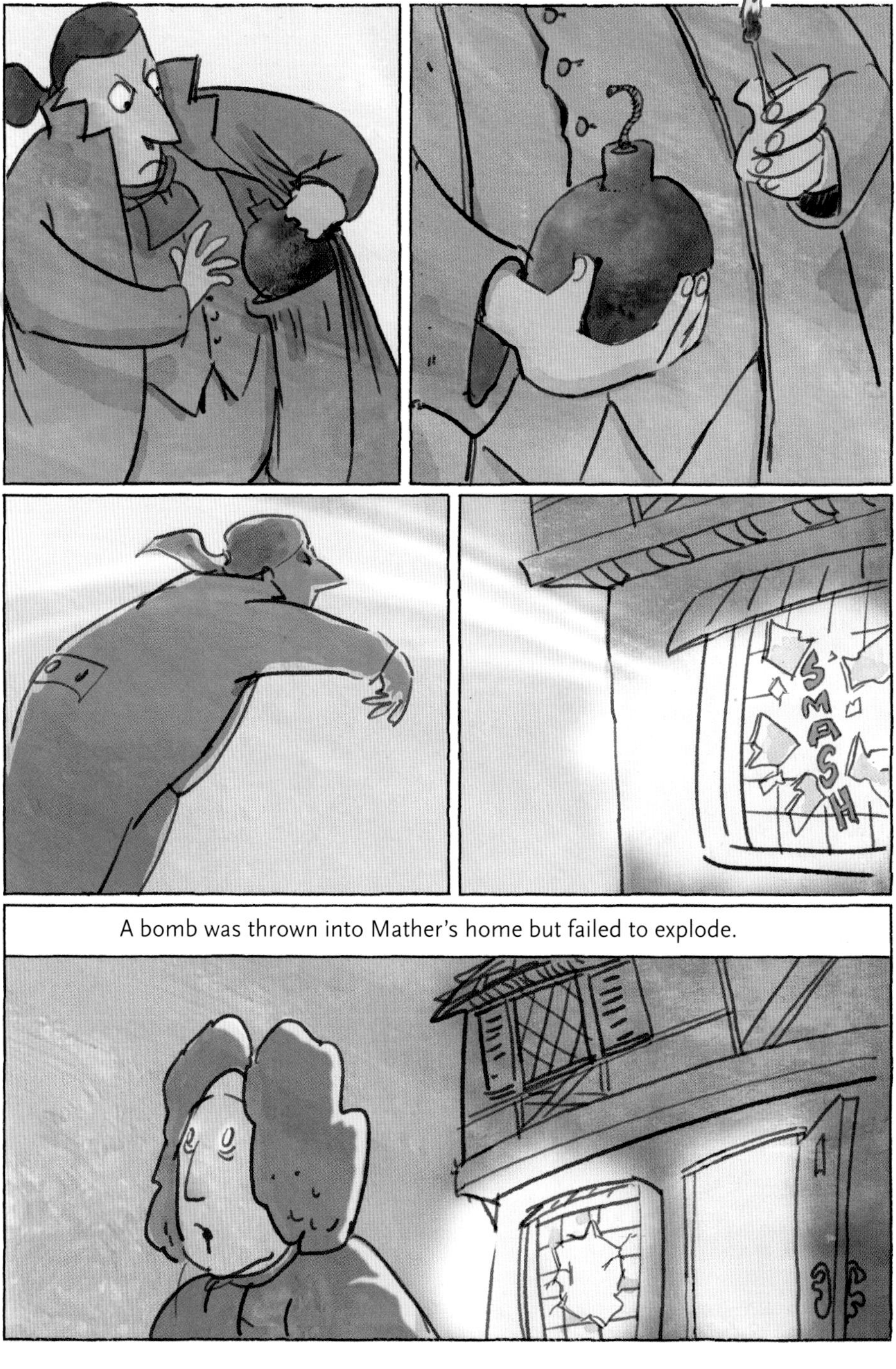
SMASH
A bomb was thrown into Mather's home but failed to explode.

By the time the smallpox epidemic ended, more than half of Boston's 11,000 residents had been sickened and 850 had died.

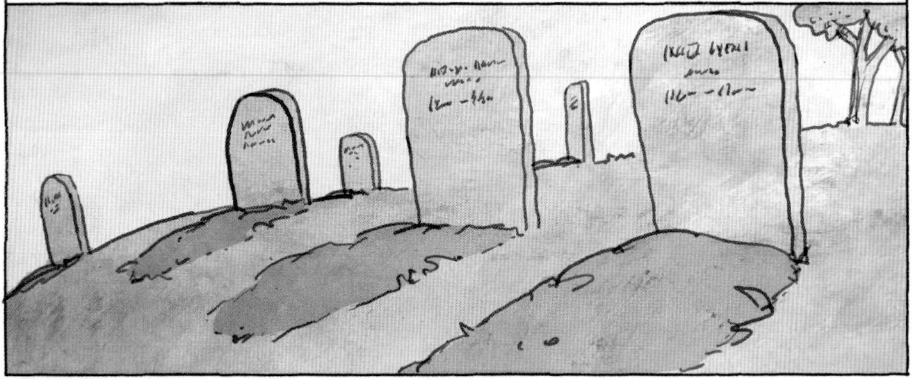

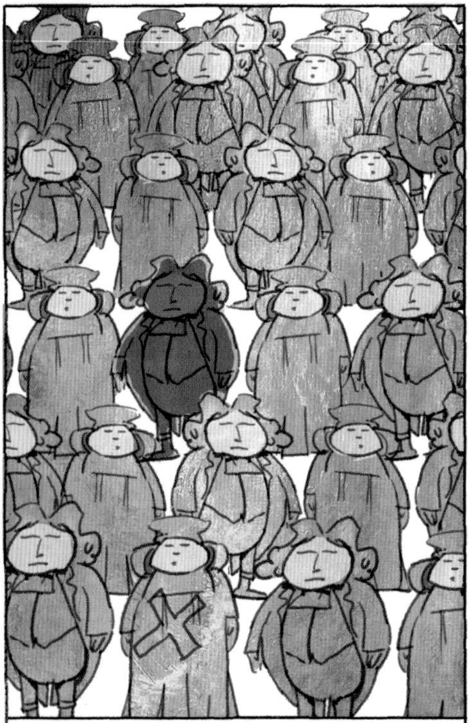

Of the approximately 240 people who had been inoculated, only 6 died, a ratio of only 1 in 40.

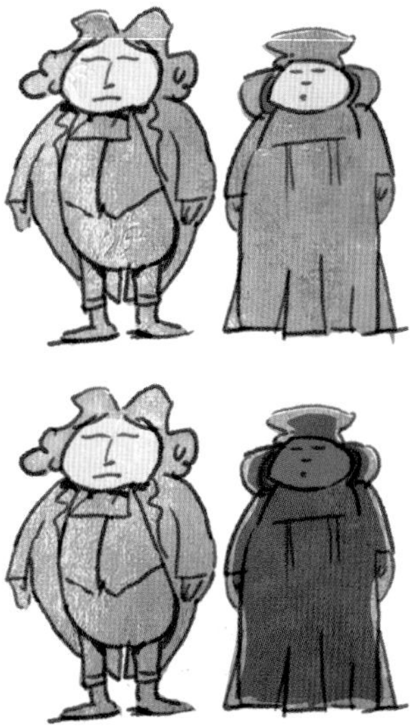

For the others, 1 in 6 died.

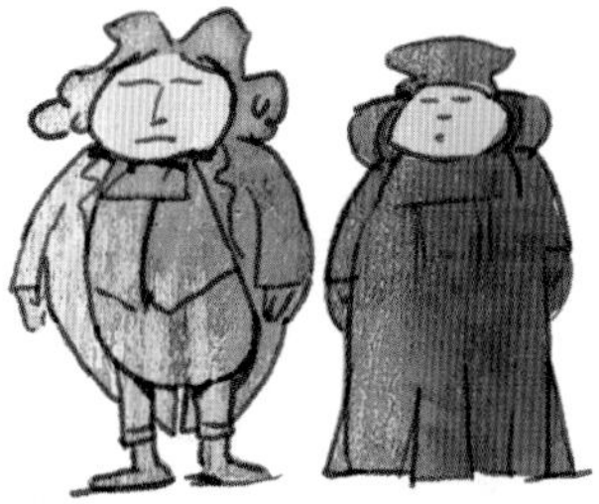

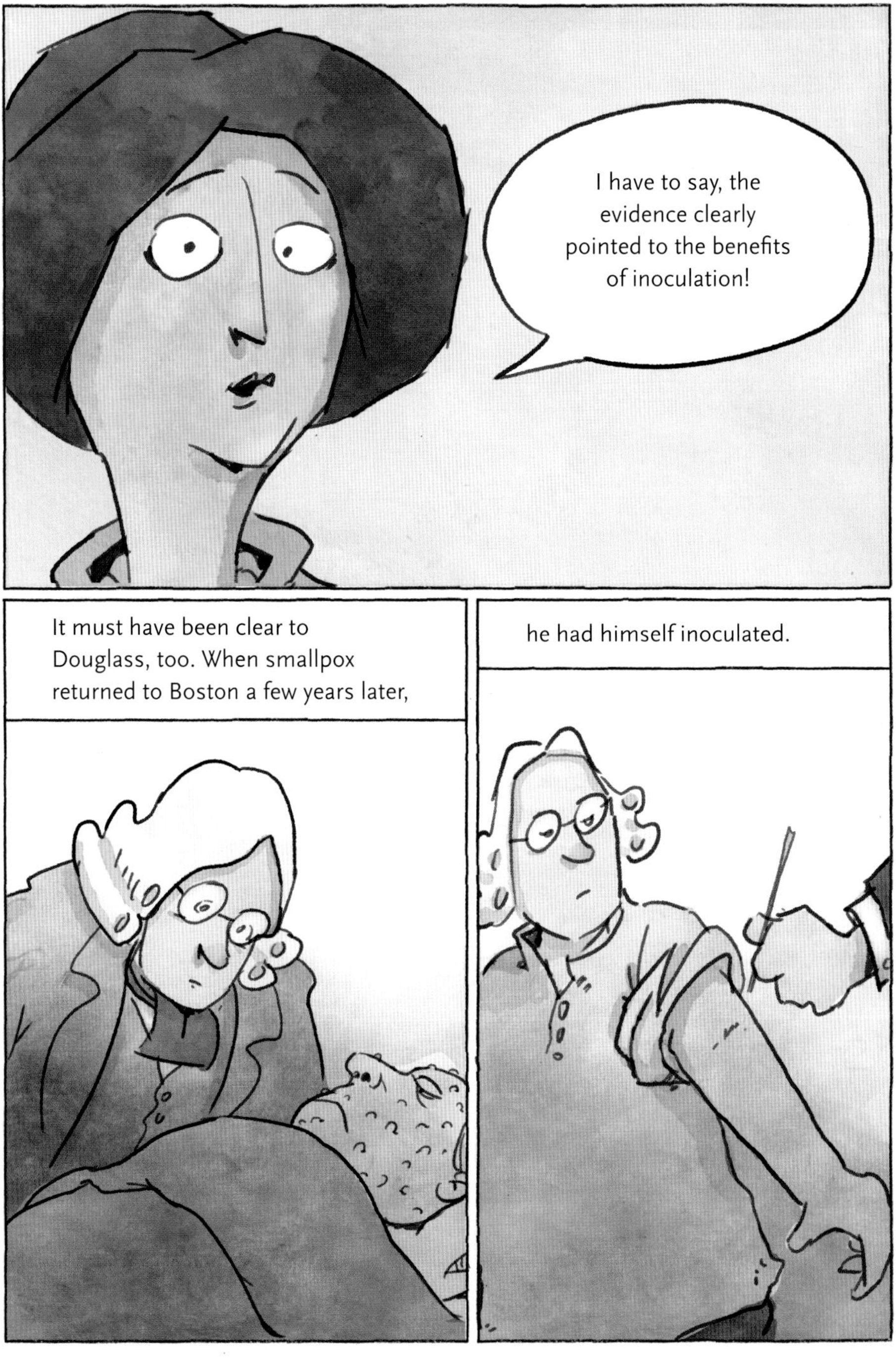
I have to say, the evidence clearly pointed to the benefits of inoculation!
It must have been clear to Douglass, too. When smallpox returned to Boston a few years later,
he had himself inoculated.

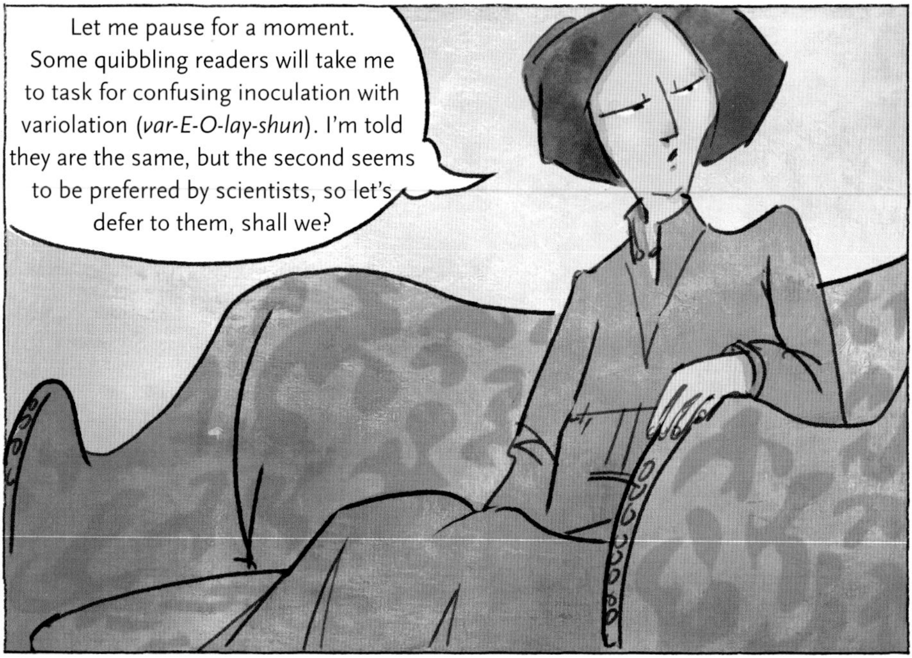
Let me pause for a moment. Some quibbling readers will take me to task for confusing inoculation with variolation (*var-E-O-lay-shun*). I'm told they are the same, but the second seems to be preferred by scientists, so let's defer to them, shall we?

Back in England, the popularity of variolation continued, making for a blossoming business for those enterprising souls who provided it.

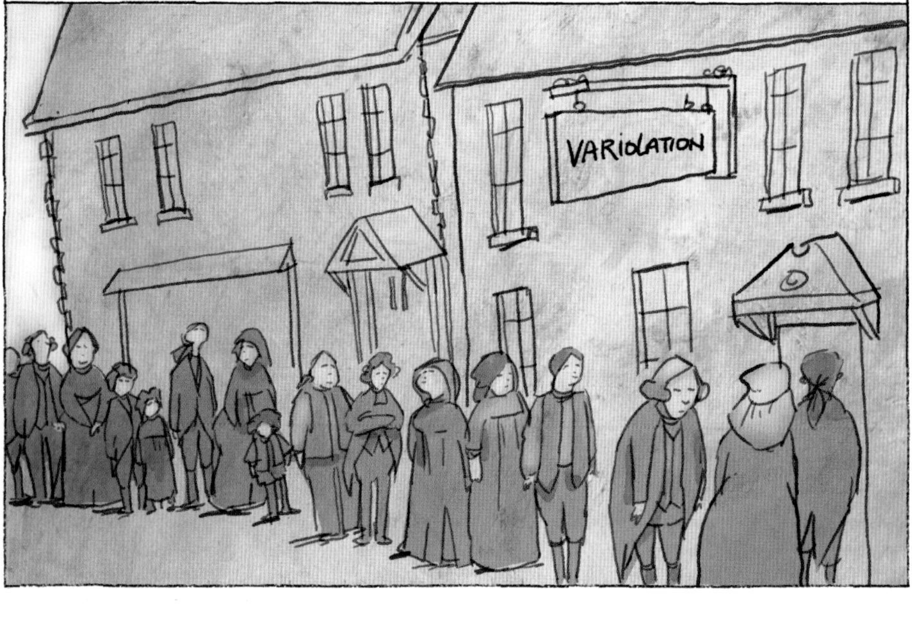
VARIOLATION

And one of them, Dr. John Fewster of the west of England, had a curious experience.

He variolated two brothers and waited for a mild case of smallpox to erupt. But nothing happened.

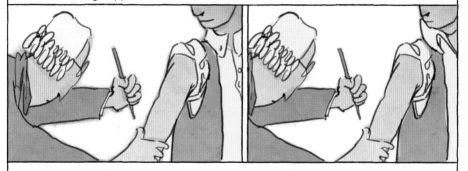

Fewster tried two more times, but still nothing.

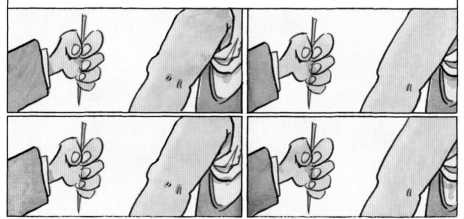

Later, Fewster joined fellow doctors at a local inn and shared his puzzling tale in which multiple variolations hadn't triggered any responses in the brothers.

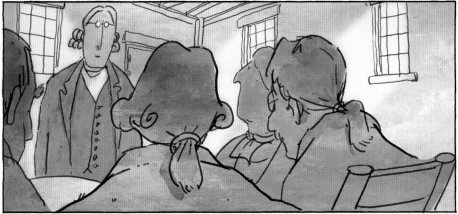

And he added a twist to the story: The brothers had said that although they'd never had smallpox before, they'd both had cowpox.

Cowpox infects cows, who then pass on it to people, mostly milkmaids—women whose job it is to milk cows. Its victims suffer a blister-like rash, but the blisters leave little scarring and, best of all, cowpox doesn't kill.

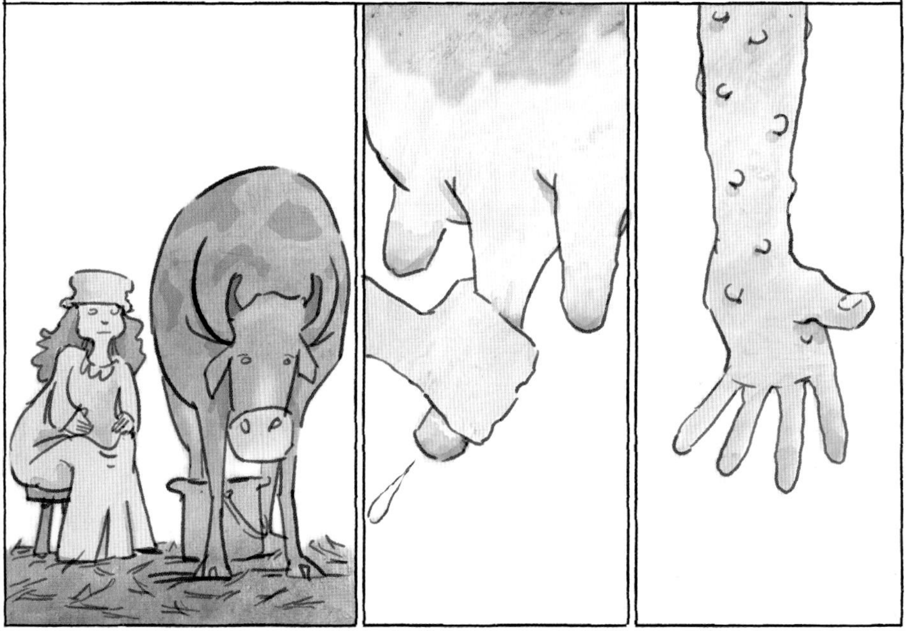

It's hard to say if Fewster's perplexing story made much of an impression on the doctors, but I can say it intrigued one of the doctor's apprentices, thirteen-year-old Edward Jenner.

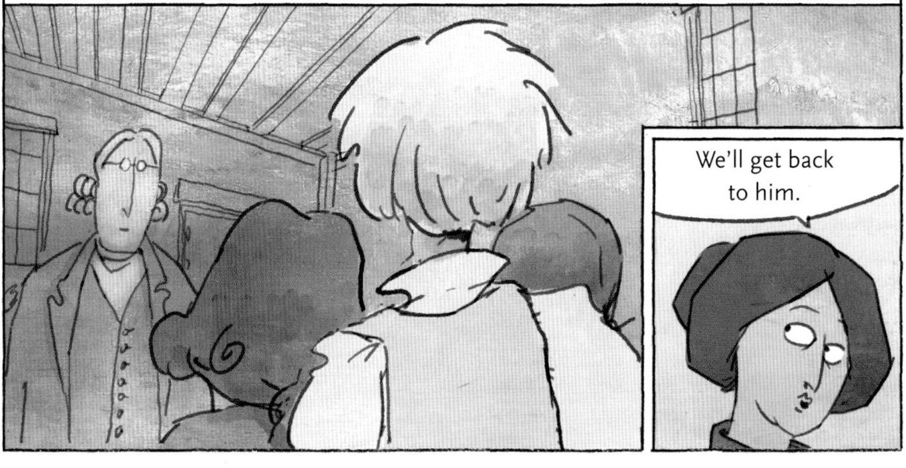
We'll get back to him.

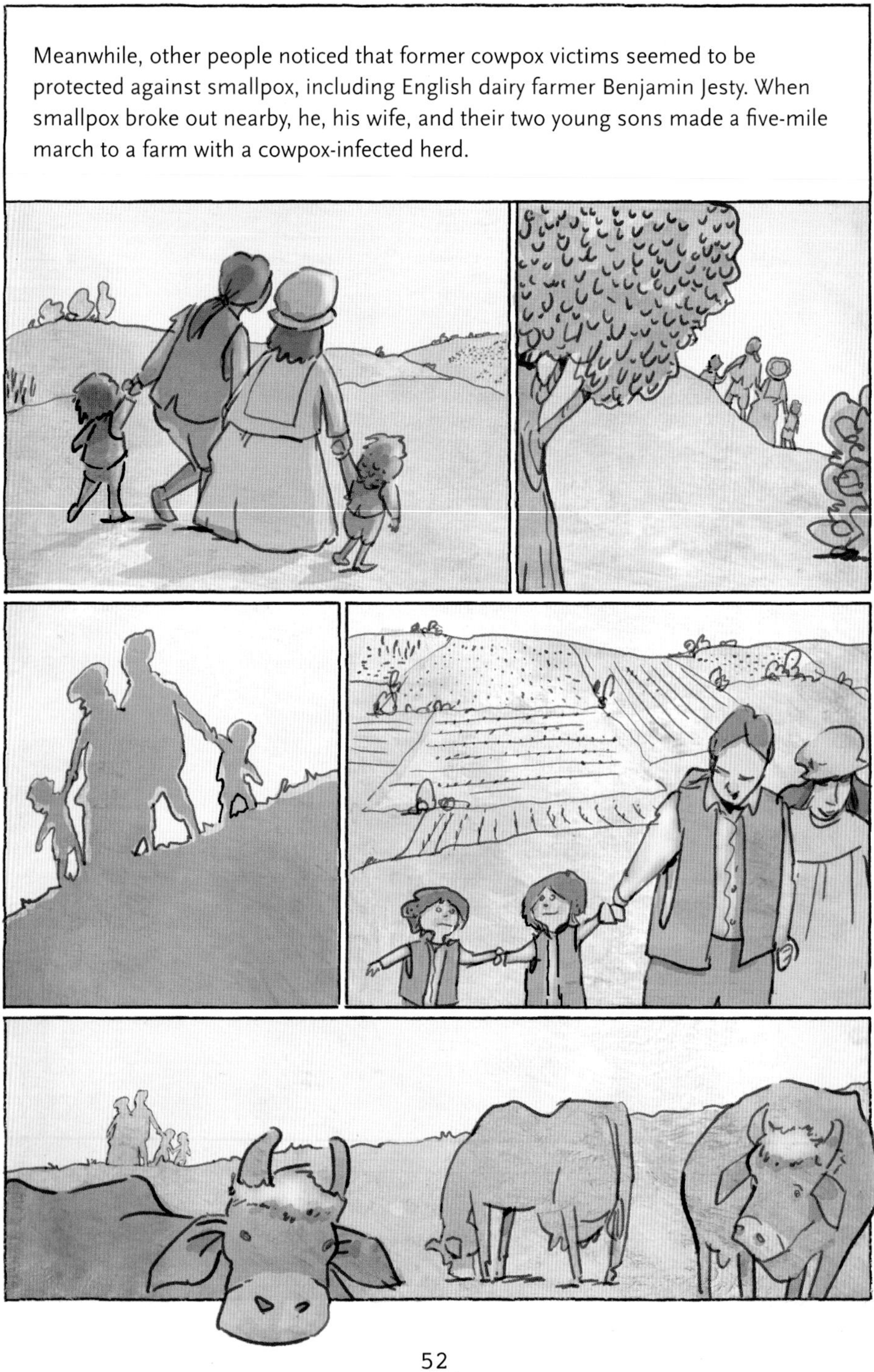
Meanwhile, other people noticed that former cowpox victims seemed to be protected against smallpox, including English dairy farmer Benjamin Jesty. When smallpox broke out nearby, he, his wife, and their two young sons made a five-mile march to a farm with a cowpox-infected herd.

Smearing a needle with the infected glop from a sick cow's udder, he scratched the arms of his family members near the elbow.

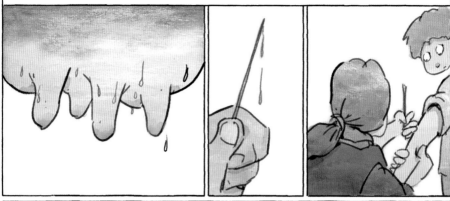

Jesty's neighbors were outraged. They tossed stones at the family, forcing them to move away.

They feared the cowpox would transform the Jestys into horned beasts, like . . . cows!

I have to say, sometimes people can be so silly. And, in the end, the Jestys escaped smallpox.

Meanwhile, in Germany, school tutor Peter Plett had learned of the protective qualities of cowpox and shared the story with two students, sisters Hedwig and Margaret. When smallpox raged around them, the girls became determined not to be disfigured by the disease.

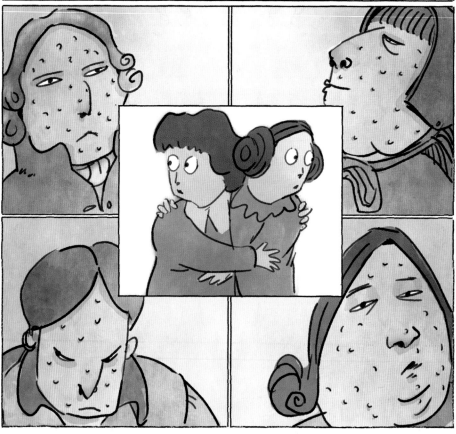

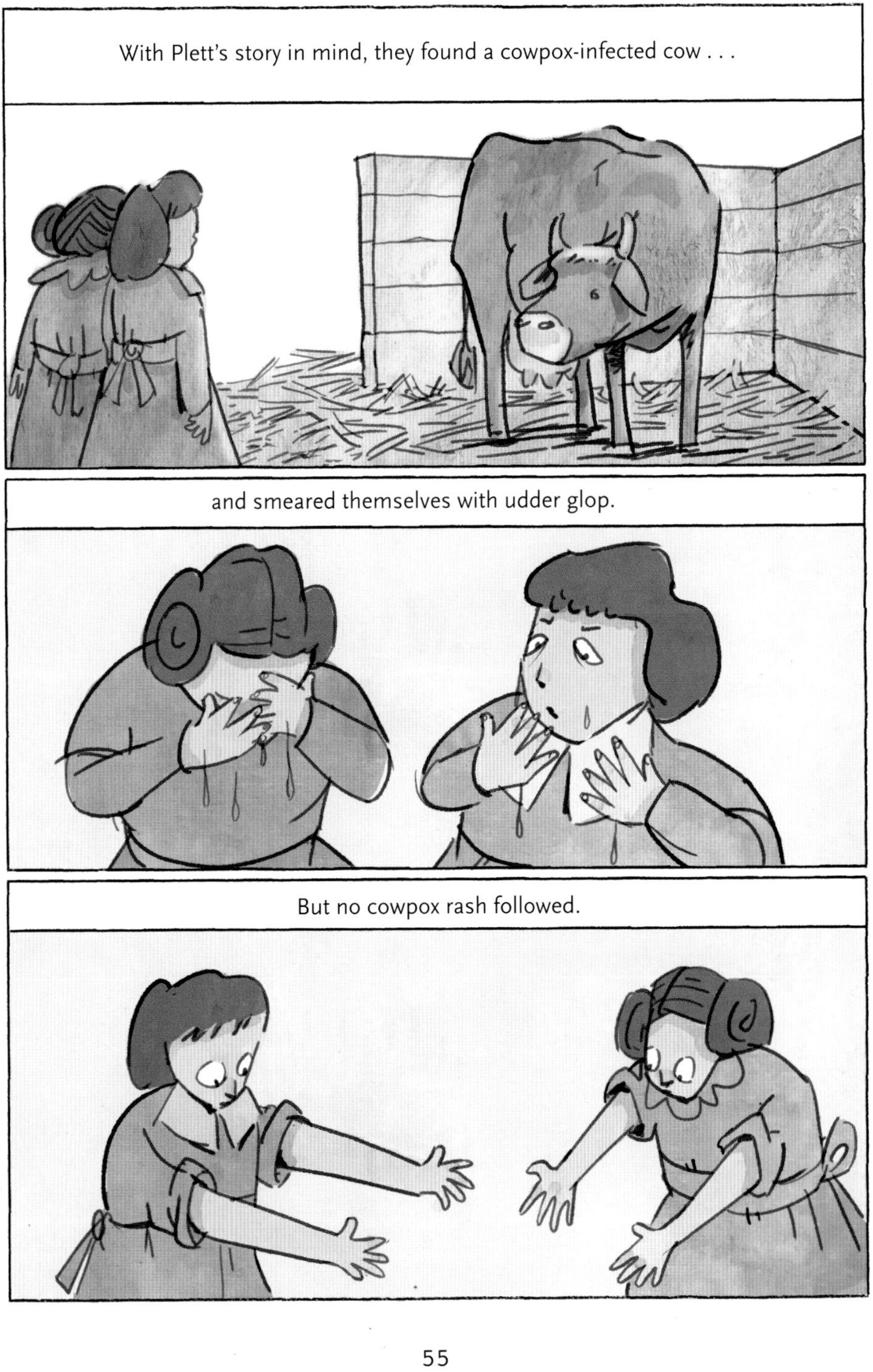
With Plett's story in mind, they found a cowpox-infected cow . . .
and smeared themselves with udder glop.
But no cowpox rash followed.

The girls appealed to Plett.

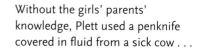

Without the girls' parents' knowledge, Plett used a penknife covered in fluid from a sick cow . . .

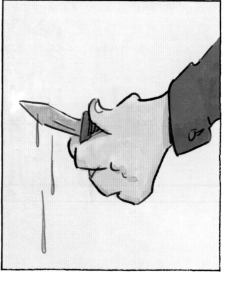

to scratch the girls' hands between the thumb and index finger.

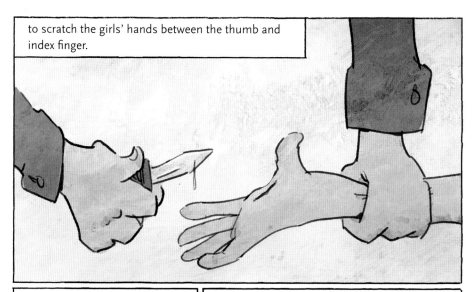

We can only guess how Hedwig and Margaret's parents received the news. How would your parents respond?

In any case, a cowpox rash appeared on each girl . . . and—more important—neither developed smallpox.

Peter Plett spoke to scholars, sharing his story of thwarting smallpox with cowpox, but they were unmoved.

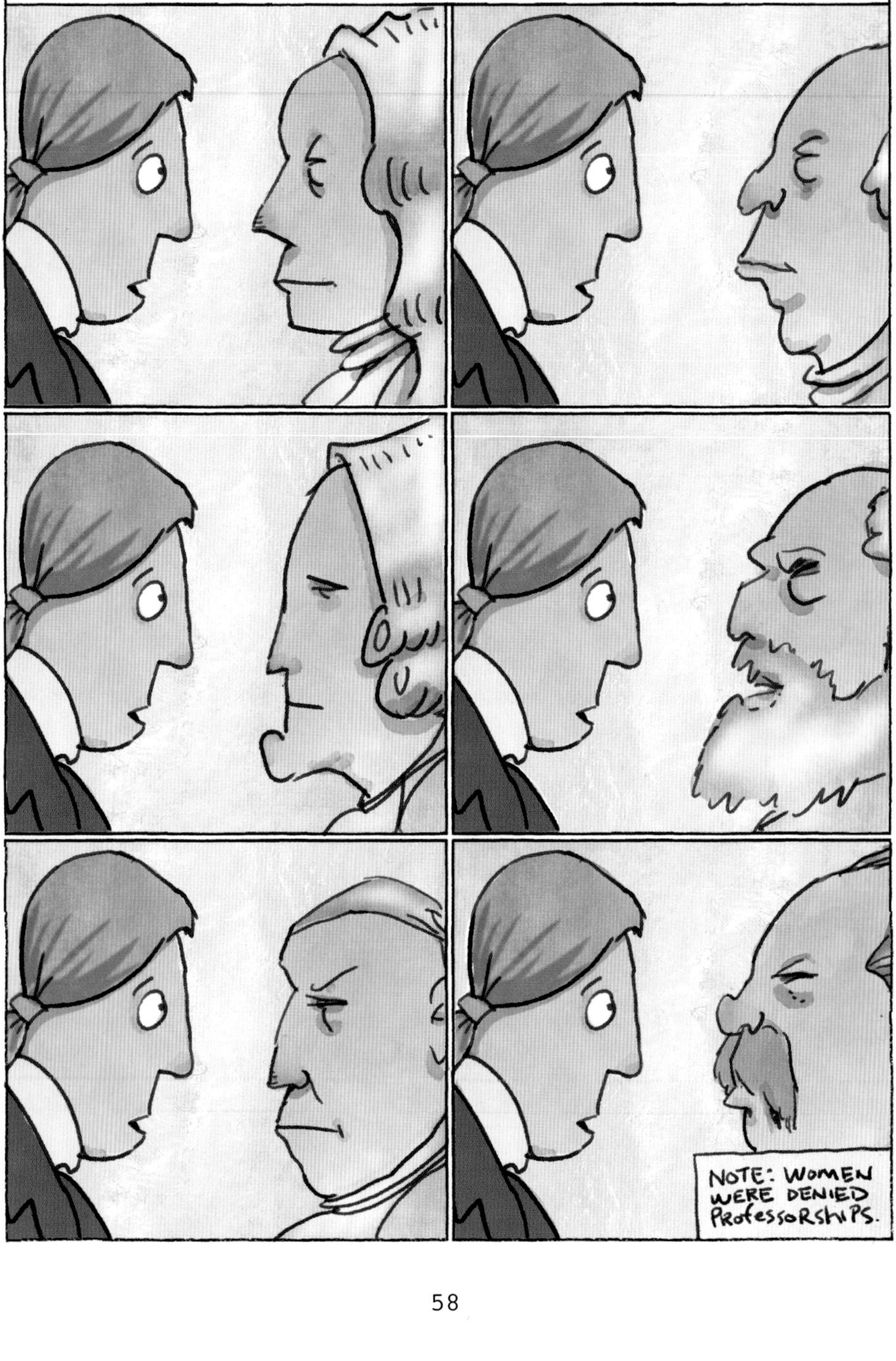
NOTE: WOMEN WERE DENIED PROFESSORSHIPS.

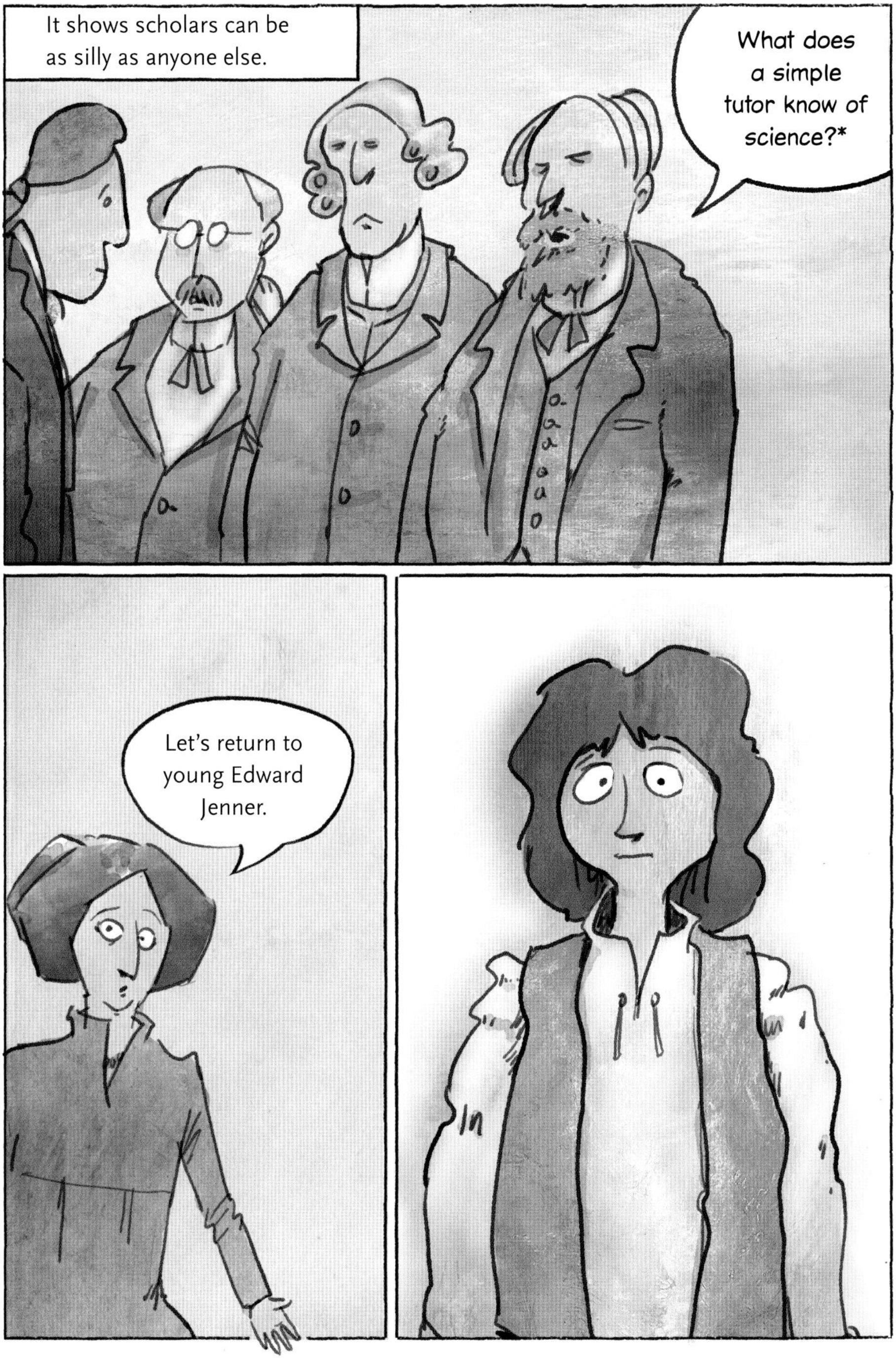
It shows scholars can be as silly as anyone else.
What does a simple tutor know of science?*
Let's return to young Edward Jenner.

No longer an apprentice, but a trained doctor,

Jenner never lost his interest in the connection between cowpox and smallpox. Practicing medicine in farm country during the late 1700s, he observed . . .

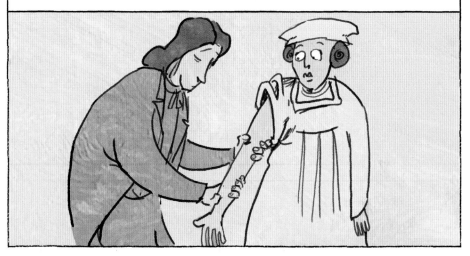

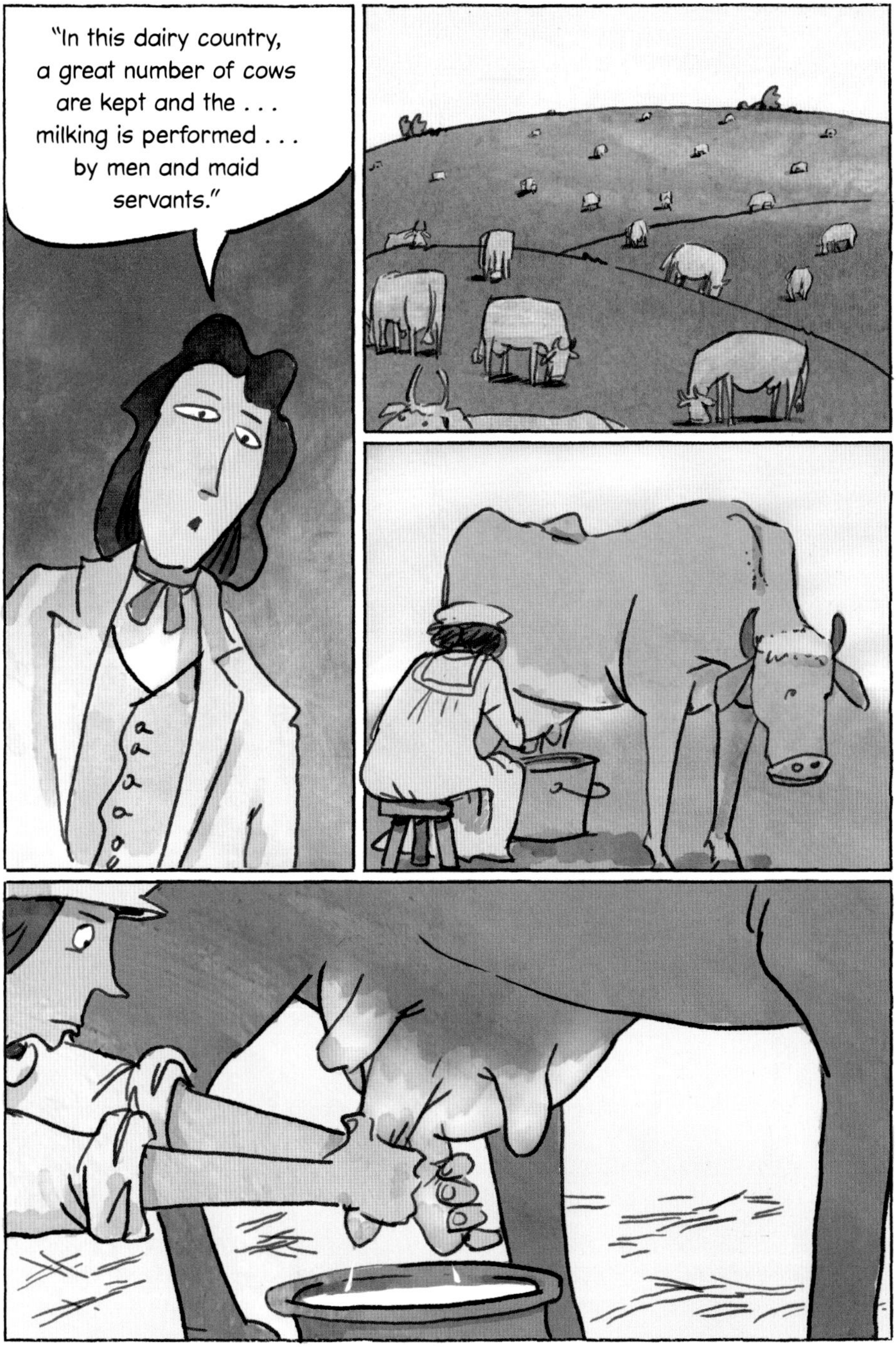
"In this dairy country, a great number of cows are kept and the . . . milking is performed . . . by men and maid servants."

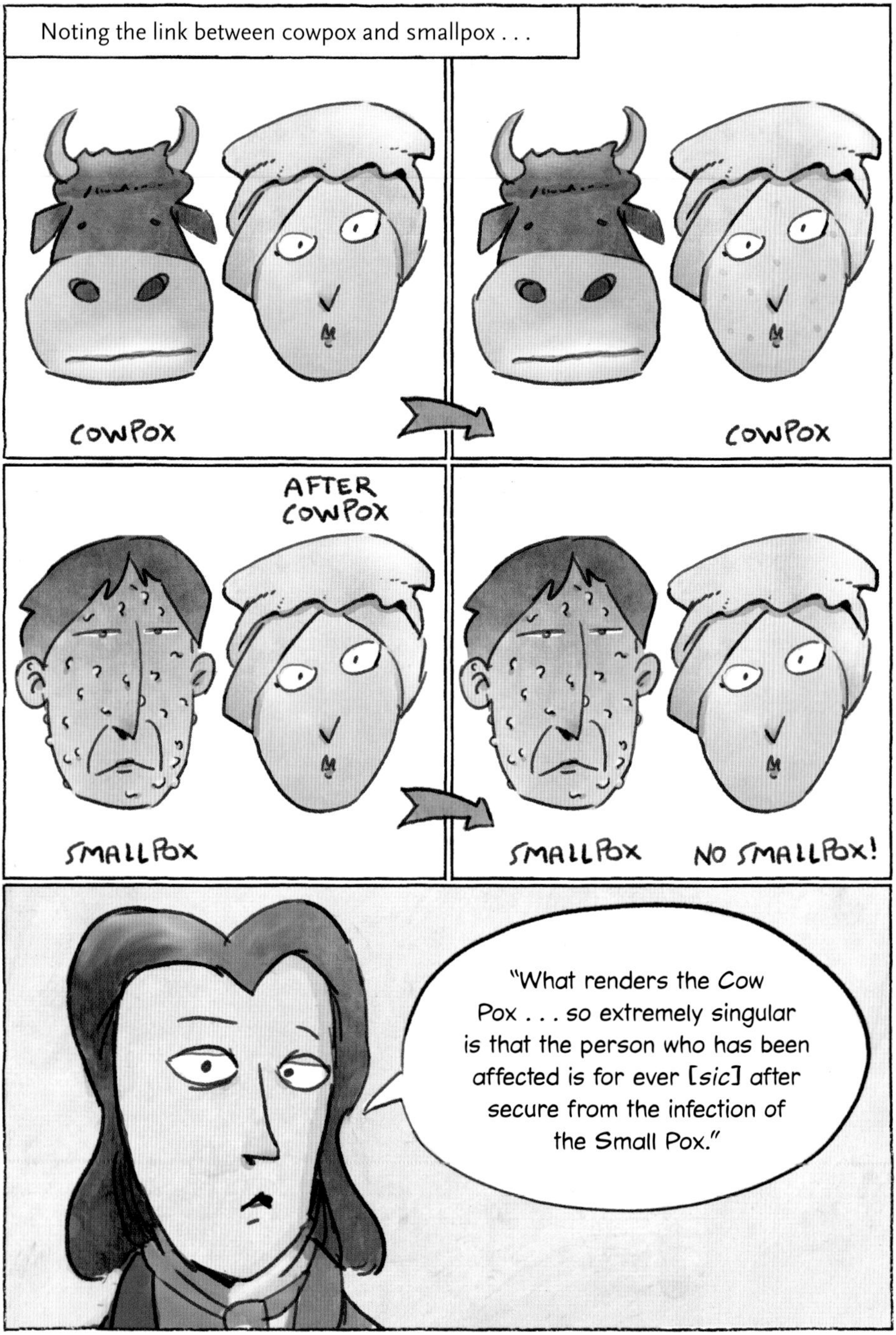
Noting the link between cowpox and smallpox . . .
COWPOX
COWPOX
AFTER COWPOX
SMALLPOX
SMALLPOX
NO SMALLPOX!
"What renders the Cow Pox . . . so extremely singular is that the person who has been affected is for ever [*sic*] after secure from the infection of the Small Pox."

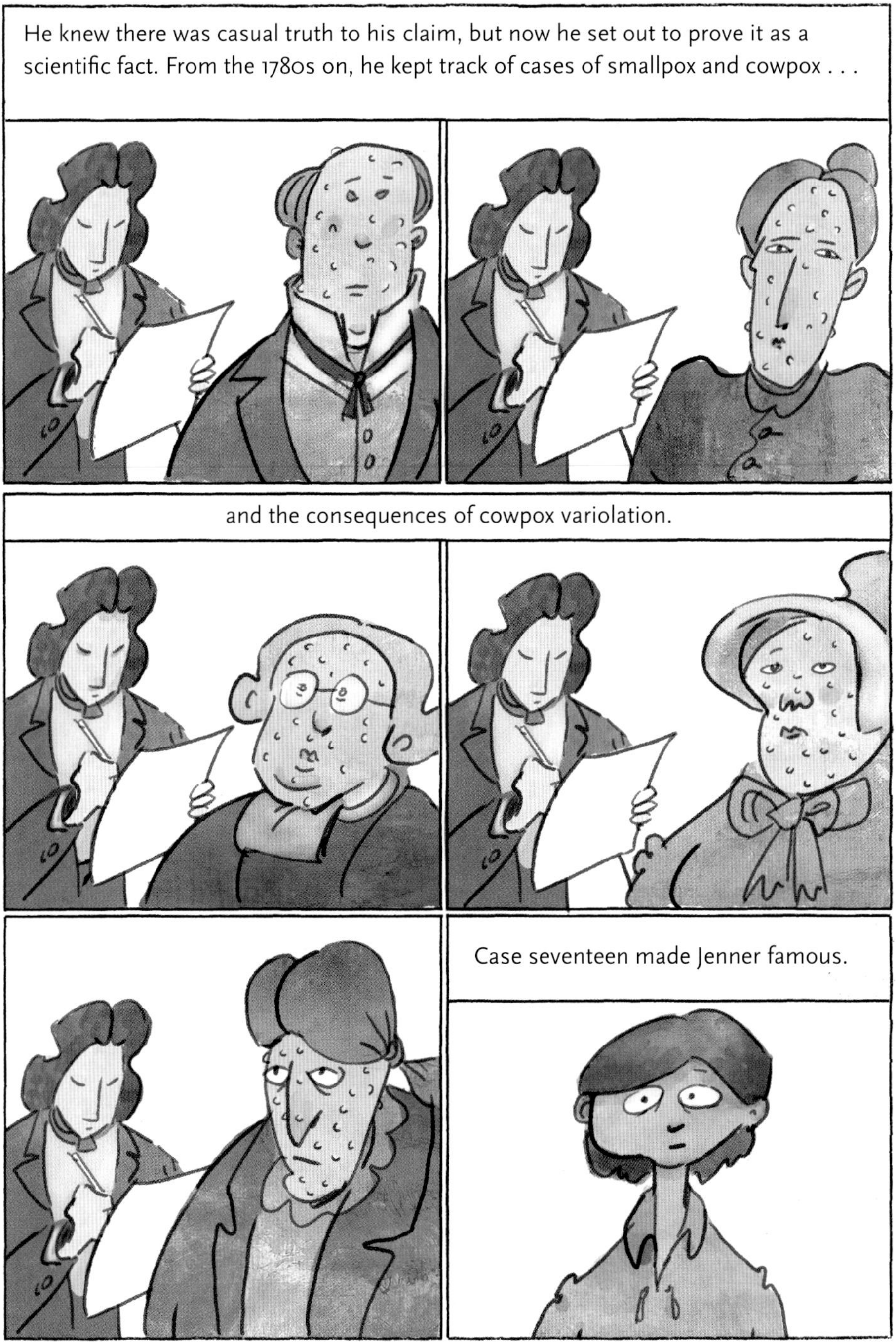
He knew there was casual truth to his claim, but now he set out to prove it as a scientific fact. From the 1780s on, he kept track of cases of smallpox and cowpox . . .
and the consequences of cowpox variolation.
Case seventeen made Jenner famous.

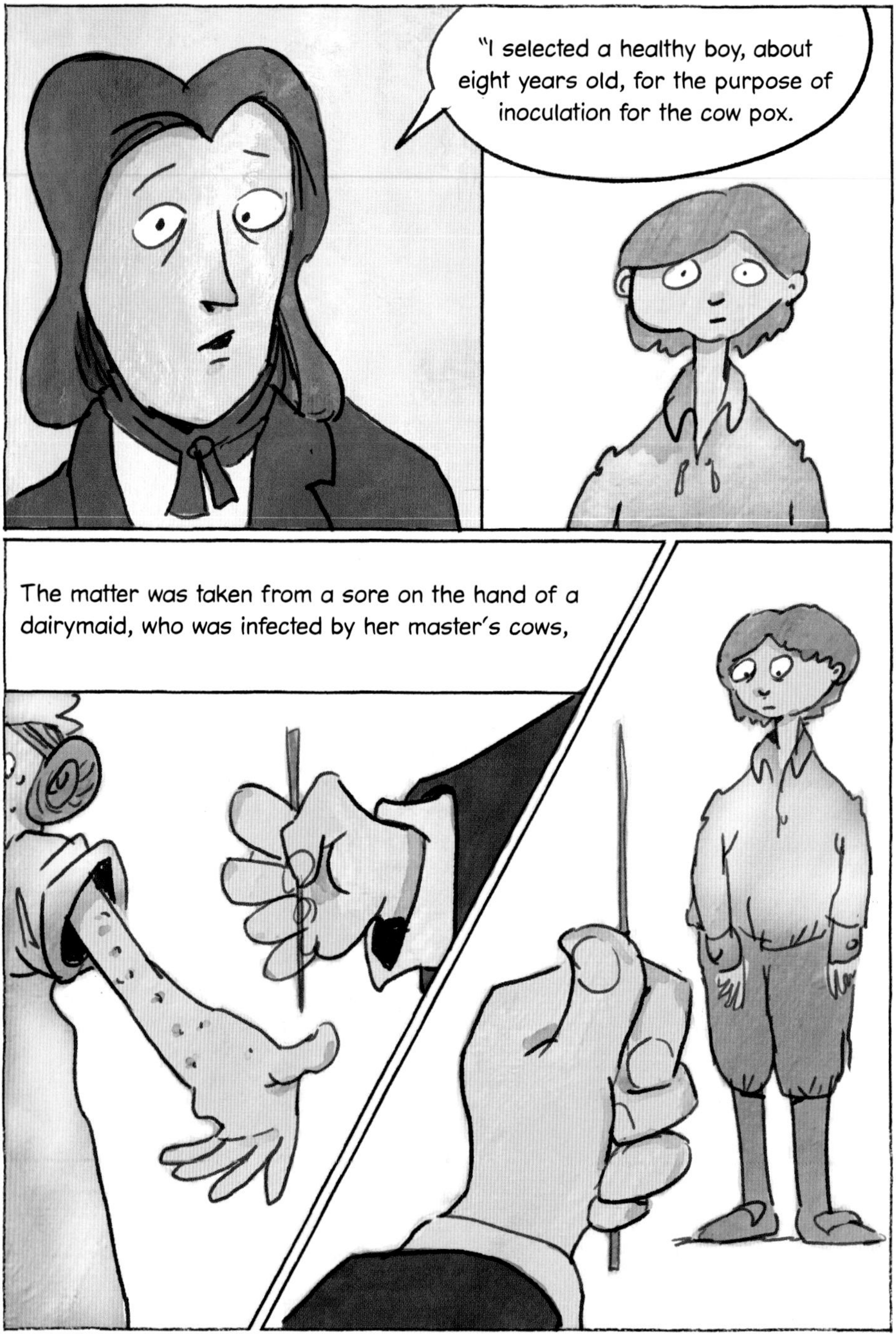
"I selected a healthy boy, about eight years old, for the purpose of inoculation for the cow pox.
The matter was taken from a sore on the hand of a dairymaid, who was infected by her master's cows,

and it was inserted, on the 14th of May, 1796, in the arm of the boy by means of two . . . incisions . . . each about half an inch along."

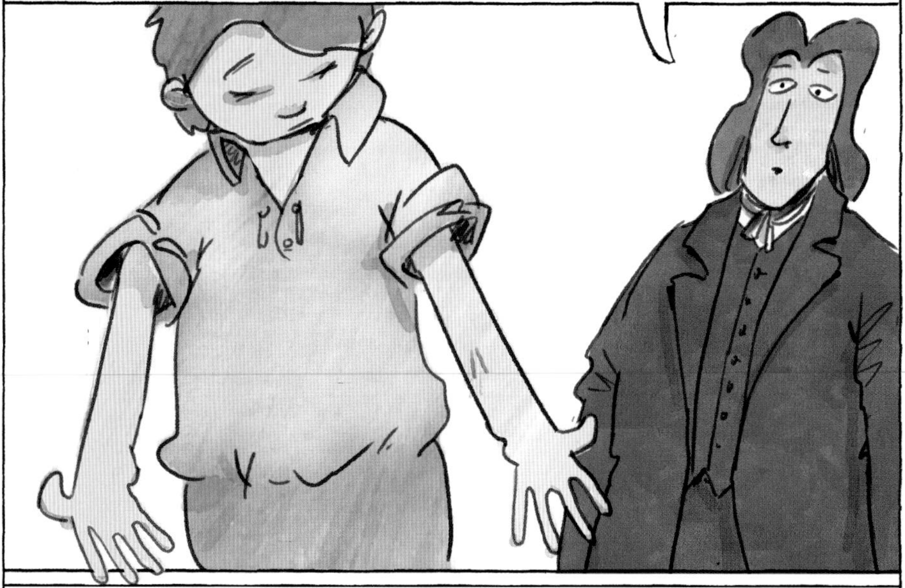

The boy, James Phipps, suffered a short-lived headache, chills, and loss of appetite. There was a bit of infection on the cuts on his arm. Then, he was inoculated with small pox taken from a pustule, but no disease followed. After several months he was inoculated again, and no disease appeared.

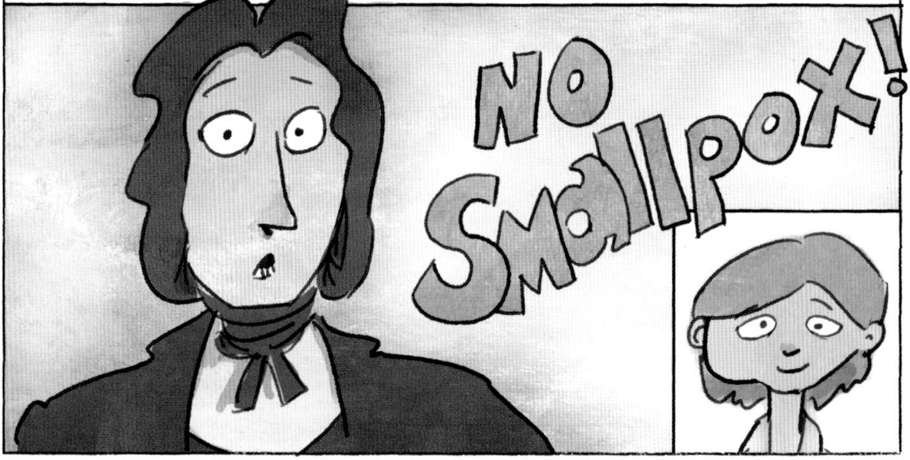
NO SMALLPOX!

Jenner proved there was a better way to protect people from dreadful smallpox!

He called his procedure *vaccination*, from the Latin word *vaccinus*, meaning "from cows."

The advantages over variolation were plain: The subject needn't suffer actual smallpox, or any risk—however small—of death and disfigurement. And since smallpox wasn't present, there was no need to isolate the person to prevent passing the disease to others.

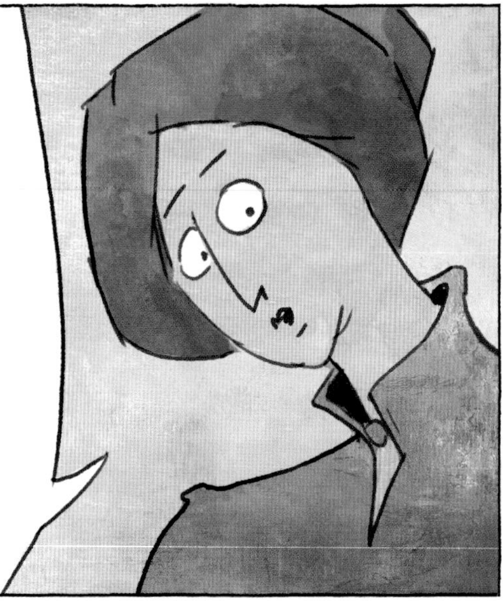

Smallpox vaccination spread in the beginning of the 1800s.

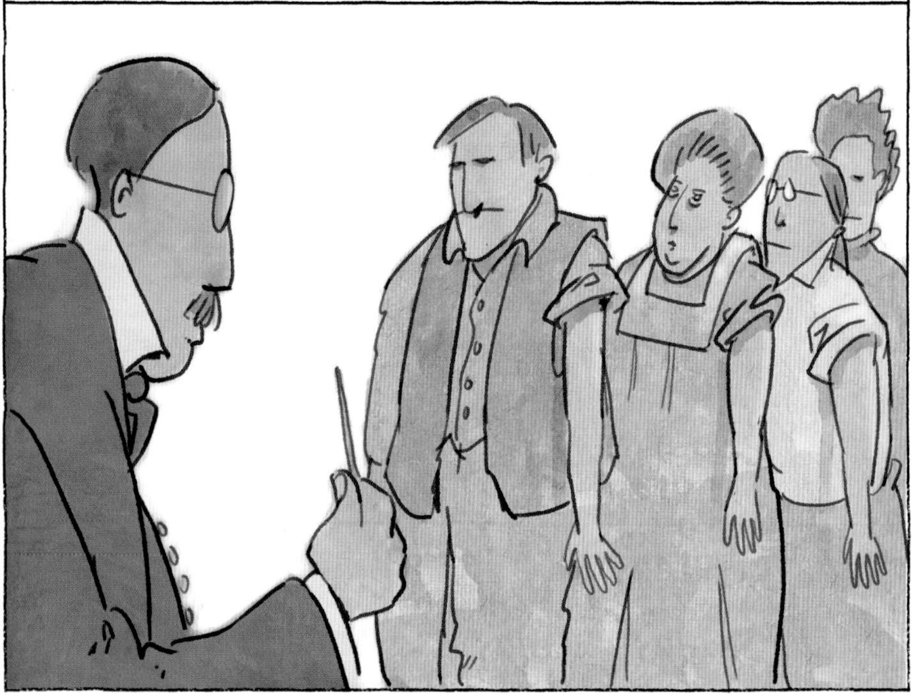

Despite its promise to destroy a wicked and hateful disease, some people objected to its use, especially after governments made it mandatory, meaning they forced everyone to get vaccinated.

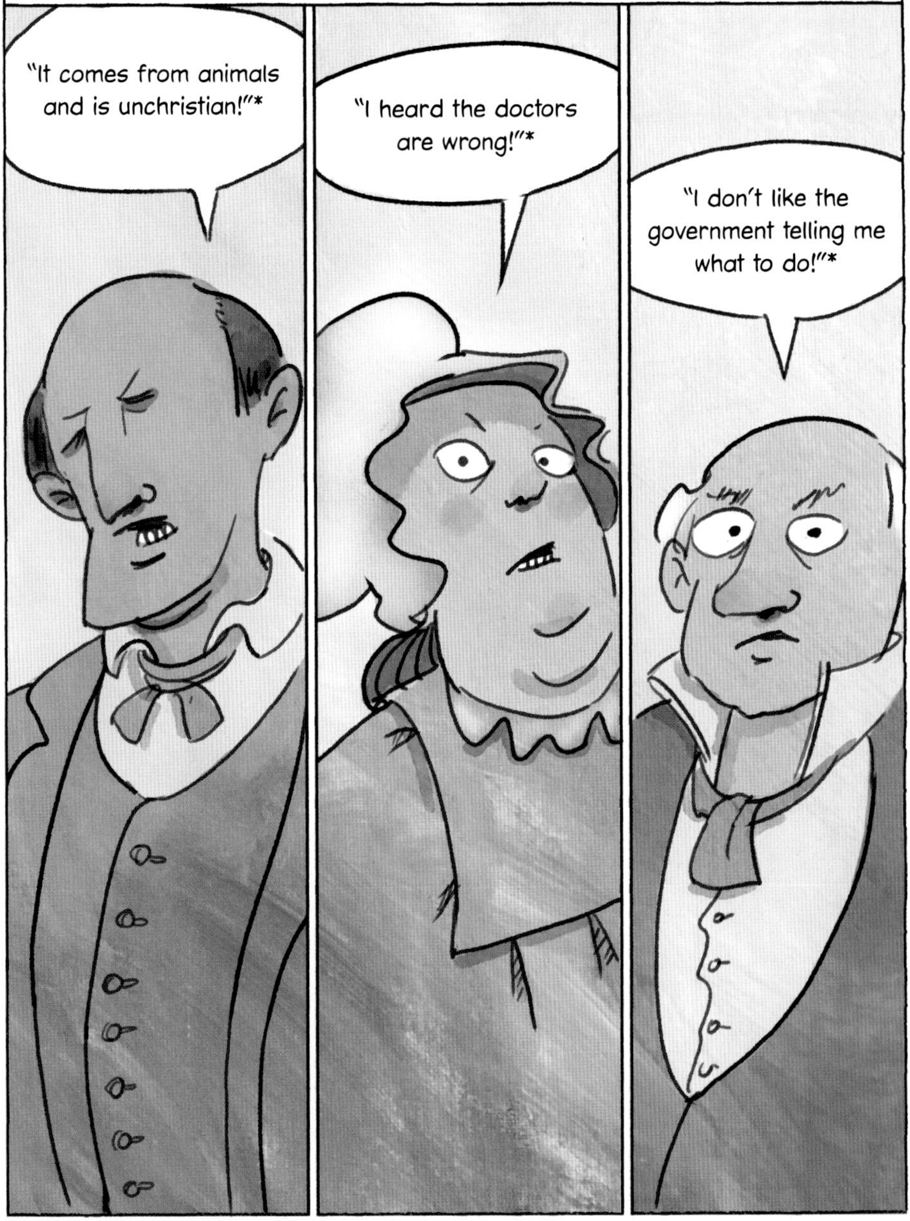
"It comes from animals and is unchristian!"*
"I heard the doctors are wrong!"*
"I don't like the government telling me what to do!"*

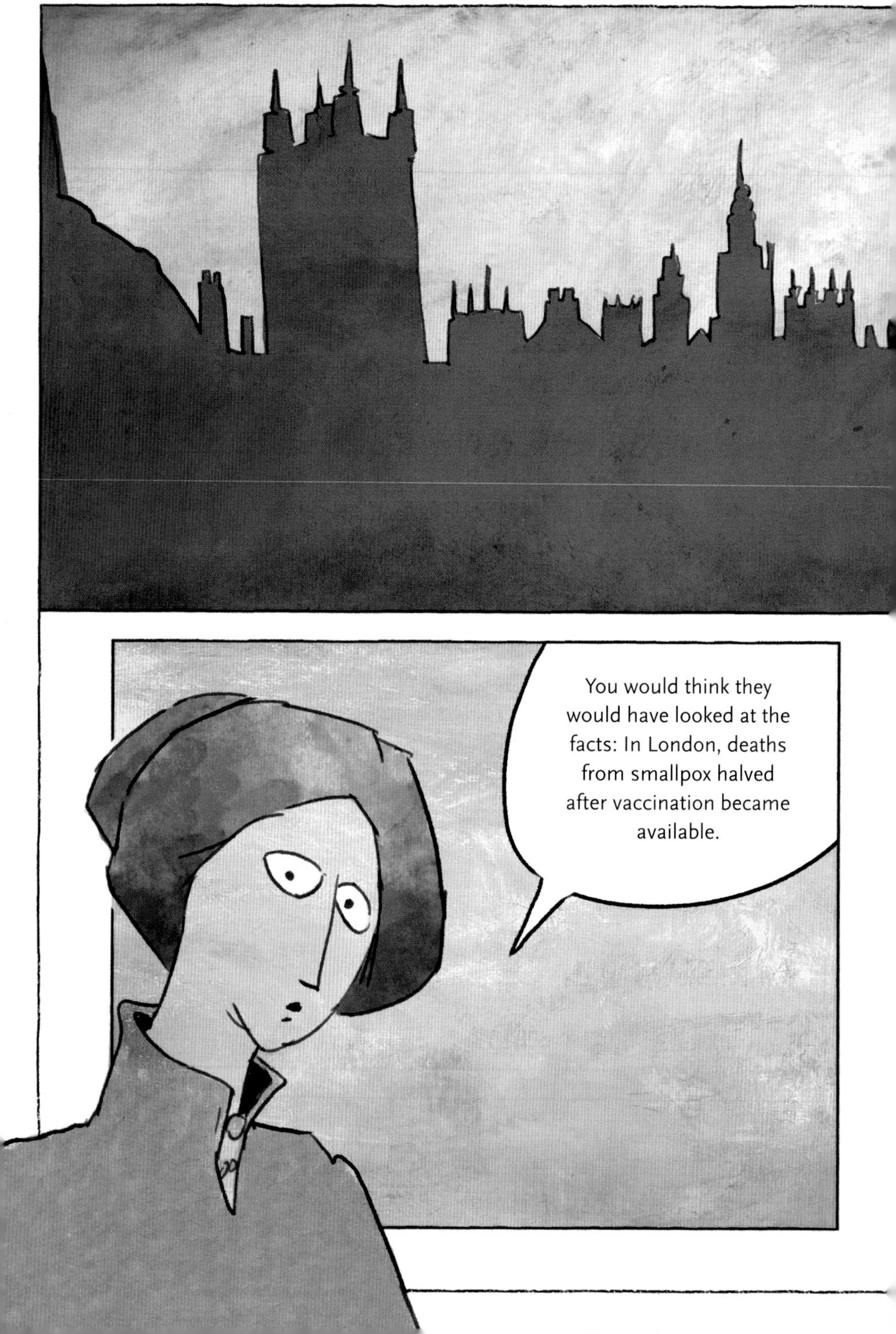
You would think they would have looked at the facts: In London, deaths from smallpox halved after vaccination became available.

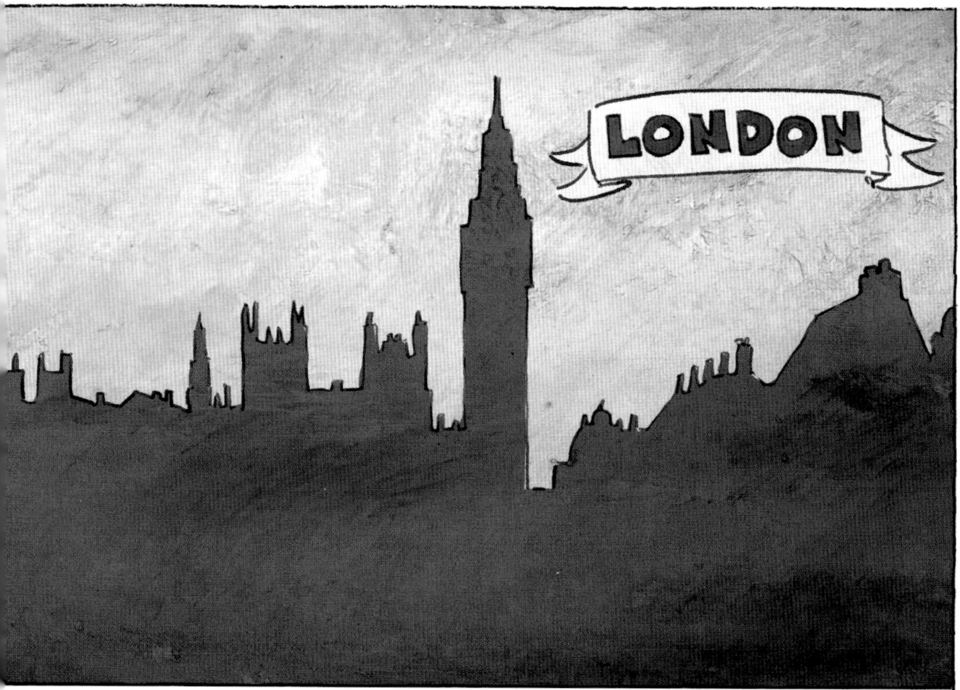
LONDON

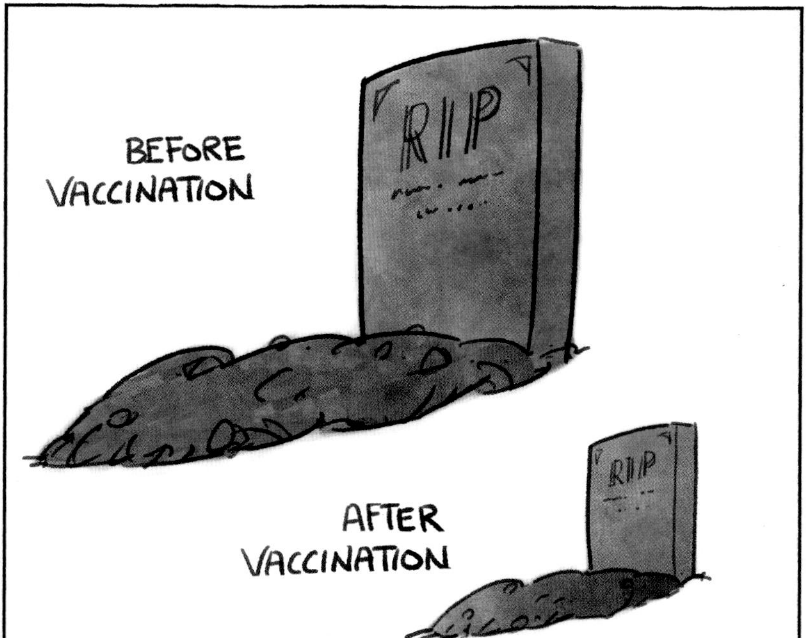
BEFORE
VACCINATION
RIP
AFTER
VACCINATION
RIP

In any case, anti-vaccination leagues formed.

In 1885, one English city saw upward of one hundred thousand people marching against vaccination.

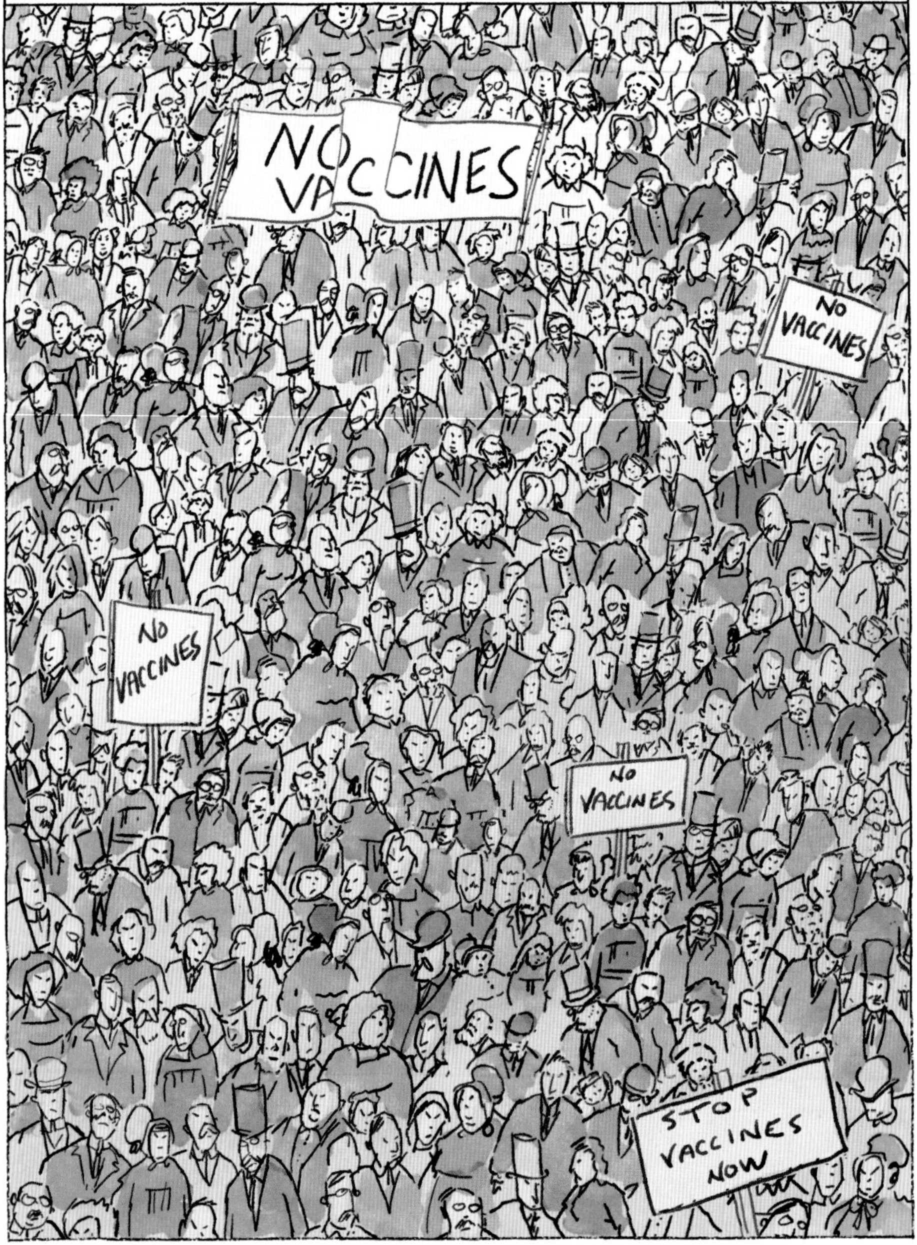
NO VACCINES
NO VACCINES
NO VACCINES
NO VACCINES
STOP VACCINES NOW

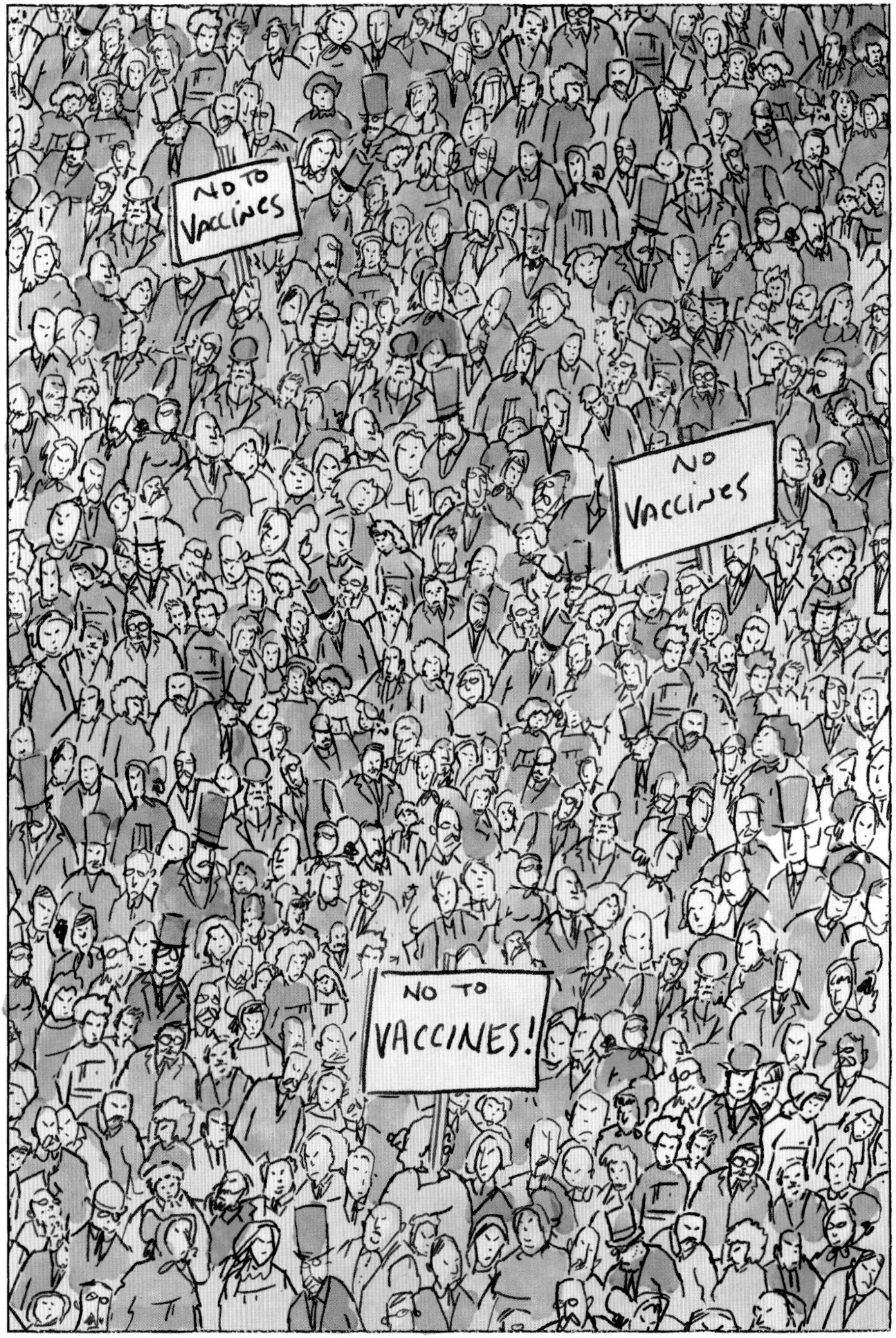
NO TO
VACCINES
NO
VACCINES
NO TO
VACCINES!

In America, the Anti-Vaccination Society was founded in 1879.

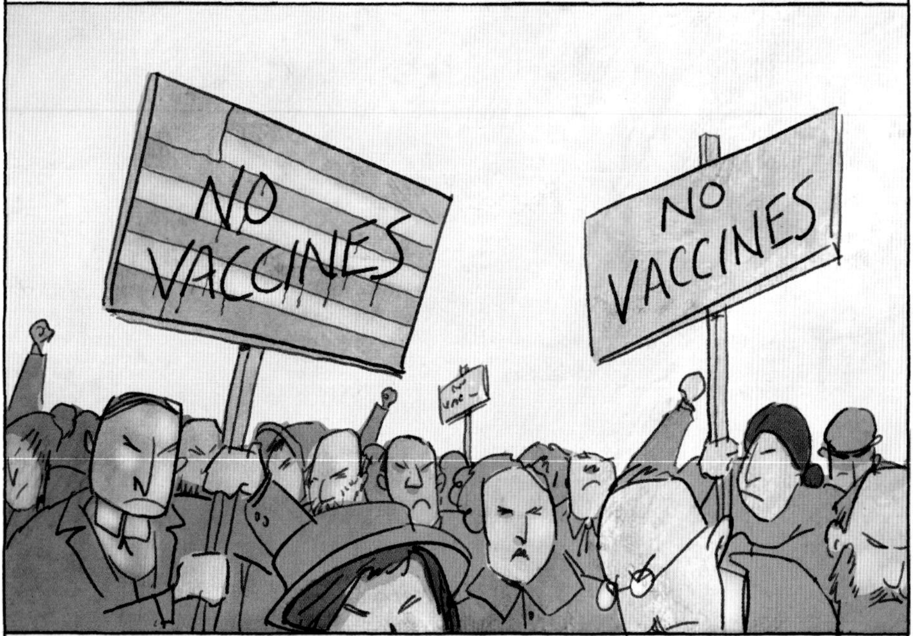
NO VACCINES
NO VACCINES

When sympathizer Henning Jacobson of Cambridge, Massachusetts, refused mandatory vaccination, the city took him to court.

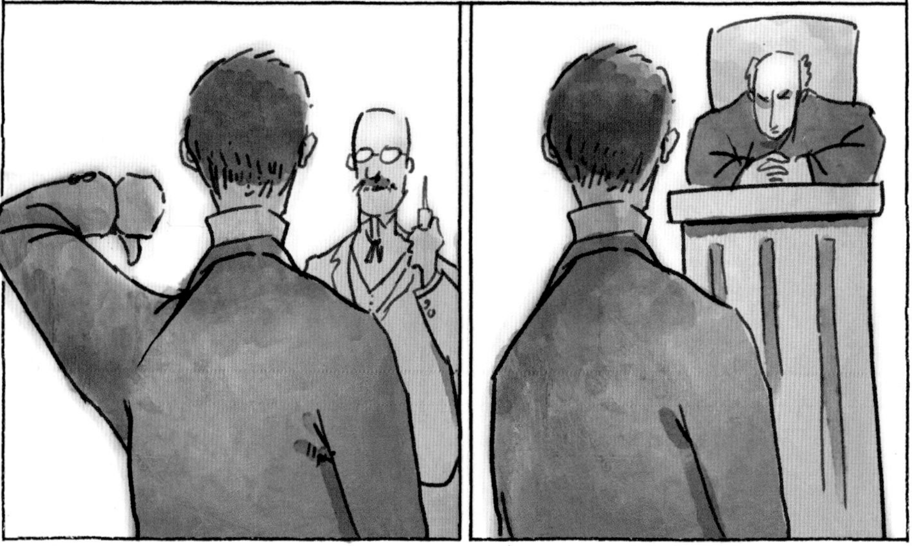

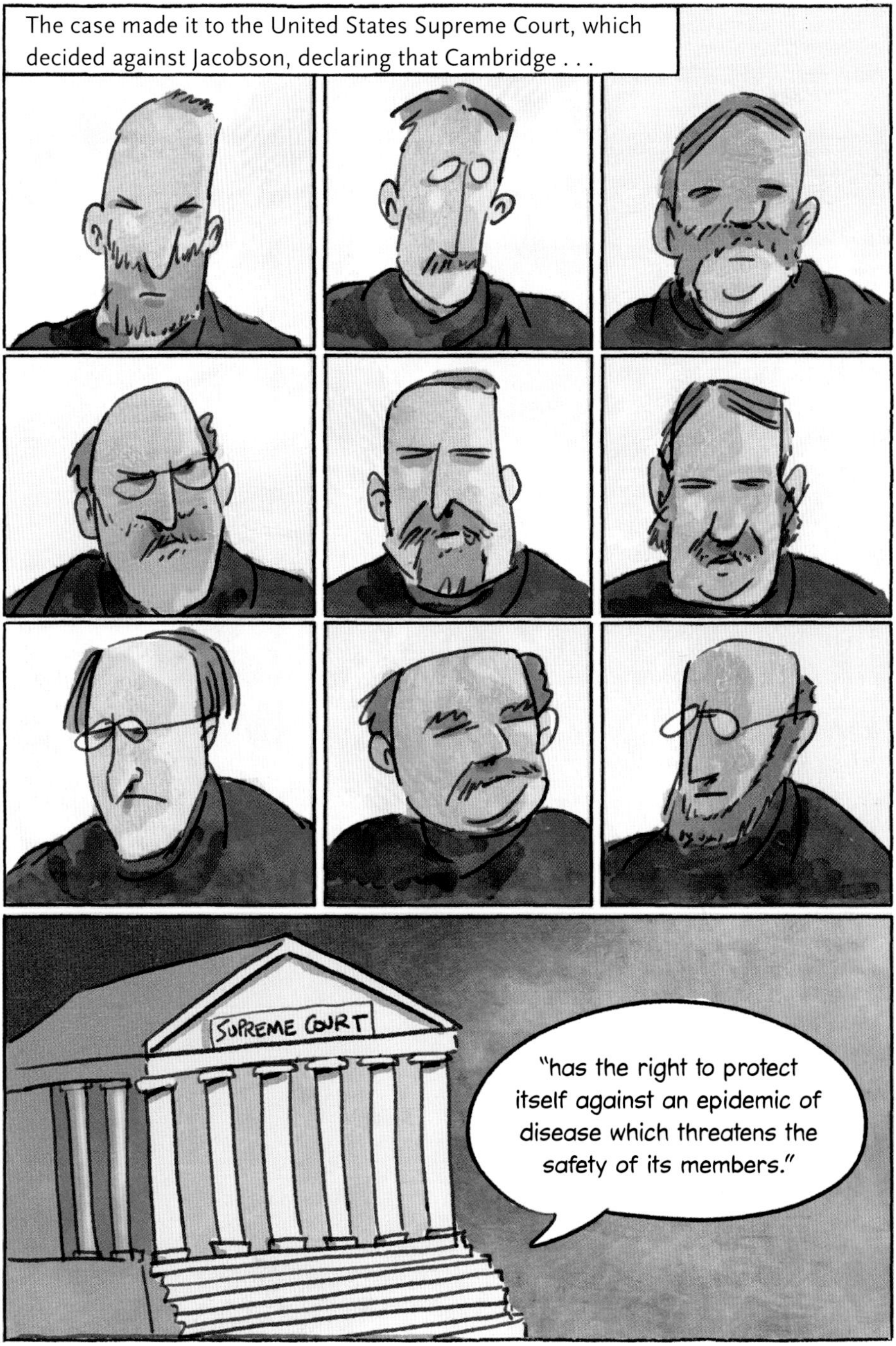
The case made it to the United States Supreme Court, which decided against Jacobson, declaring that Cambridge . . .
SUPREME COURT
"has the right to protect itself against an epidemic of disease which threatens the safety of its members."

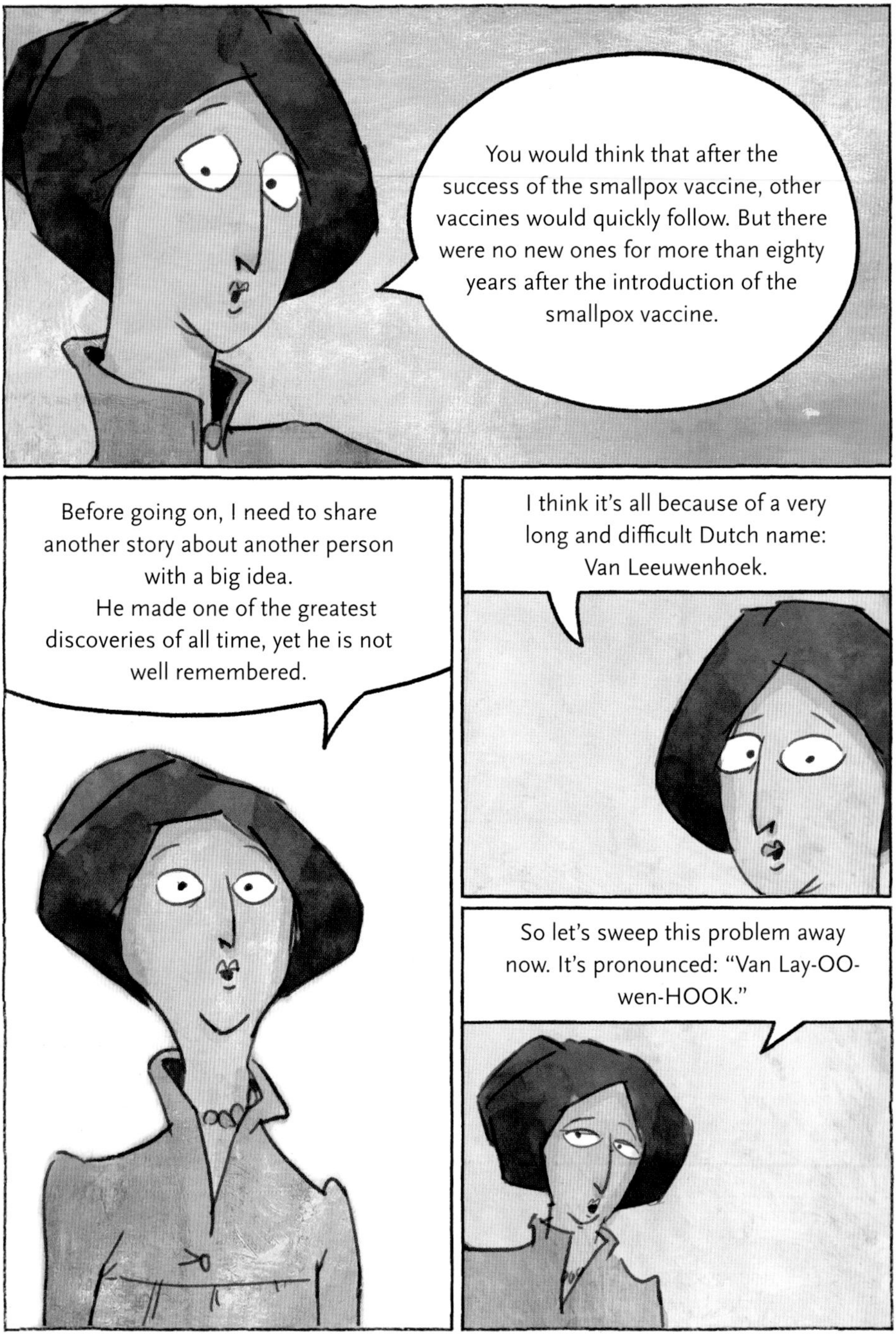
You would think that after the success of the smallpox vaccine, other vaccines would quickly follow. But there were no new ones for more than eighty years after the introduction of the smallpox vaccine.
Before going on, I need to share another story about another person with a big idea.
He made one of the greatest discoveries of all time, yet he is not well remembered.
I think it's all because of a very long and difficult Dutch name: Van Leeuwenhoek.
So let's sweep this problem away now. It's pronounced: "Van Lay-OO-wen-HOOK."

Around 1654, Antony van Leeuwenhoek lived in the city of Delft in the Netherlands. He had worked as a fabric merchant, a surveyor, and a government official.

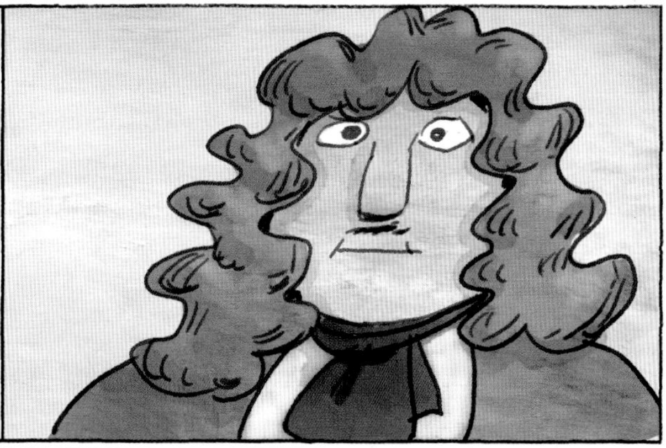

It's not for his jobs that we remember him, but rather his interest in microscopes. He ground his own lenses and made about five hundred of them.

Oh, they weren't the compound microscopes that had been invented sixty years earlier and the ones we are familiar with today, but instead very powerful magnifying glasses.

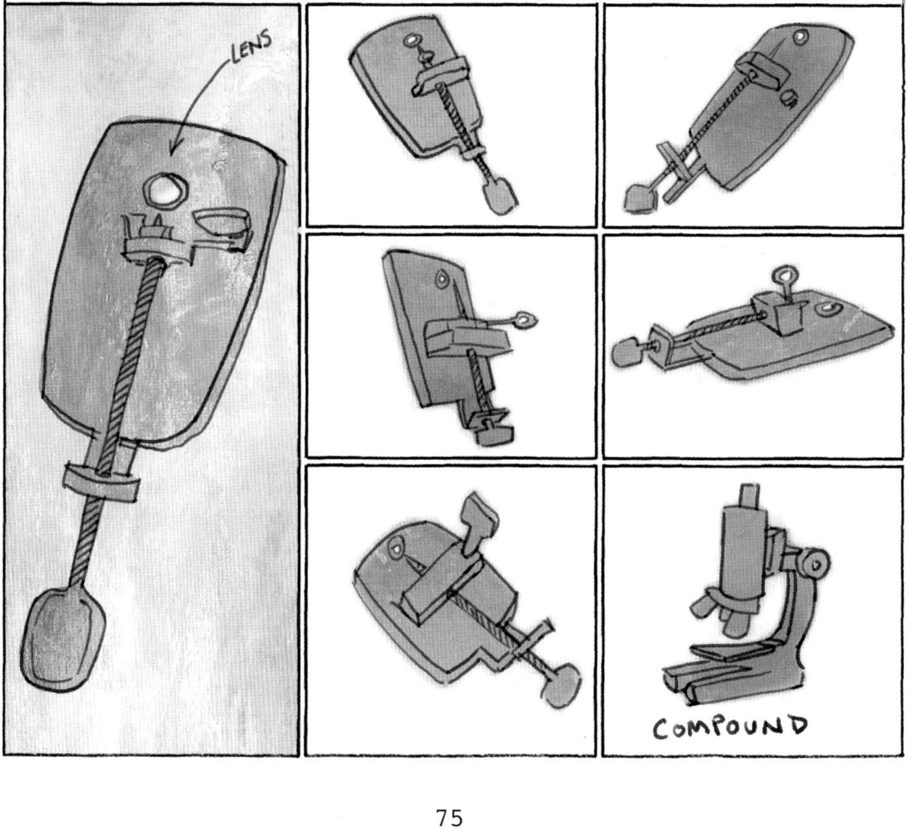
LENS
COMPOUND

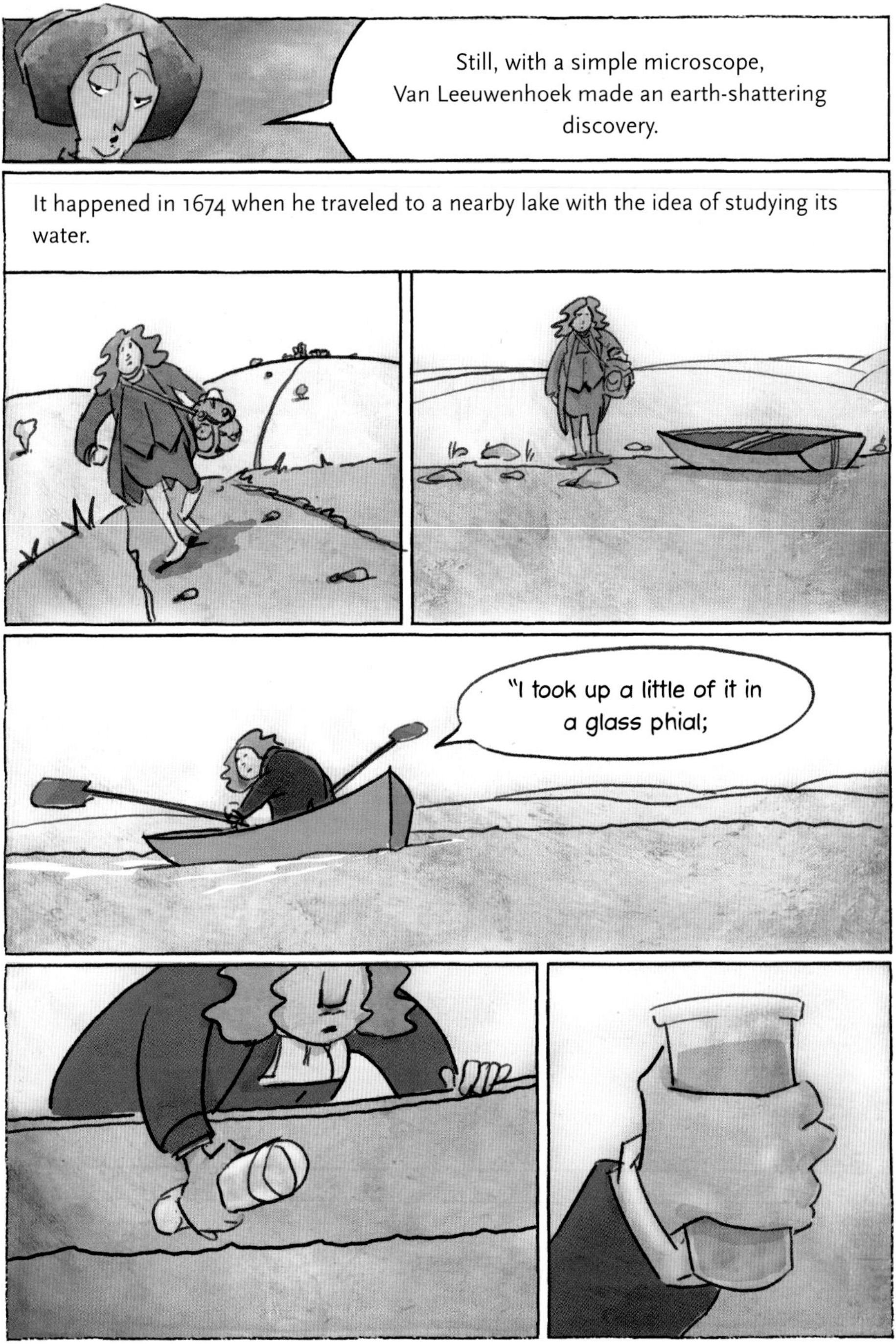
Still, with a simple microscope, Van Leeuwenhoek made an earth-shattering discovery.
It happened in 1674 when he traveled to a nearby lake with the idea of studying its water.
"I took up a little of it in a glass phial;

and examining this water the next day, I found floating therein . . .

very many little animalcules . . . I saw two little legs near the head and two little fins at the hindmost end of the body . . . the motion of most of these animalcules in the water was so swift . . . I judge that some of these little creatures were . . . a thousand times smaller than the smallest ones I have ever seen."

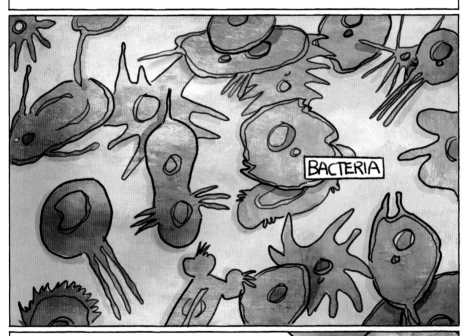

BACTERIA

Antony van Leeuwenhoek had discovered bacteria, those tiny creatures that are all around us, on us, and *in* us. The world hasn't been the same since.

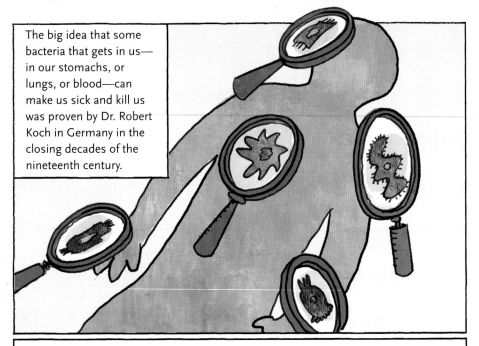

The big idea that some bacteria that gets in us—in our stomachs, or lungs, or blood—can make us sick and kill us was proven by Dr. Robert Koch in Germany in the closing decades of the nineteenth century.

Working from his tiny house, he studied anthrax, a vicious disease that kills animals and people alike.

KOCH

Risking his own life, he worked with infected blood and proved a particular bacterium caused the disease. He went on to discover the specific bacteria that caused tuberculosis, cholera, and anthrax, to name just a few.

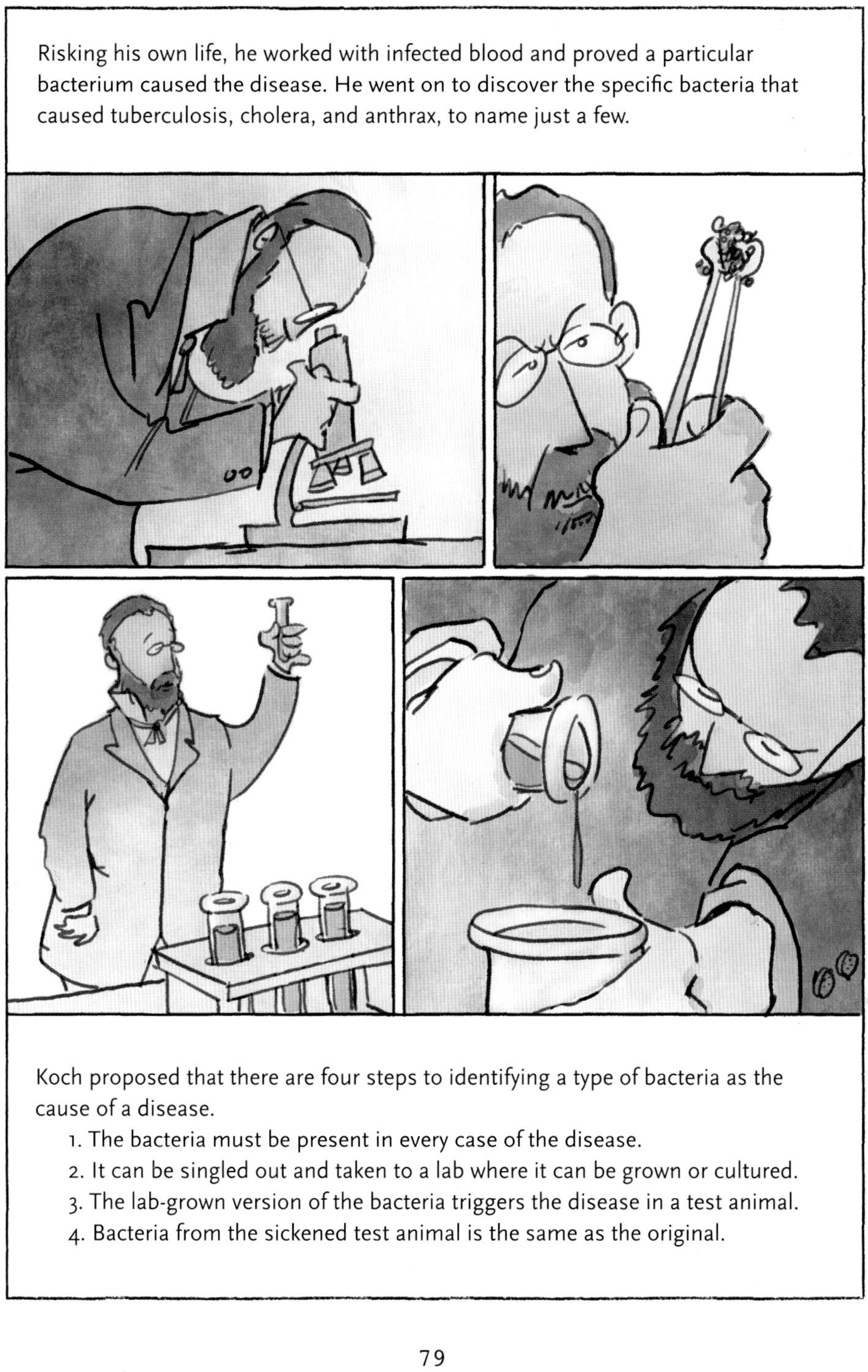

Koch proposed that there are four steps to identifying a type of bacteria as the cause of a disease.

1. The bacteria must be present in every case of the disease.
2. It can be singled out and taken to a lab where it can be grown or cultured.
3. The lab-grown version of the bacteria triggers the disease in a test animal.
4. Bacteria from the sickened test animal is the same as the original.

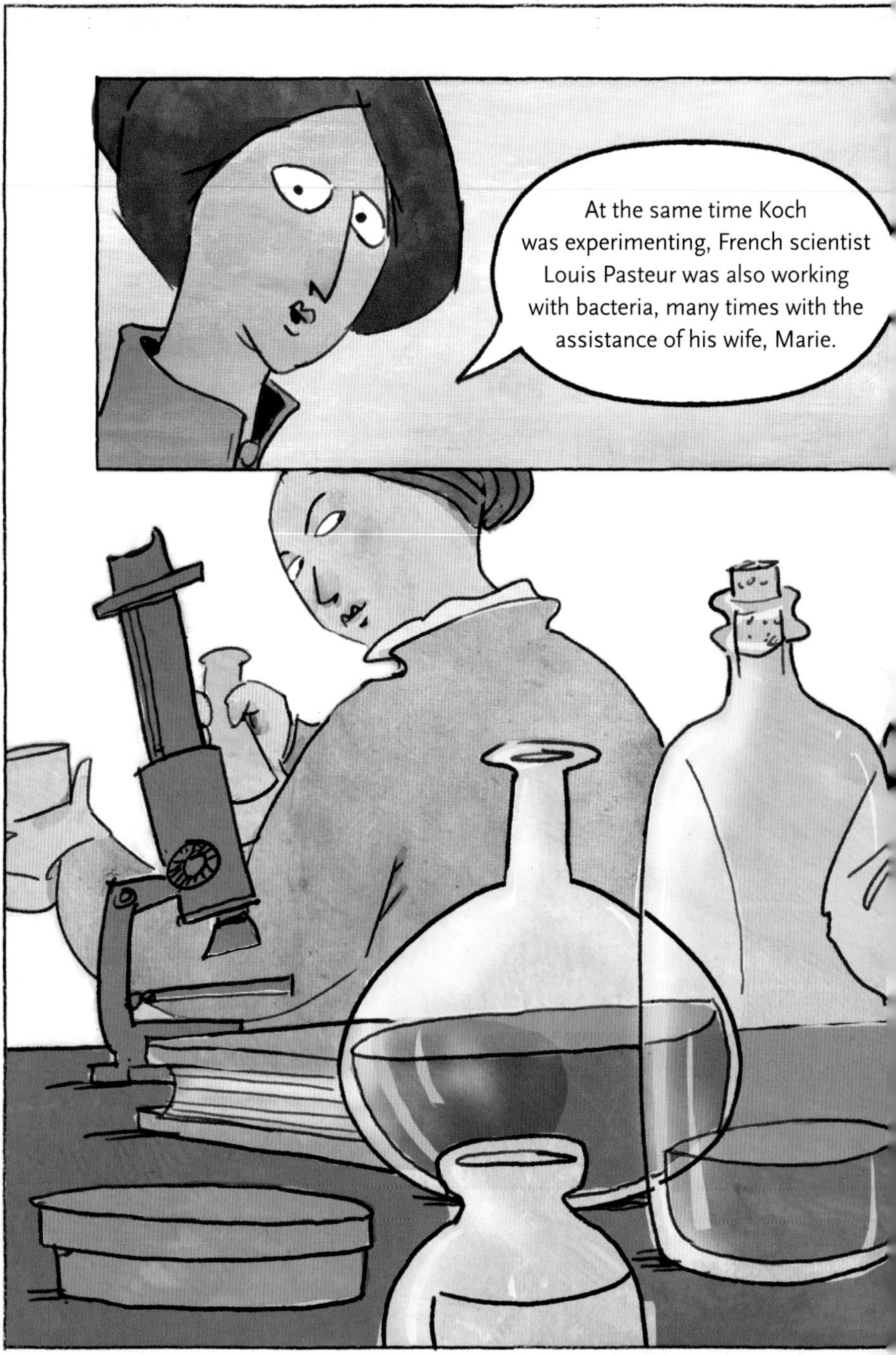
At the same time Koch was experimenting, French scientist Louis Pasteur was also working with bacteria, many times with the assistance of his wife, Marie.

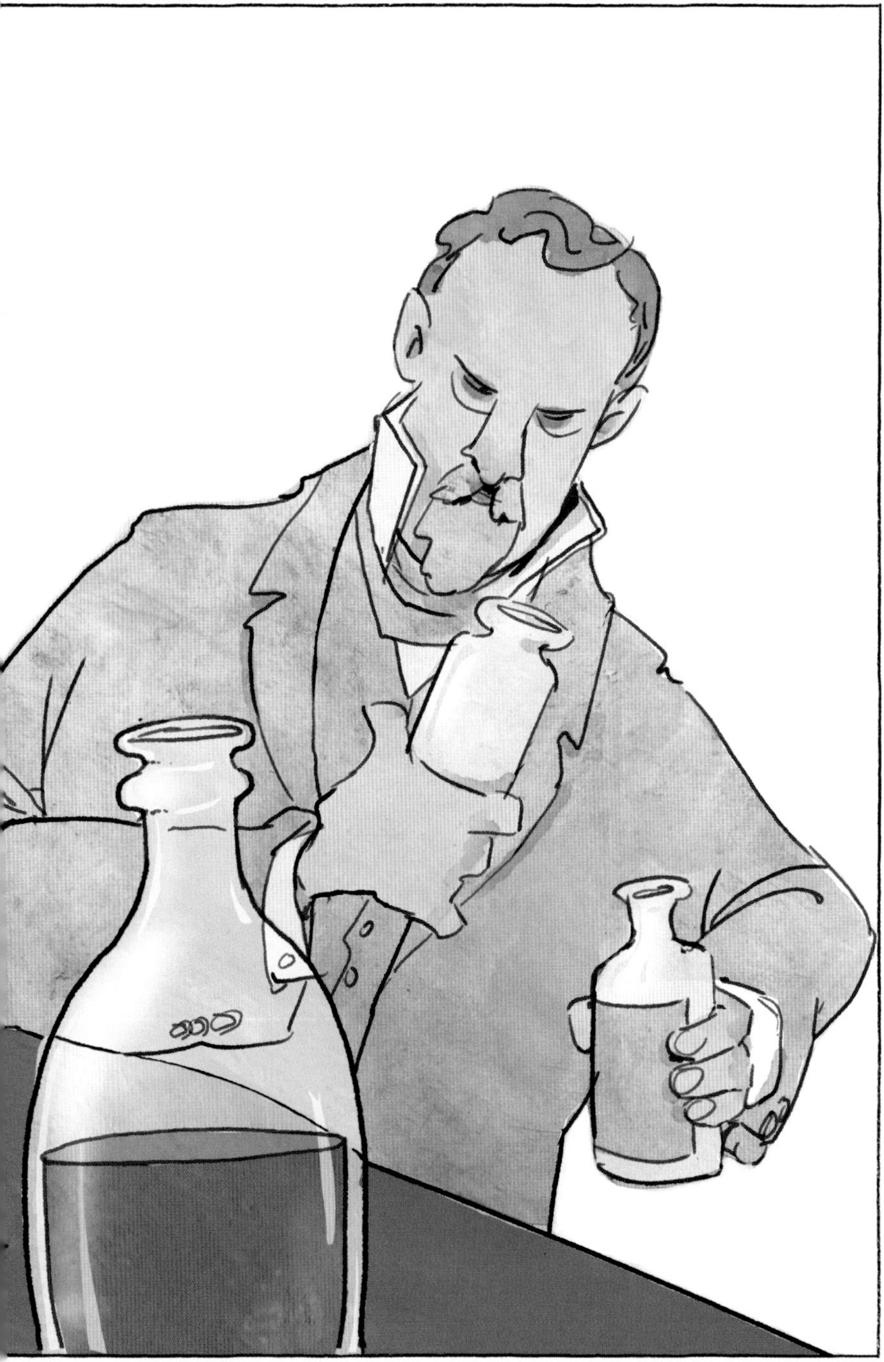

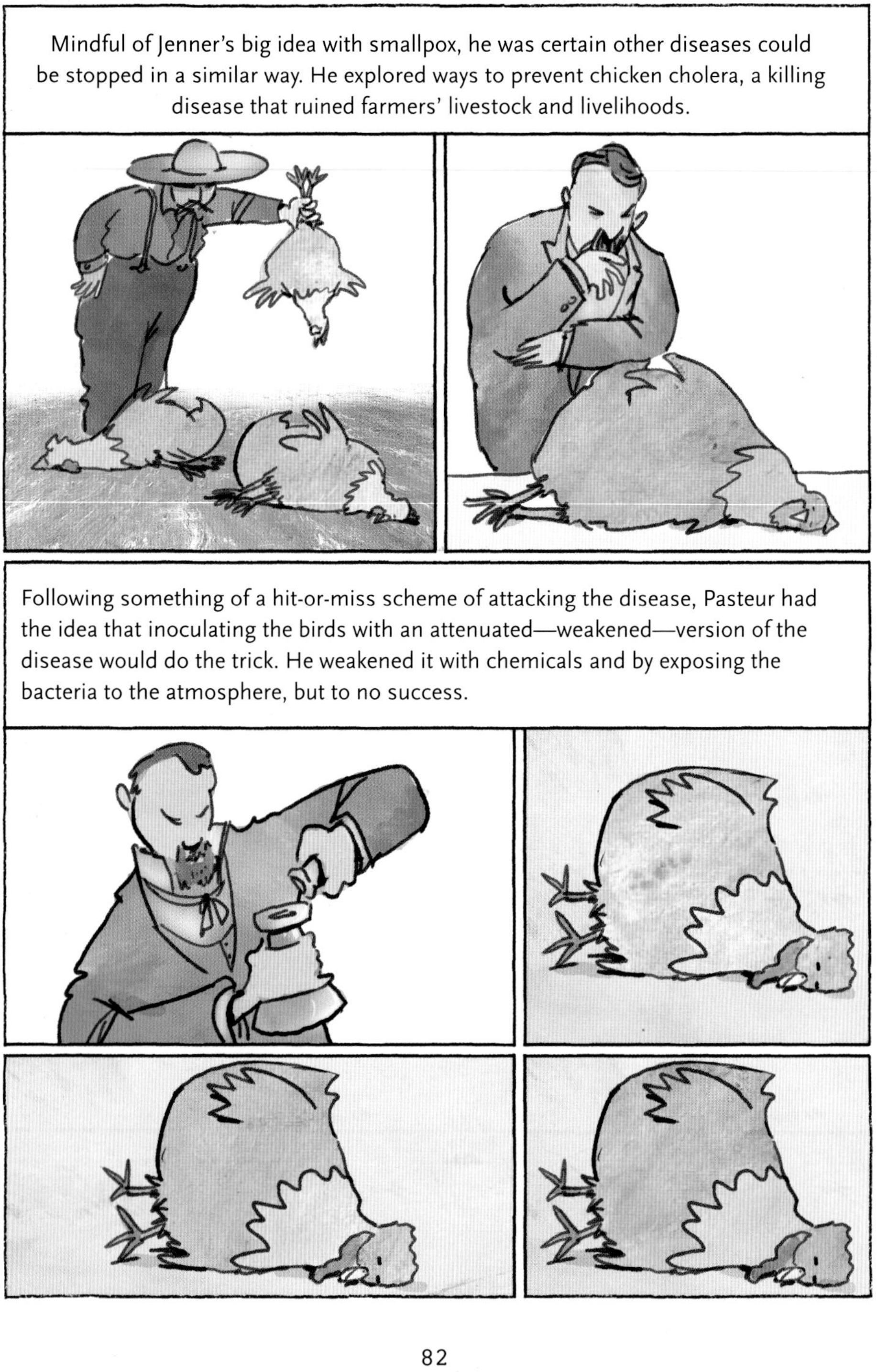
Mindful of Jenner's big idea with smallpox, he was certain other diseases could be stopped in a similar way. He explored ways to prevent chicken cholera, a killing disease that ruined farmers' livestock and livelihoods.
Following something of a hit-or-miss scheme of attacking the disease, Pasteur had the idea that inoculating the birds with an attenuated—weakened—version of the disease would do the trick. He weakened it with chemicals and by exposing the bacteria to the atmosphere, but to no success.

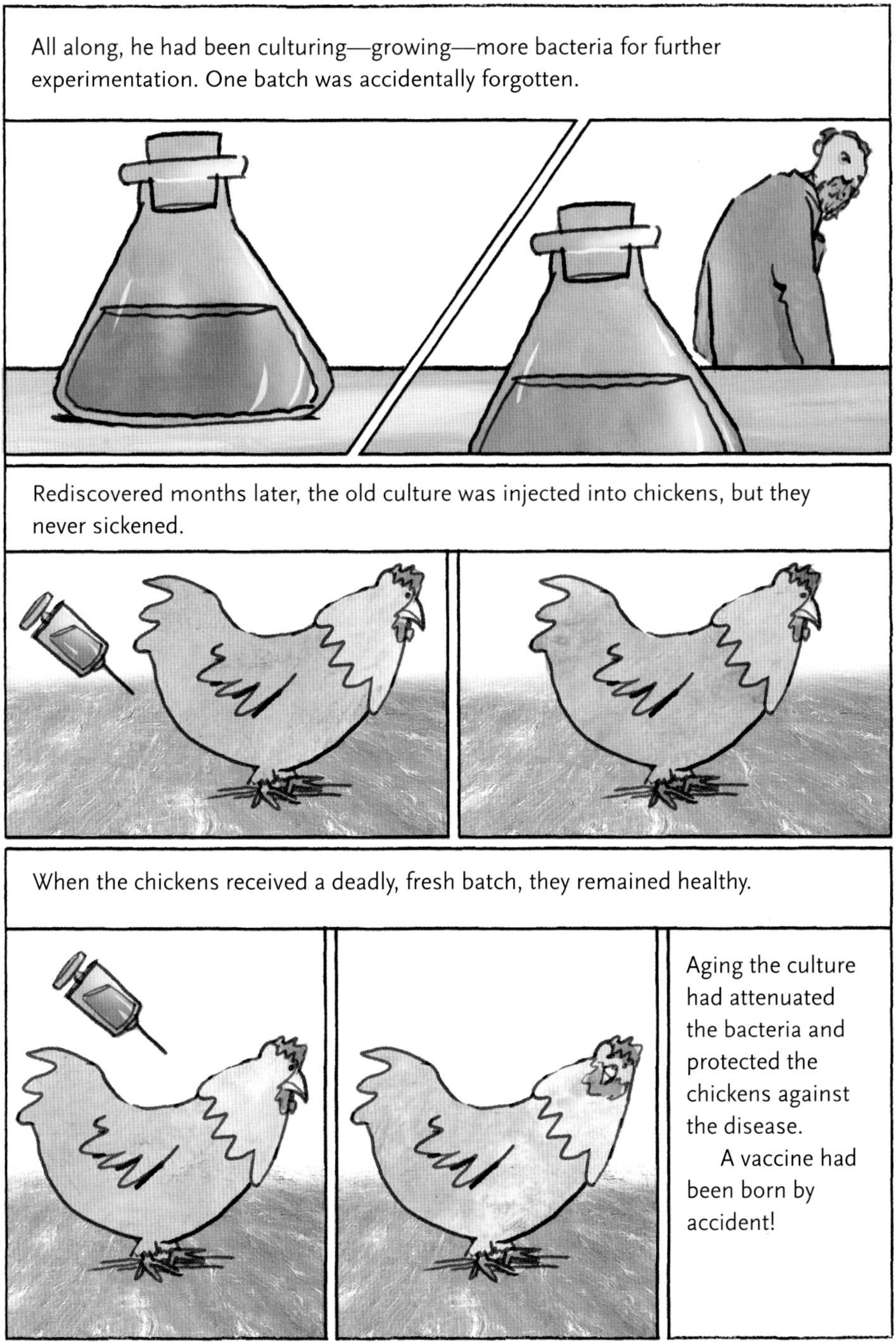
All along, he had been culturing—growing—more bacteria for further experimentation. One batch was accidentally forgotten.
Rediscovered months later, the old culture was injected into chickens, but they never sickened.
When the chickens received a deadly, fresh batch, they remained healthy.
Aging the culture had attenuated the bacteria and protected the chickens against the disease.
A vaccine had been born by accident!

Building on the work of Koch, Pasteur turned to anthrax. Again, after much trial and error, he discovered anthrax cultures could be weakened by chemicals.

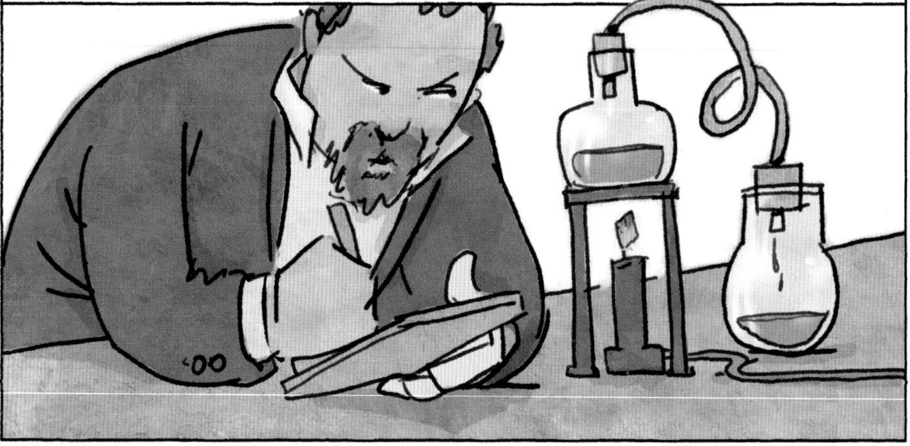

In 1881, Pasteur performed a public experiment of anthrax *vaccination*—a term he applied in honor of Jenner—on two groups of farm animals.

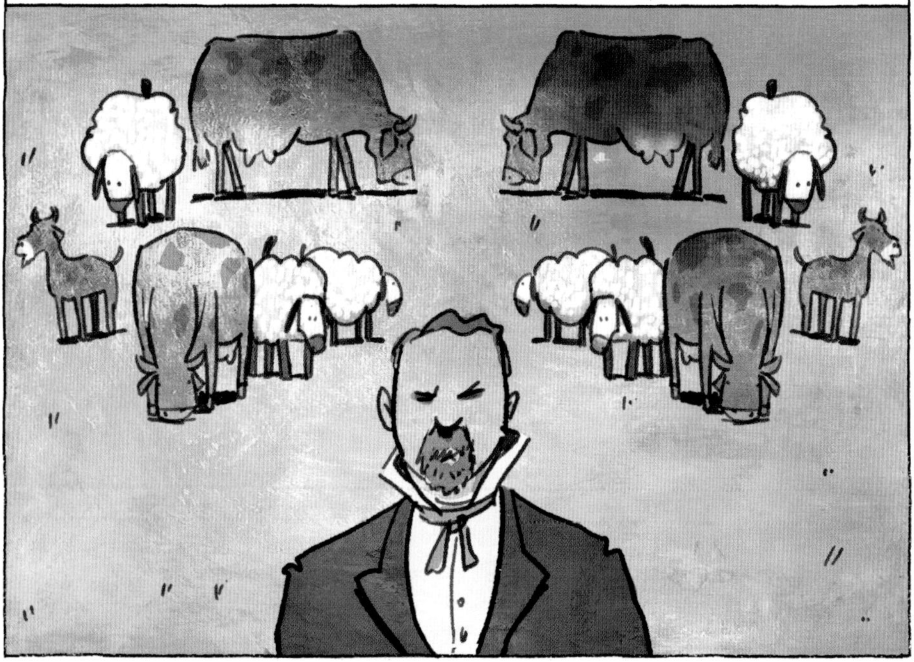

Mindful of the deadly disease, he carefully injected the animals with anthrax. All the animals—sheep, cows, one goat—that had been previously vaccinated, survived. The untreated group sickened, and most died.

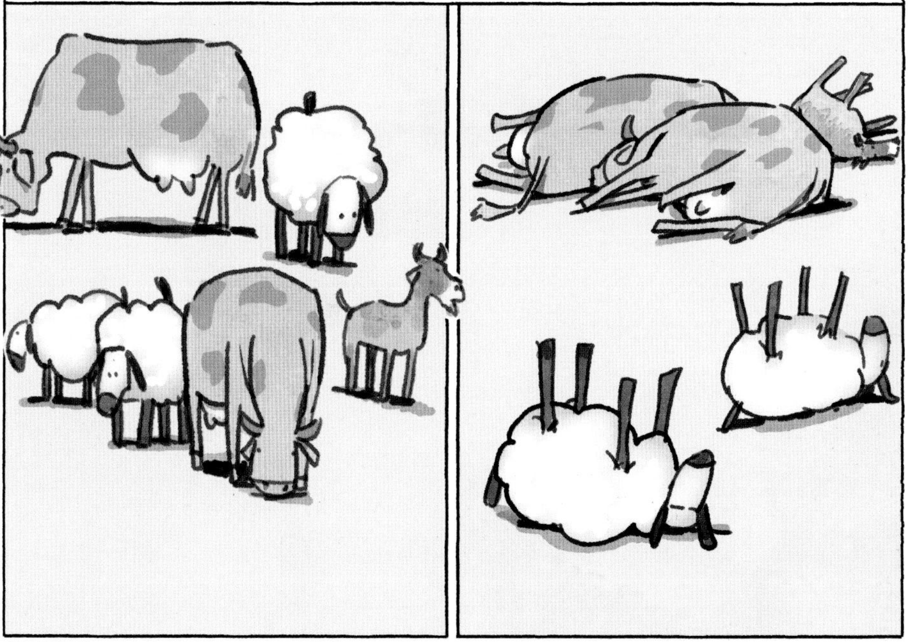

Soon, millions of French cows were vaccinated against anthrax, nearly eliminating the disease.

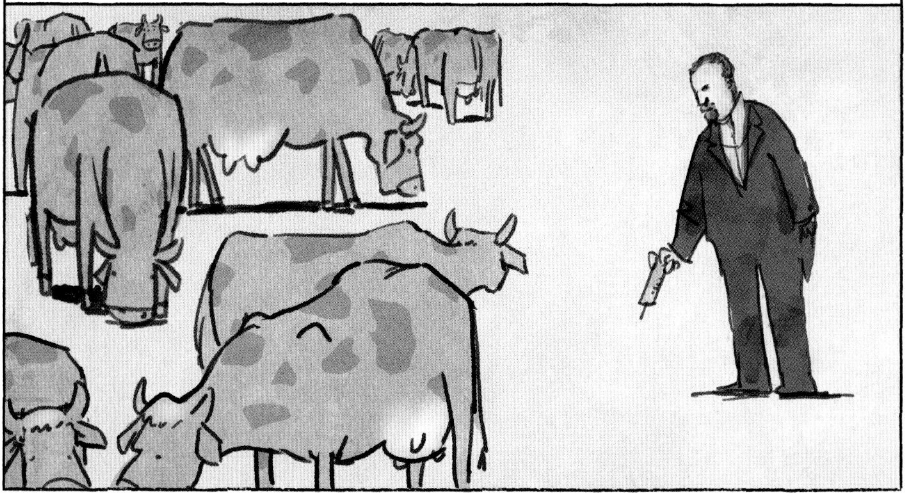

But Pasteur's most dramatic success was against rabies.

People bitten by an infected animal acquire rabies from its saliva. Rabies attacks the brain, leaving the victim confused, excited, and agitated.

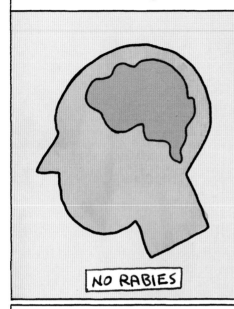

NO RABIES

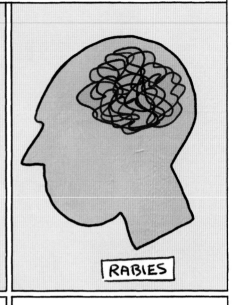

RABIES

Most victims die.

"Mad dog" was a way of describing a rabid dog . . .

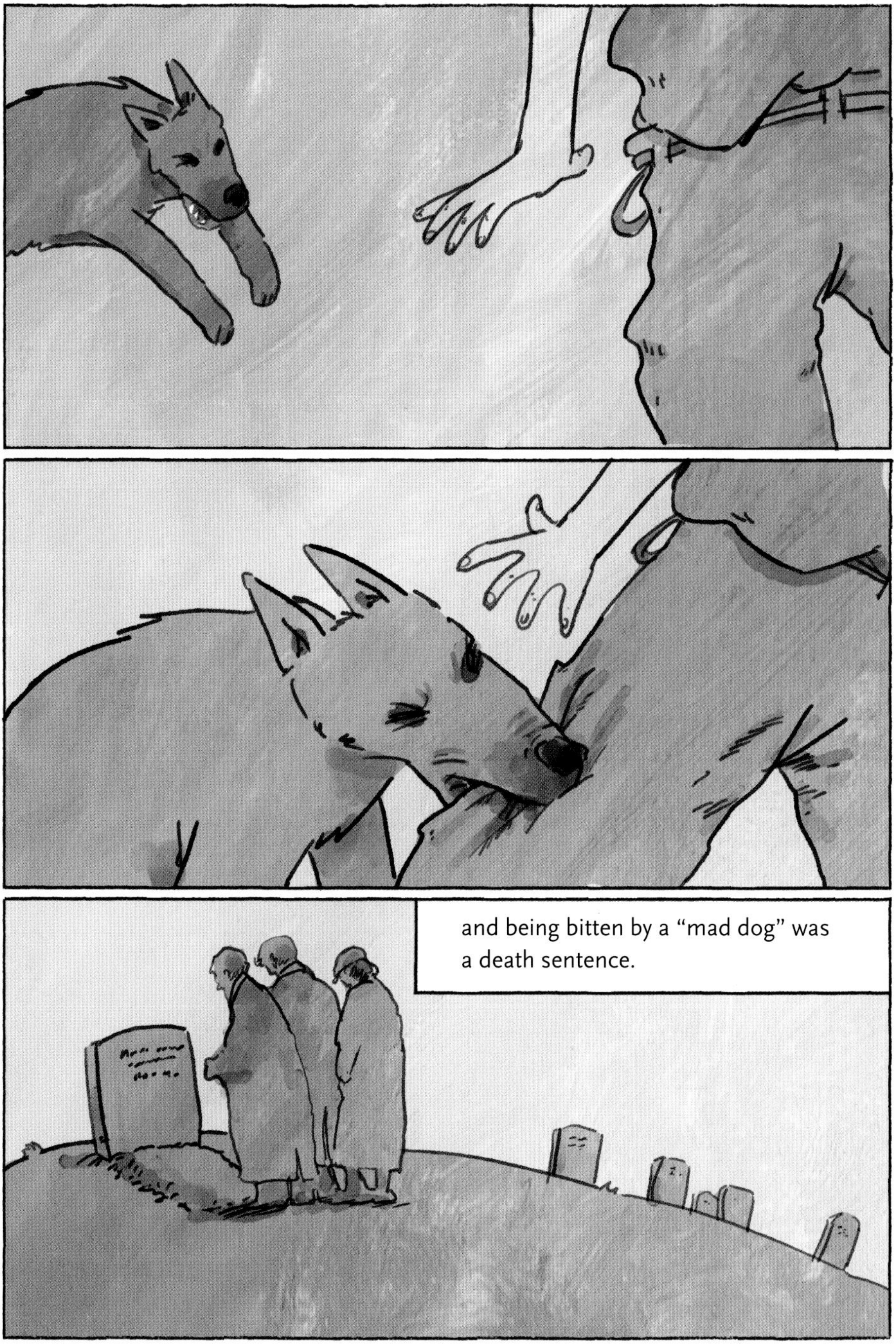
and being bitten by a "mad dog" was a death sentence.

Pasteur couldn't identity a bacteria that caused rabies. It would later be identified as a virus, of which Pasteur knew nearly nothing. Viruses are much, much tinier than bacteria and are odd things that don't even seem to be alive. For example, they don't poo and can only reproduce by hijacking the genetic machinery of a host cell. Still, Pasteur believed attenuating or weakening the disease as he had with chicken cholera and anthrax was the path to a rabies vaccine.

So, how did Pasteur make his rabies vaccine?

It is here that I believe a lady—or gentleman—must exercise some restraint. Let's just say Pasteur experimented with the spines of dead, rabies-infected rabbits and leave it at that . . .

Pasteur concocted a vaccine against rabies that appeared to work, or did so on dogs. But then in 1885, nine-year-old Joseph Meister was brought to Pasteur. The boy had suffered savage bites from a rabid dog.

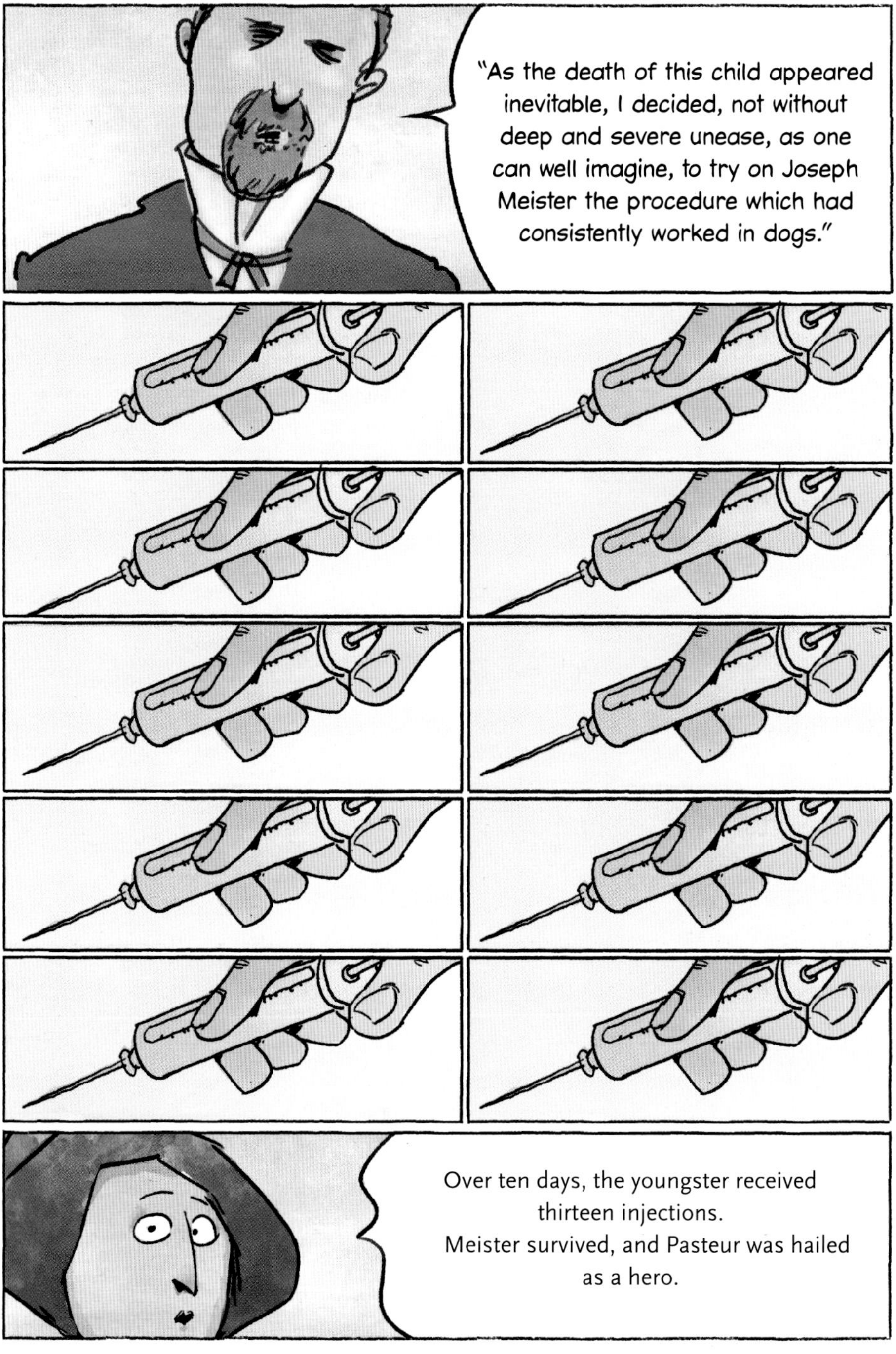
"As the death of this child appeared inevitable, I decided, not without deep and severe unease, as one can well imagine, to try on Joseph Meister the procedure which had consistently worked in dogs."
Over ten days, the youngster received thirteen injections.
Meister survived, and Pasteur was hailed as a hero.

In the following years, scientists' ideas resulted in vaccines for diphtheria, tetanus, plague, typhoid, pertussis, yellow fever, and tuberculosis, saving people from misery and death.

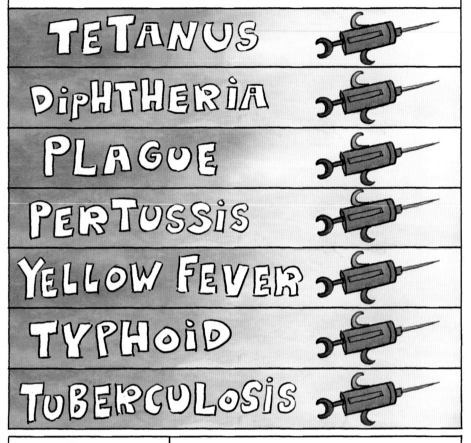

TETANUS

DIPHTHERIA

PLAGUE

PERTUSSIS

YELLOW FEVER

TYPHOID

TUBERCULOSIS

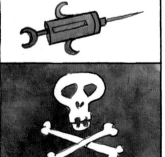

But the path of success was not always smooth.

In 1901, children in Missouri and New Jersey died from poorly made vaccines. The United States government stepped in and eventually passed the Biologics Control Act and the Pure Food and Drug Act, which were laws to ensure the quality of vaccines.

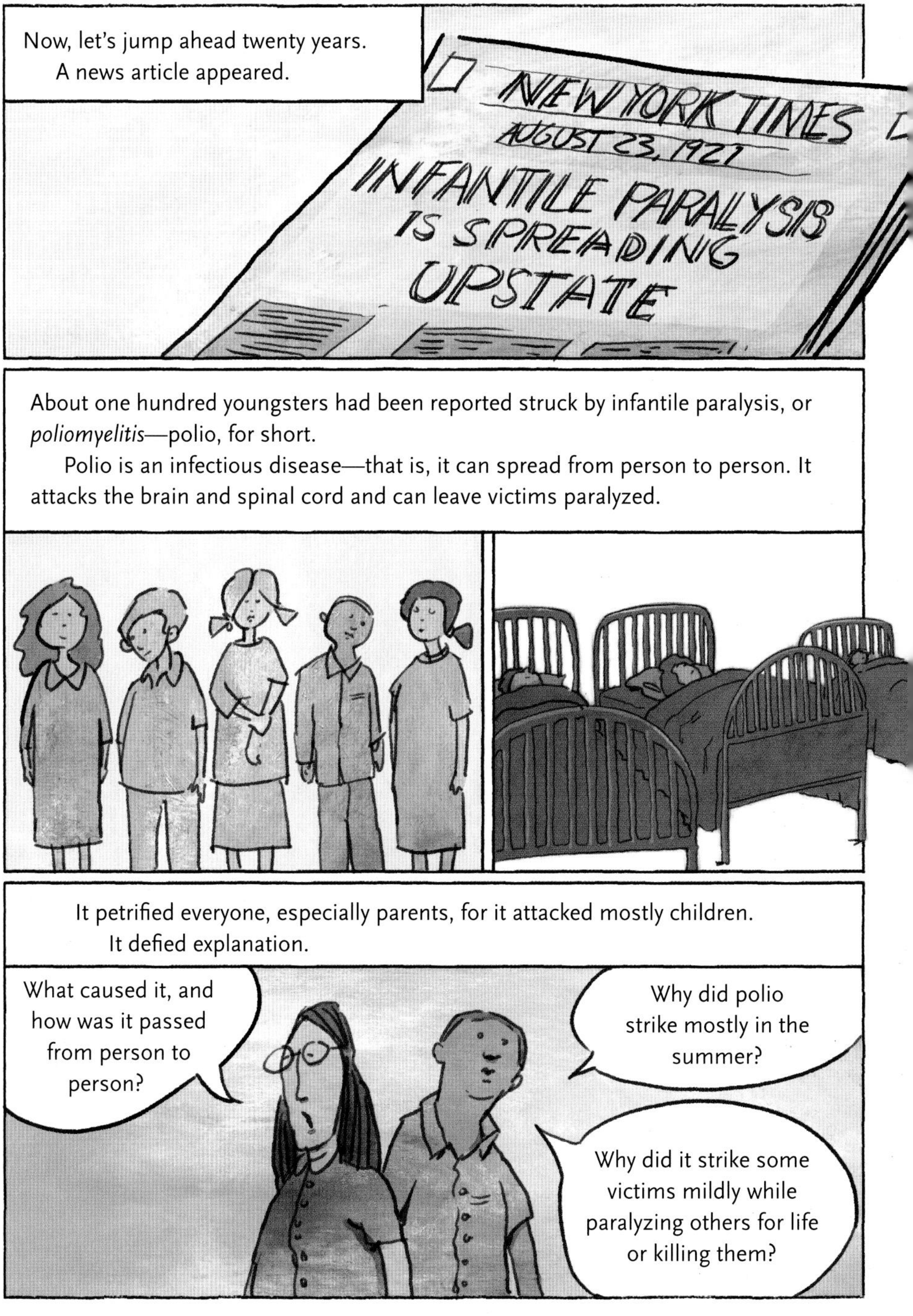
Now, let's jump ahead twenty years.
A news article appeared.
NEW YORK TIMES
AUGUST 23, 1921
INFANTILE PARALYSIS IS SPREADING UPSTATE
About one hundred youngsters had been reported struck by infantile paralysis, or *poliomyelitis*—polio, for short.
Polio is an infectious disease—that is, it can spread from person to person. It attacks the brain and spinal cord and can leave victims paralyzed.
It petrified everyone, especially parents, for it attacked mostly children.
It defied explanation.
What caused it, and how was it passed from person to person?
Why did polio strike mostly in the summer?
Why did it strike some victims mildly while paralyzing others for life or killing them?

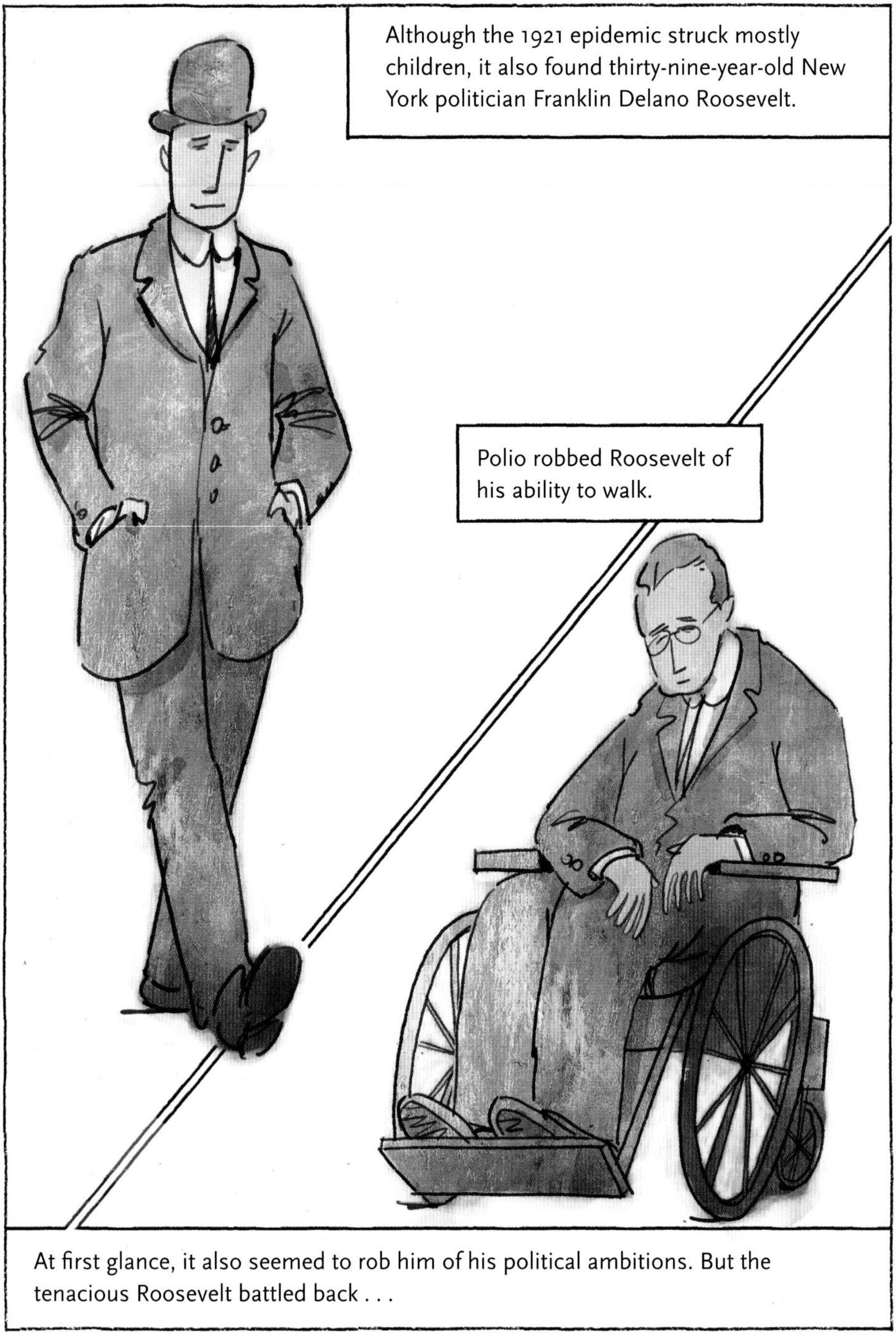
Although the 1921 epidemic struck mostly children, it also found thirty-nine-year-old New York politician Franklin Delano Roosevelt.
Polio robbed Roosevelt of his ability to walk.
At first glance, it also seemed to rob him of his political ambitions. But the tenacious Roosevelt battled back . . .

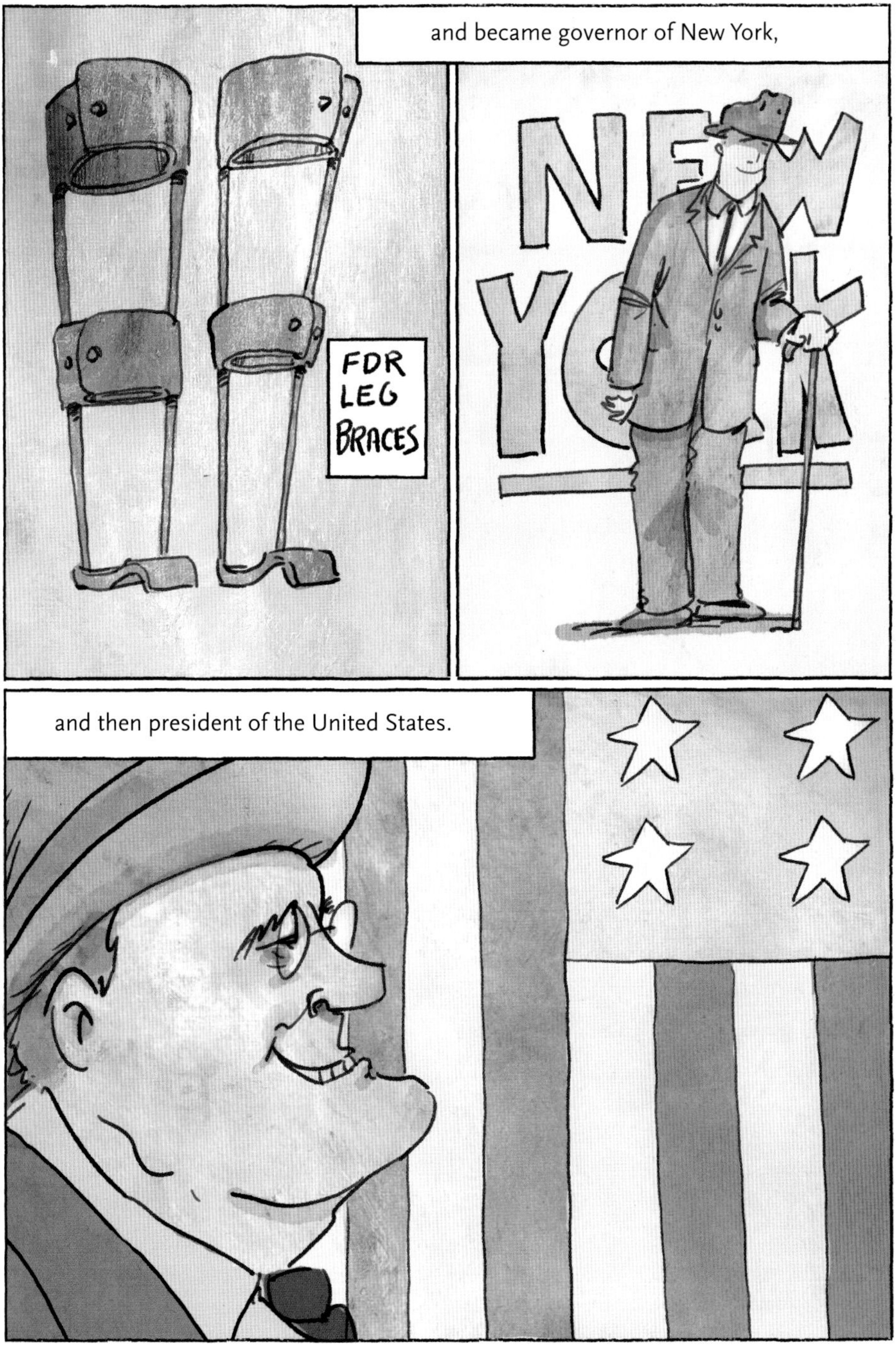
and became governor of New York,
FDR
LEG
BRACES
and then president of the United States.

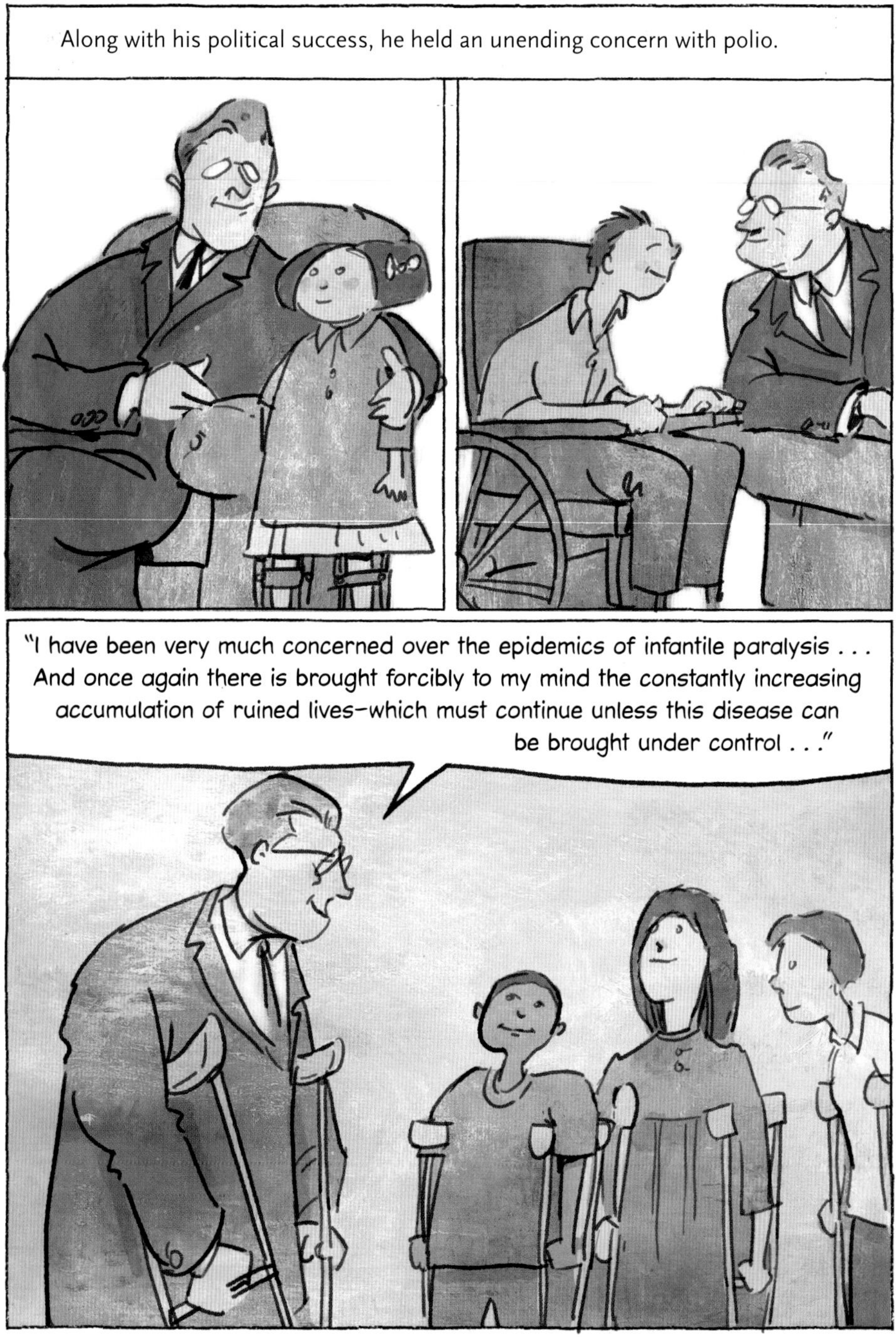
Along with his political success, he held an unending concern with polio.
"I have been very much concerned over the epidemics of infantile paralysis . . . And once again there is brought forcibly to my mind the constantly increasing accumulation of ruined lives–which must continue unless this disease can be brought under control . . ."

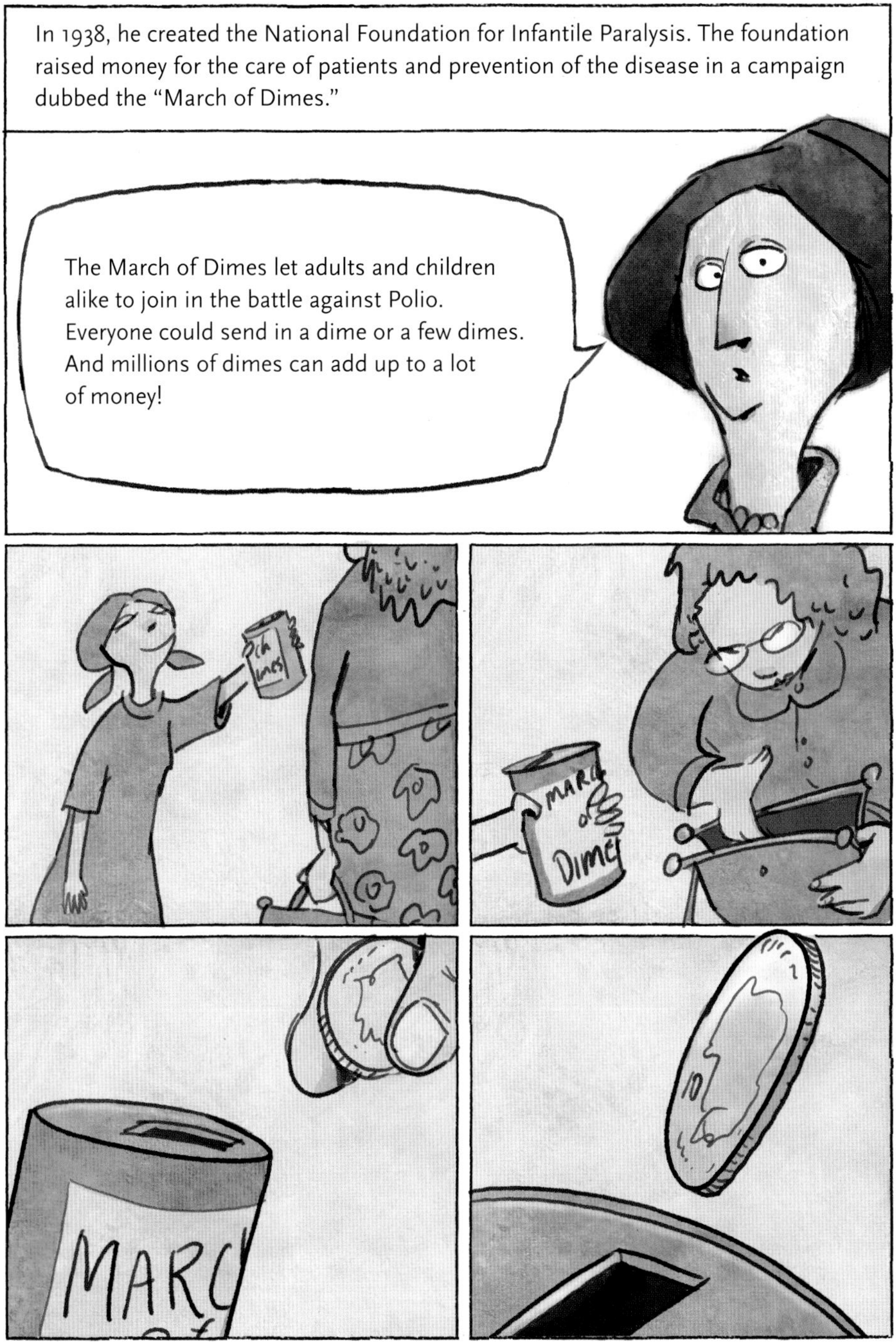
In 1938, he created the National Foundation for Infantile Paralysis. The foundation raised money for the care of patients and prevention of the disease in a campaign dubbed the "March of Dimes."
The March of Dimes let adults and children alike to join in the battle against Polio. Everyone could send in a dime or a few dimes. And millions of dimes can add up to a lot of money!
MARC

Within weeks, tens of thousands of letters bearing dimes arrived at the White House.

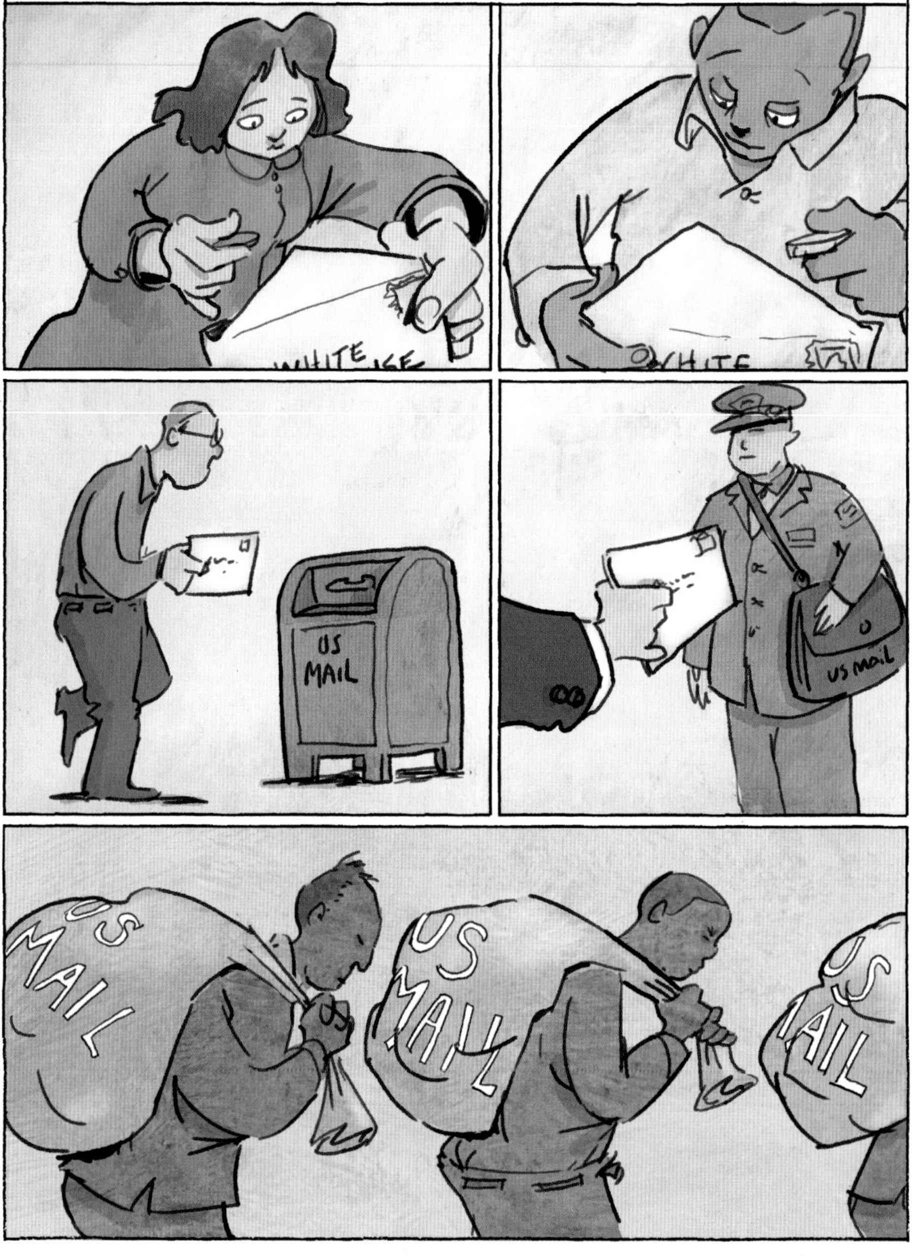
US MAIL
US MAIL
US MAIL
US MAIL

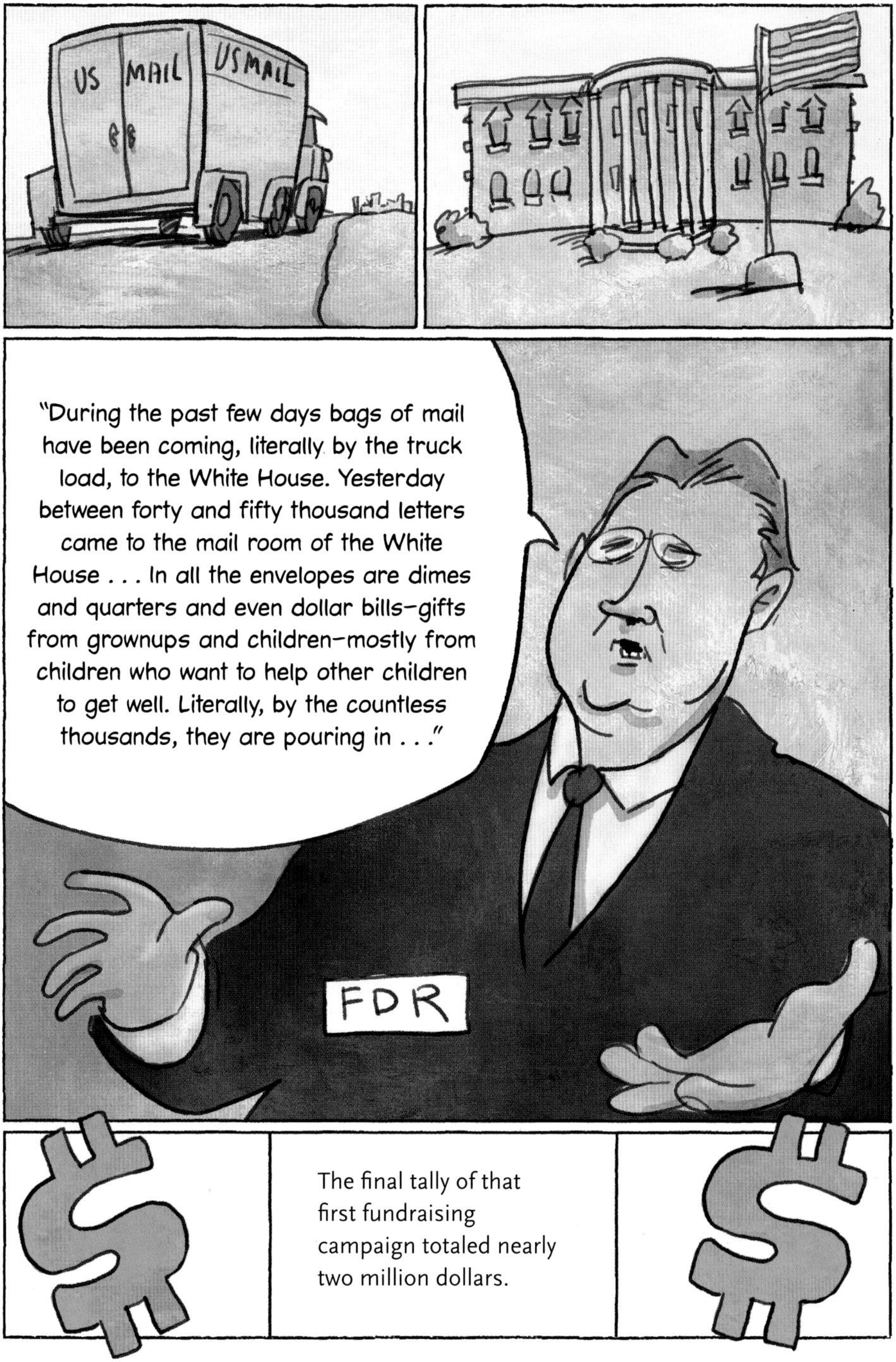
US MAIL
USMAIL
"During the past few days bags of mail have been coming, literally by the truck load, to the White House. Yesterday between forty and fifty thousand letters came to the mail room of the White House . . . In all the envelopes are dimes and quarters and even dollar bills—gifts from grownups and children—mostly from children who want to help other children to get well. Literally, by the countless thousands, they are pouring in . . ."
FDR
The final tally of that first fundraising campaign totaled nearly two million dollars.

The March of Dimes became a fixture of American life and raised millions of dollars. Some of it found its way to Dr. Jonas Salk, a vaccine scientist who had an idea about a polio vaccine.

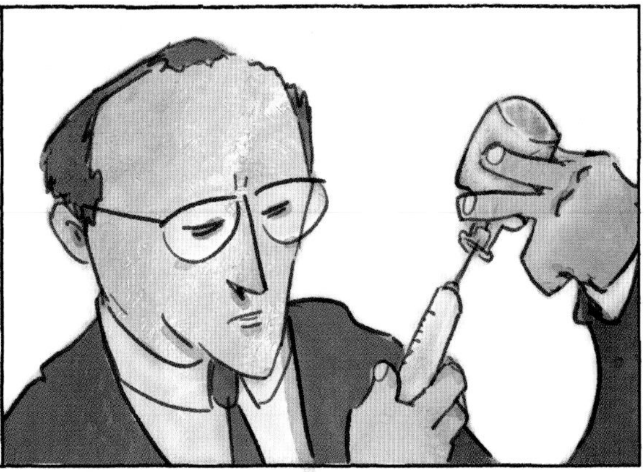

In 1952, in a strategy that would be rejected today, he tested his vaccine on crippled and mentally challenged children. Then he vaccinated himself and his own family.

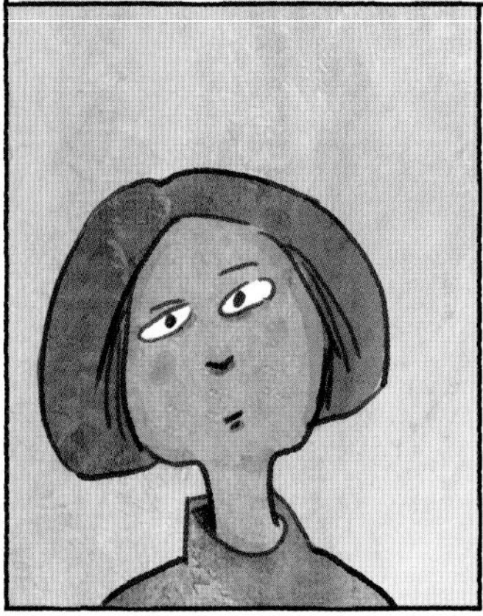

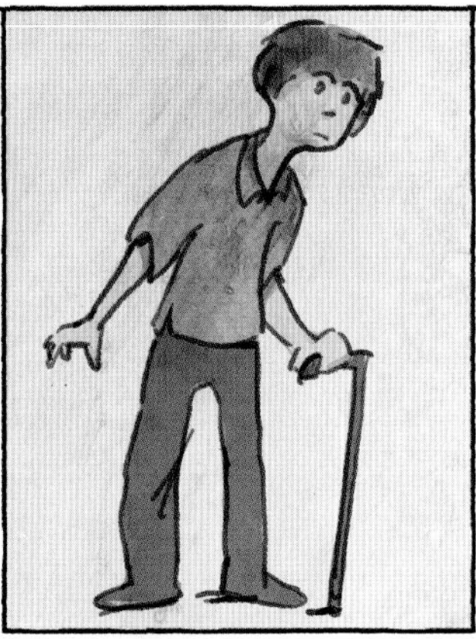

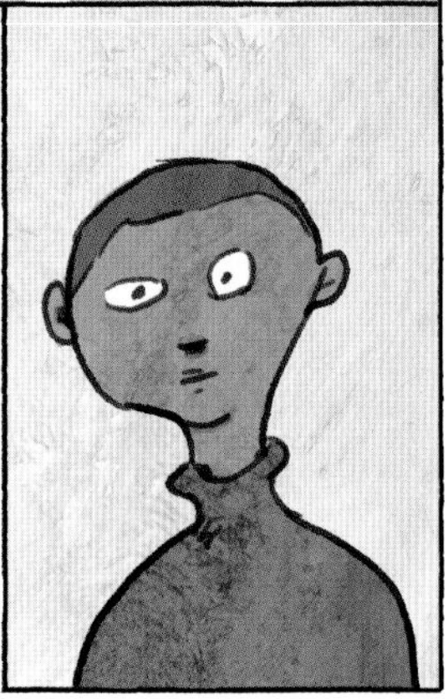

The vaccine seemed to work.

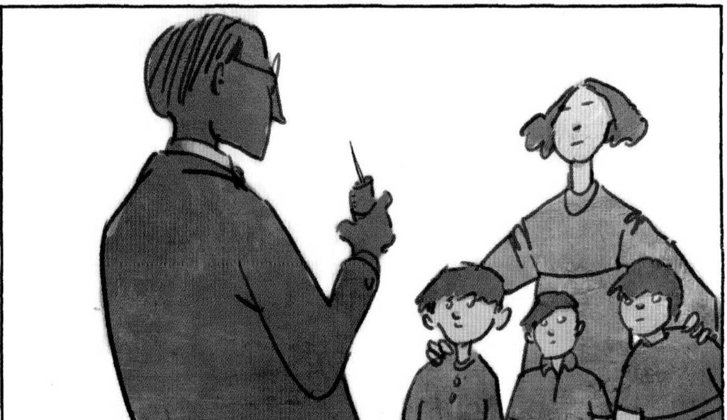

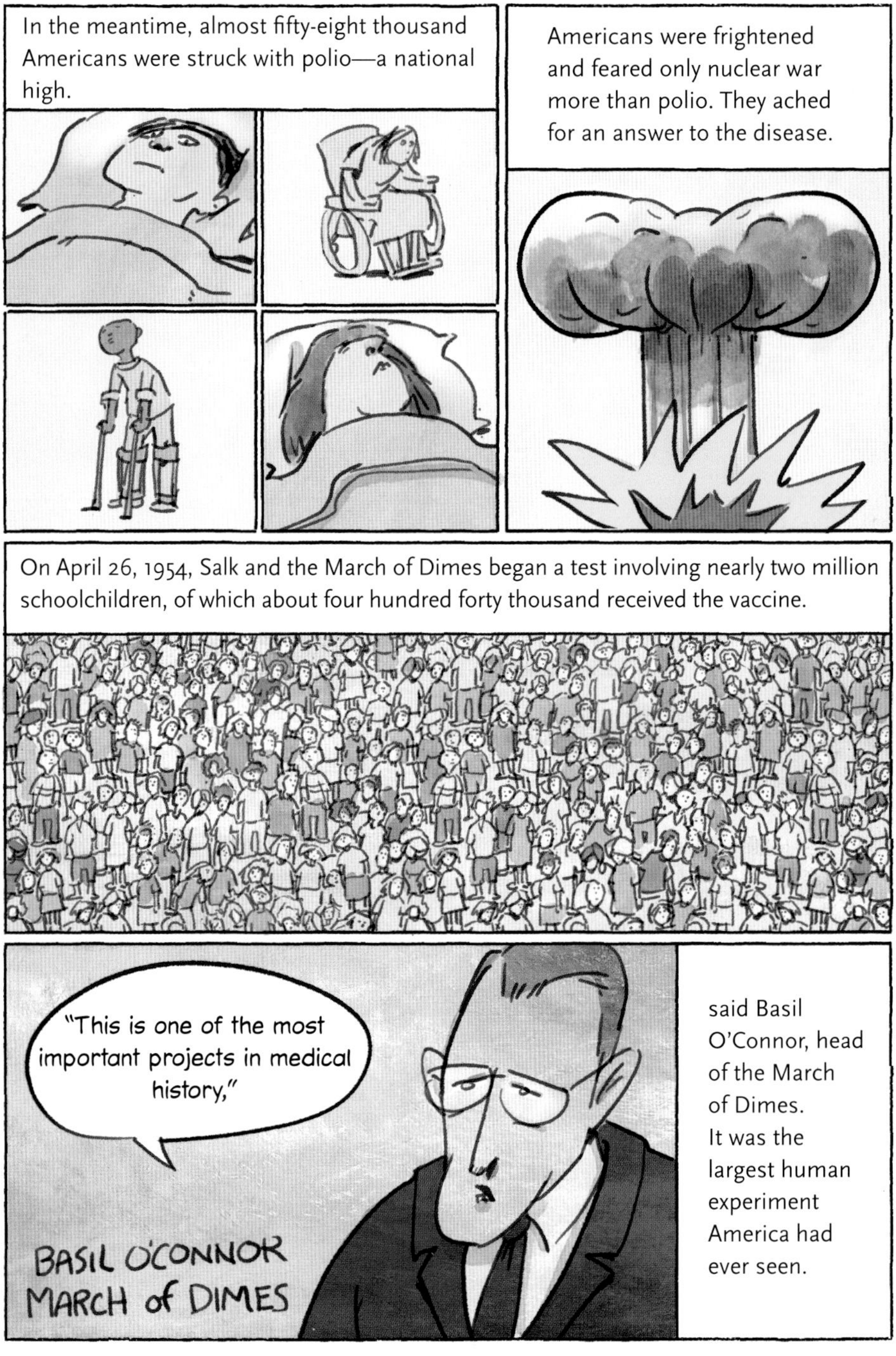
In the meantime, almost fifty-eight thousand Americans were struck with polio—a national high.
Americans were frightened and feared only nuclear war more than polio. They ached for an answer to the disease.
On April 26, 1954, Salk and the March of Dimes began a test involving nearly two million schoolchildren, of which about four hundred forty thousand received the vaccine.
"This is one of the most important projects in medical history,"
BASIL O'CONNOR
MARCH of DIMES
said Basil O'Connor, head of the March of Dimes.
It was the largest human experiment America had ever seen.

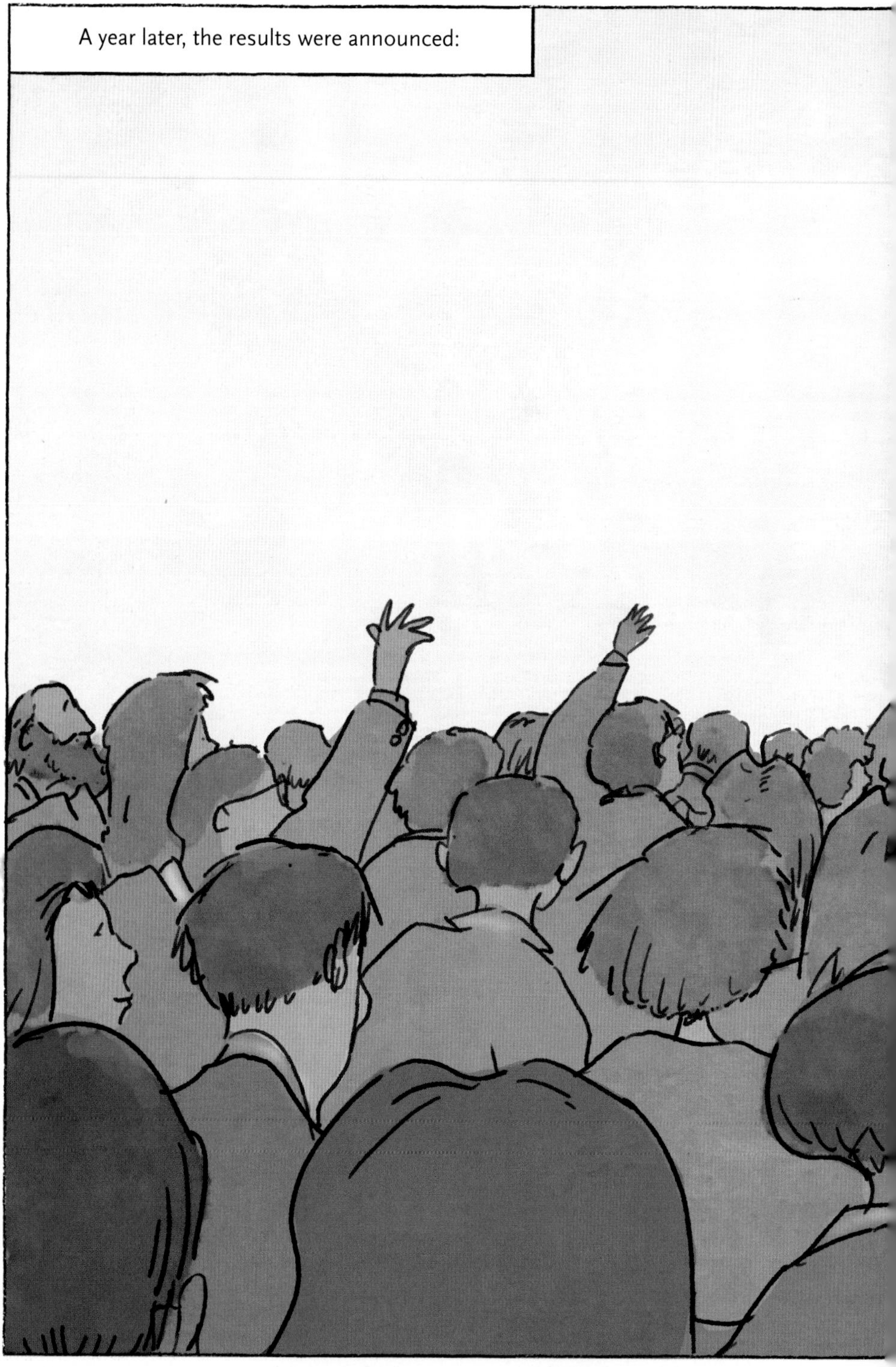
A year later, the results were announced:

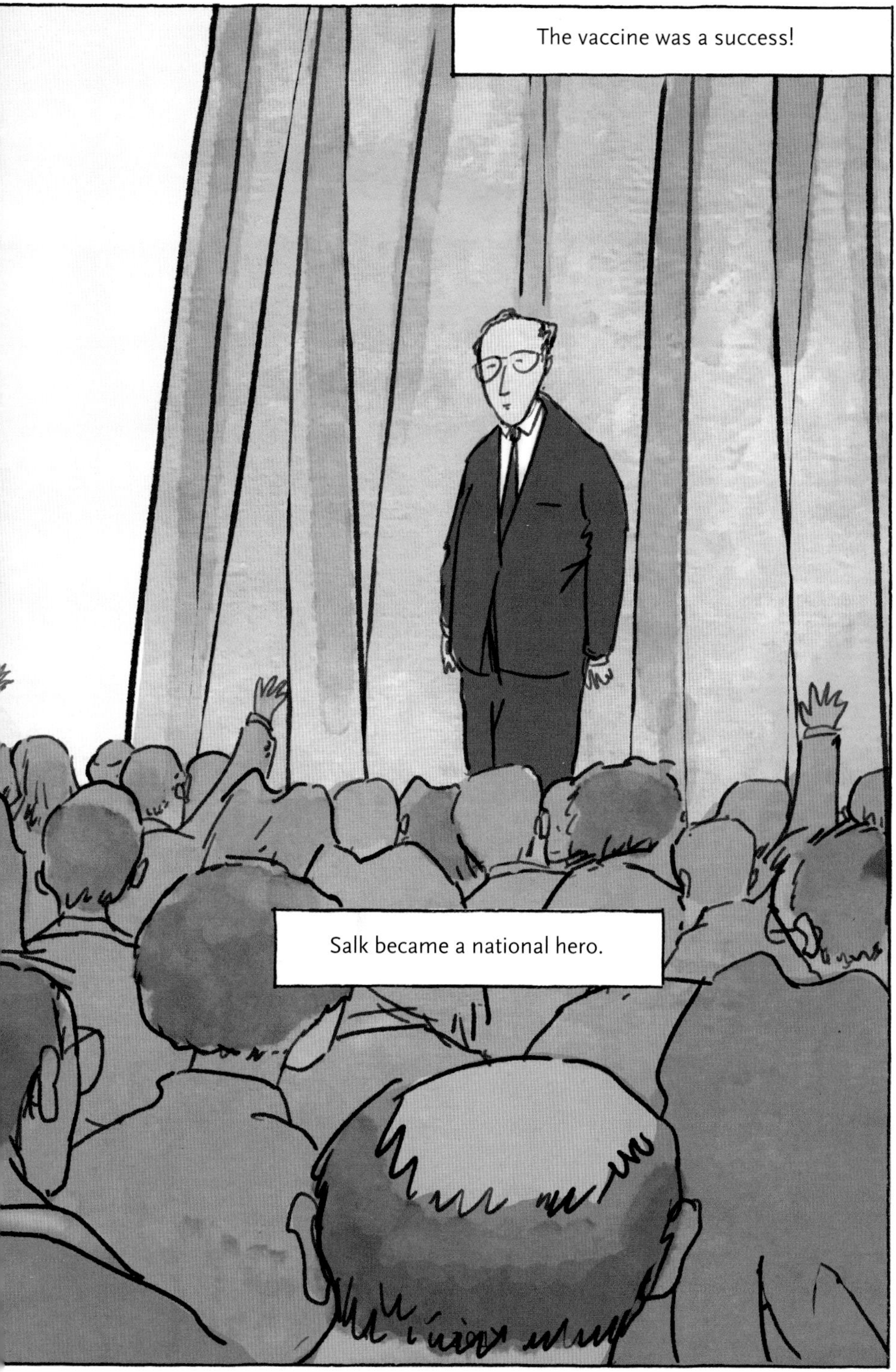
The vaccine was a success!
Salk became a national hero.

A hopeful campaign of national polio vaccinations began . . . and then tragedy struck.

Two hundred thousand children were injected with mismanufactured vaccines. Forty thousand fell victim to polio. Two hundred were crippled and ten died.

The government stepped in to ensure future vaccines would be safe.

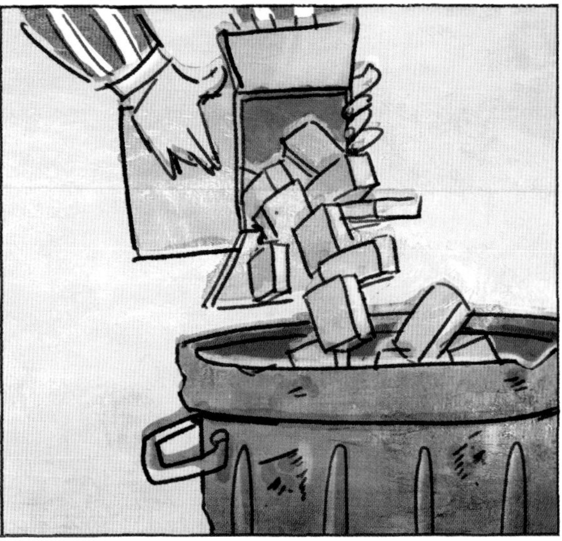

On the heels of Salk's vaccine, Dr. Albert Sabin introduced his vaccine. Sabin had the idea for a cheaper vaccine that could be taken orally and would provide lifetime protection against polio, features Salk could not match.

And Sabin's could provide immunity—the ability for the body to remember and kill reappearing microbes—to people who hadn't received the vaccine.

How is that possible?

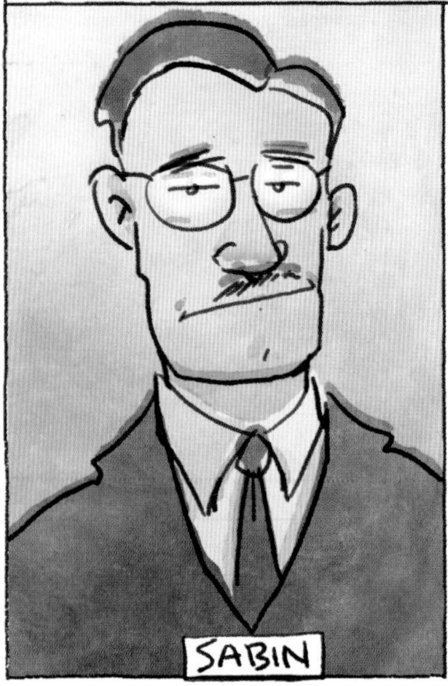
SABIN

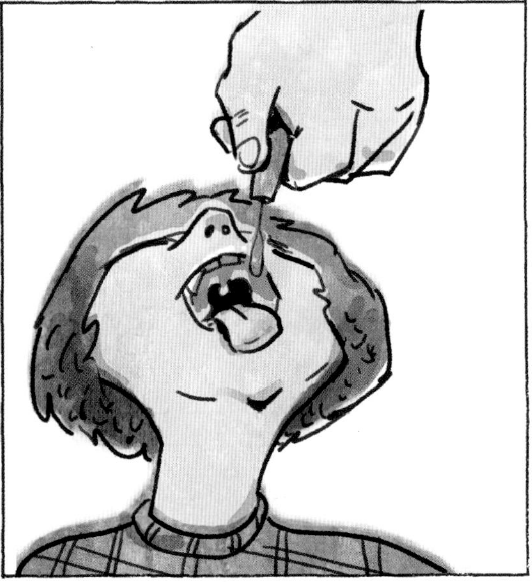

Salk used dead polio virus in his vaccine, but Sabin used an attenuated—weakened—virus. The Sabin vaccine evoked the body's natural defenses to defeat the weak virus, providing the recipient with immunity against polio. Sometimes, however, the vaccine—the weakened polio virus—was transmitted from the vaccinated person to someone who wasn't. The unvaccinated person's immune system then created his or her own immunity from polio.

DEAD VIRUS
WEAK LIVE VIRUS
IMMUNE
IMMUNE
CONTAGIOUS
IMMUNE

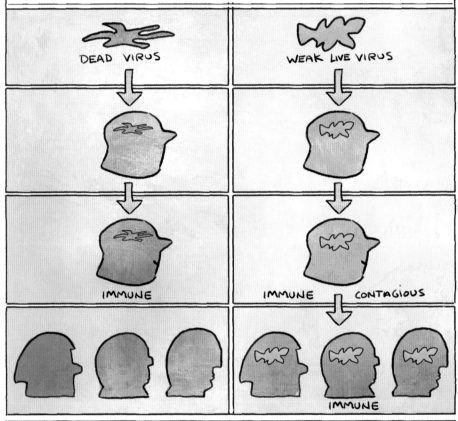

But here's a troubling note: Although polio vaccines had nearly wiped out the disease, for some people, especially those with naturally faulty immune systems, the oral version of the vaccine could trigger full-blown, crippling polio. In the United States, that meant eight to ten cases a year. For that reason, many people prefer the Salk dead-virus vaccine, which cannot spark the disease. As of 2000, America's guardian of the country's health, the Centers for Disease Control and Prevention, has permitted only a dead-virus vaccine.

By now, you must be wondering just how a vaccine works. First you have to learn about our immune system, the body's natural defense against disease.

There are trillions of bacteria and viruses on and in your body . . . yes, I said trillions.

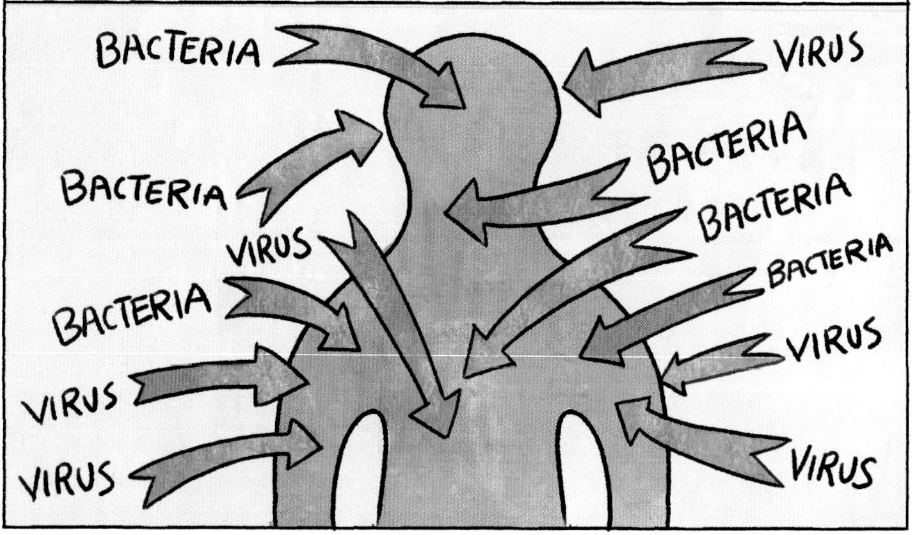
BACTERIA
VIRUS
BACTERIA
BACTERIA
BACTERIA
VIRUS
BACTERIA
BACTERIA
VIRUS
VIRUS
VIRUS
VIRUS

When destructive bacteria or viruses enter the body and begin to multiply . . .

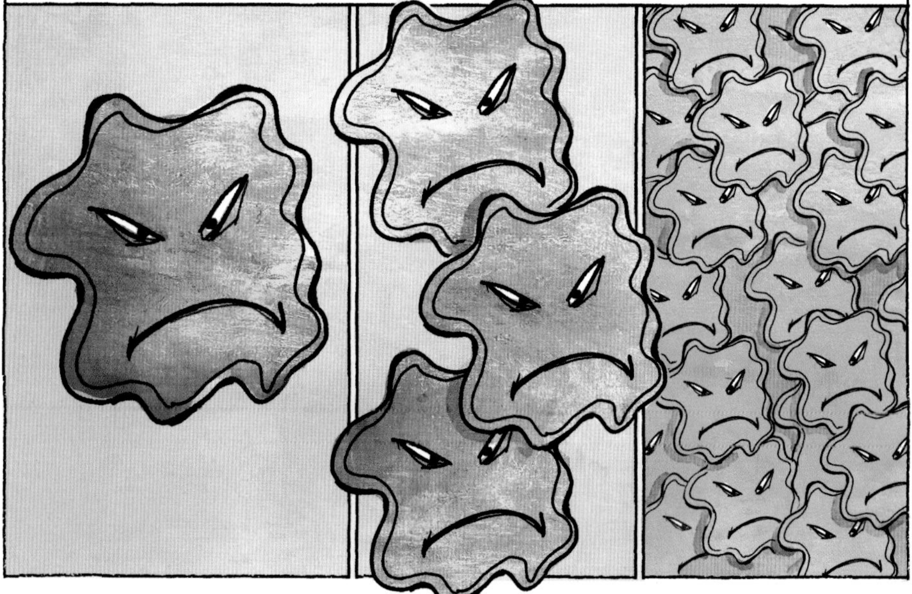

white cells—the body's natural guardians—jump into action.

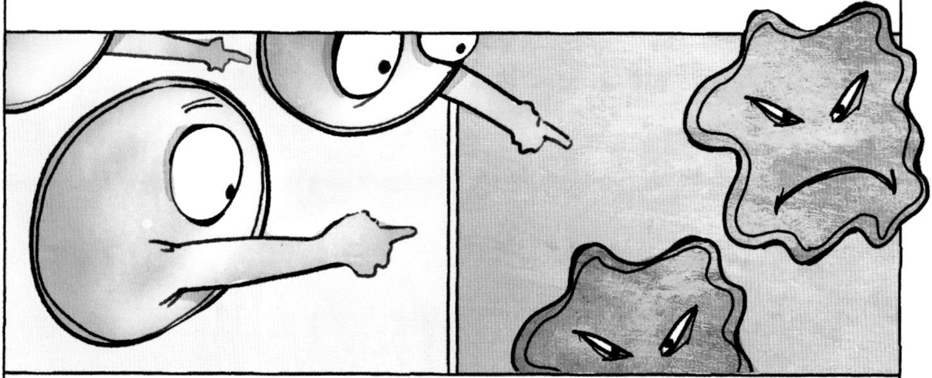

First they have to figure out which type of white cell, of which there are lots, is best designed to attack the invaders.

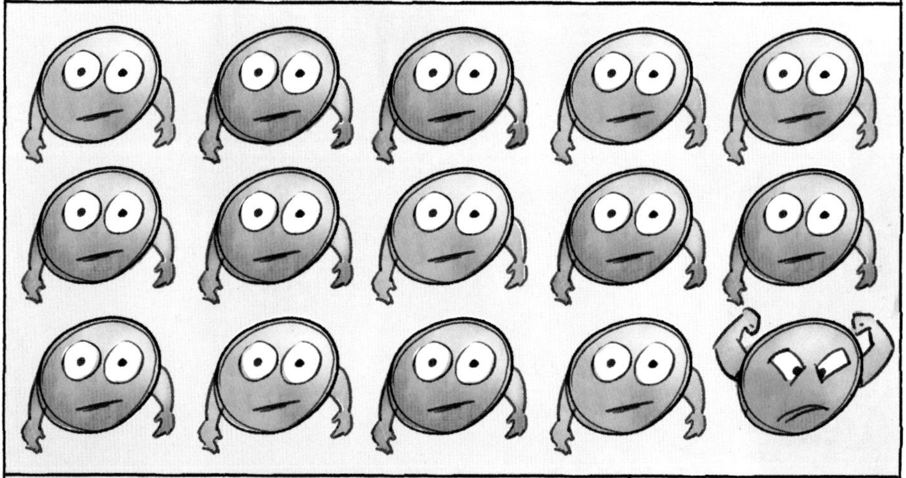

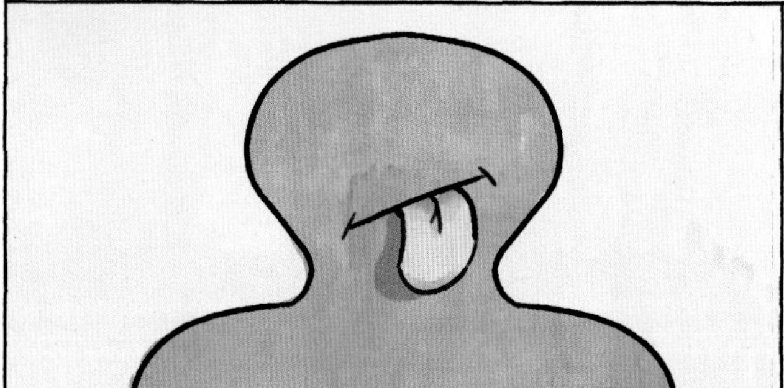

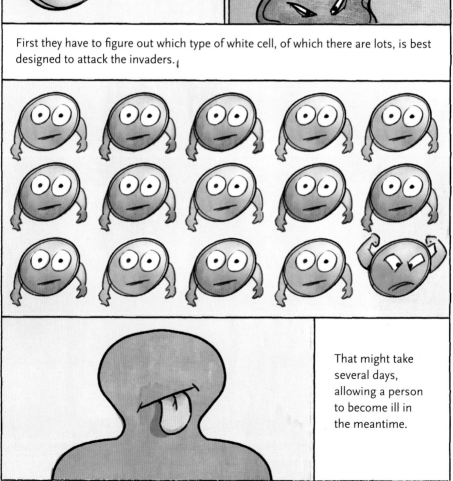

That might take several days, allowing a person to become ill in the meantime.

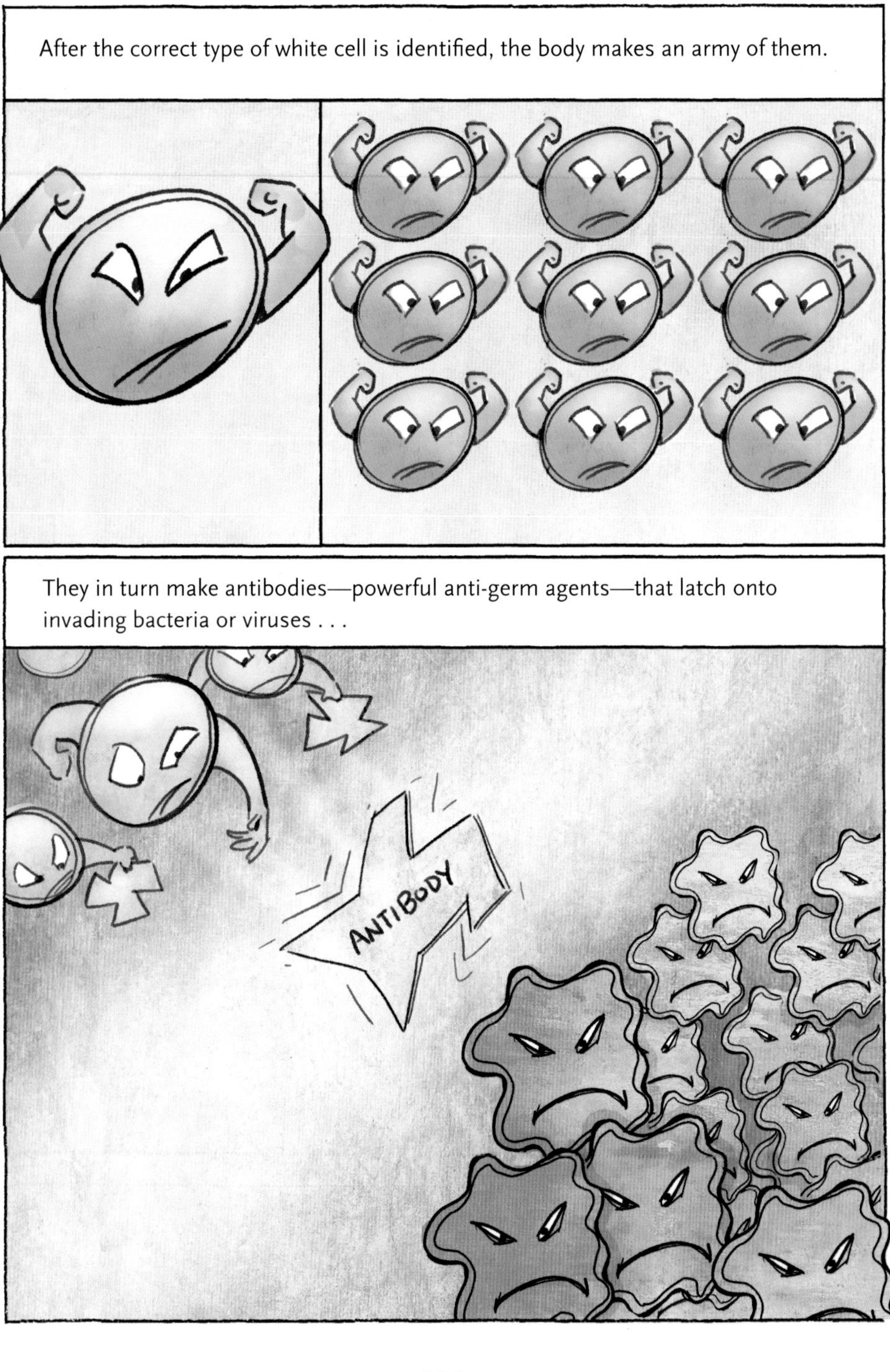
After the correct type of white cell is identified, the body makes an army of them.
They in turn make antibodies—powerful anti-germ agents—that latch onto invading bacteria or viruses . . .
ANTIBODY

killing them.

Afterward, memory cells remain on the lookout for the offending bacteria or virus.

If it's spotted again, the body jumps to immediate action and attacks without having to wait several days, sparing the person of sickness.

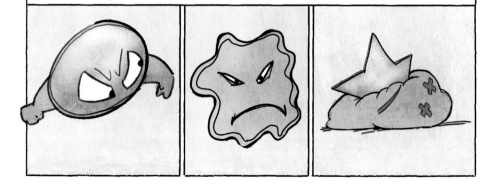

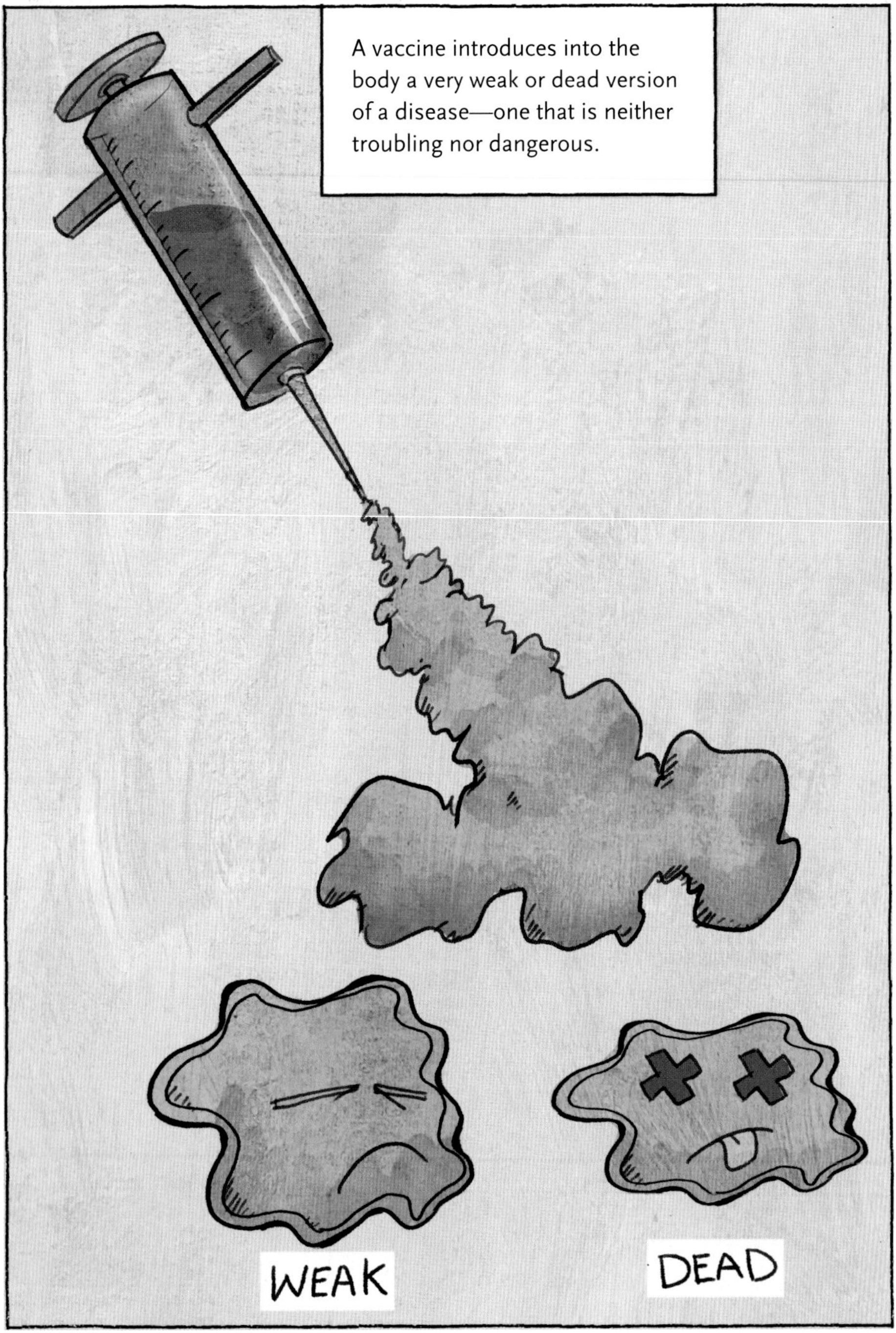
A vaccine introduces into the body a very weak or dead version of a disease—one that is neither troubling nor dangerous.
WEAK
DEAD

Feeble or not, the body's white cells go into action and meet the invader. Best of all, memory cells are created . . .

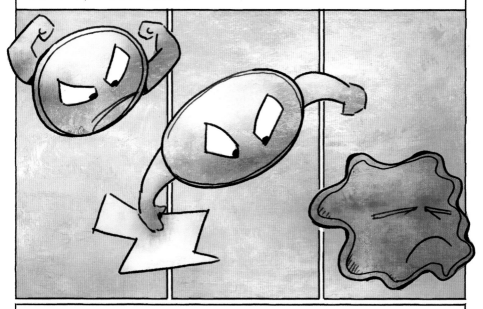

so that if the disease returns in the future . . .

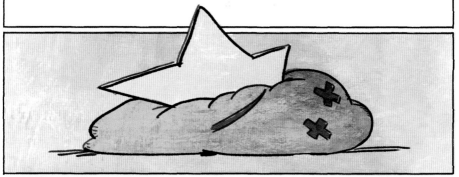

the body can spot it and get rid of it . . . all without you even knowing it's there!

In 1958, the World Health Organization, an arm of the United Nations concerned with international public health, had the very big idea to eradicate—wipe out—smallpox.

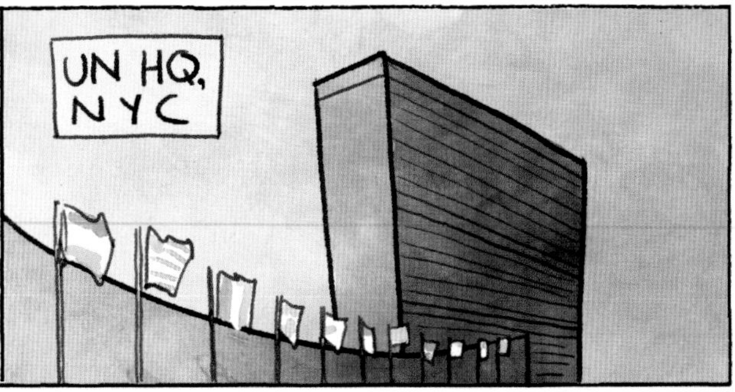
UN HQ,
NYC

In 1966, the Smallpox Eradication Program began attacking the disease in the forty-four countries that still reported cases.

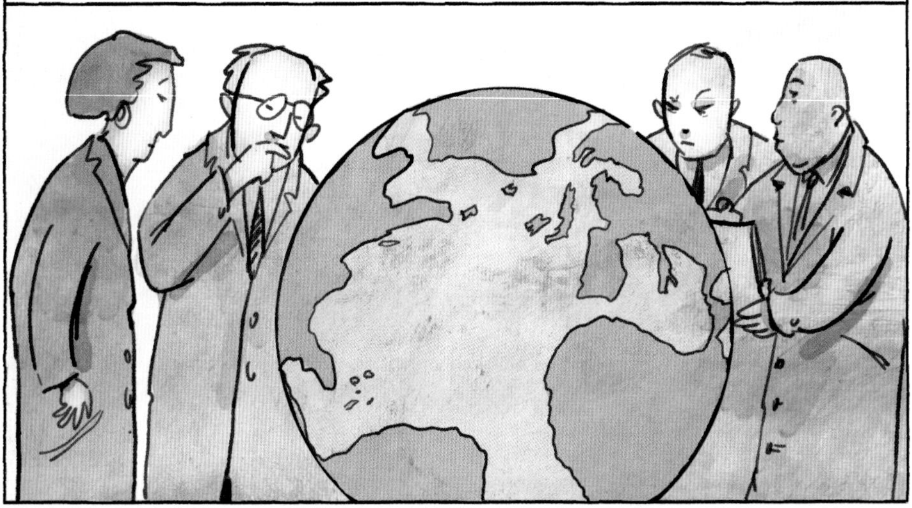

Vaccines did their job, and in 1977, Ali Maow Maalin, a hospital cook in Somalia, survived the last naturally occurring case of smallpox.

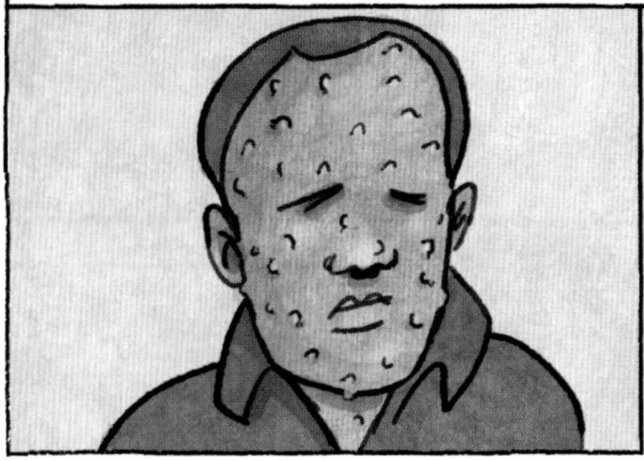

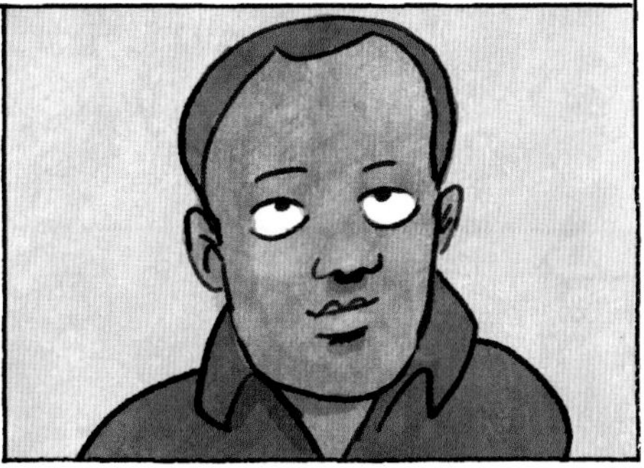

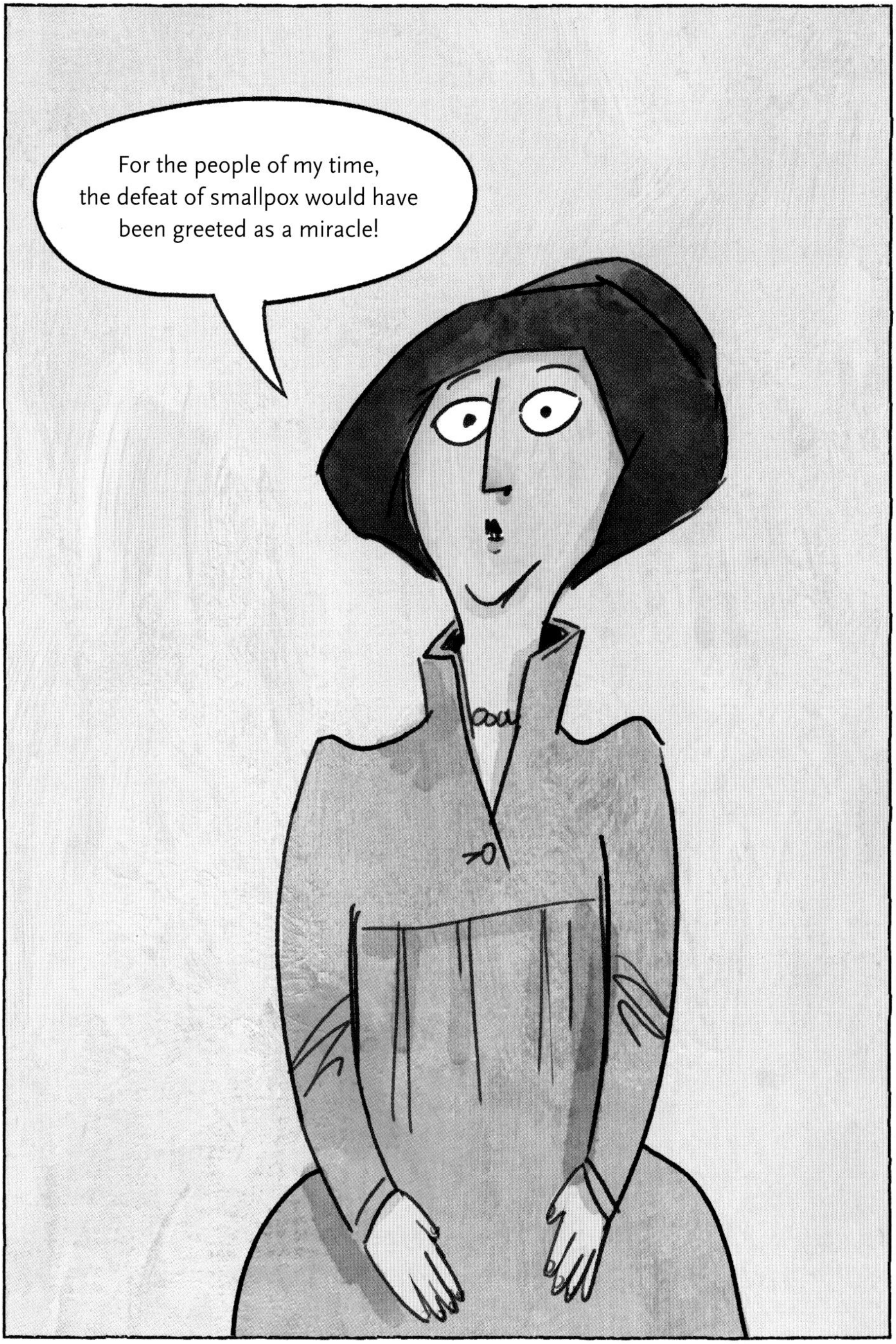
For the people of my time, the defeat of smallpox would have been greeted as a miracle!

Public health officials looked for more diseases to eradicate. Scientists eyed measles as a likely target. Measles is an easily spread disease that results in fever, runny nose, and a rash. But for some victims, the disease can blind and kill.

Then in 1998, someone had a big idea: British doctor and researcher Andrew Wakefield linked the commonly used measles, mumps, and rubella (MMR) vaccine to autism, a developmental disorder.

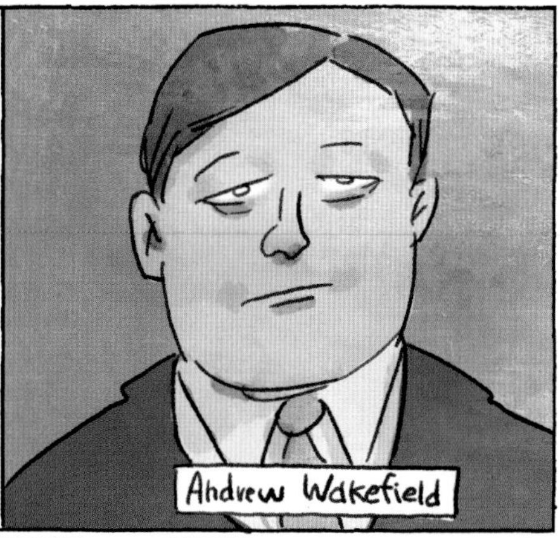
Andrew Wakefield

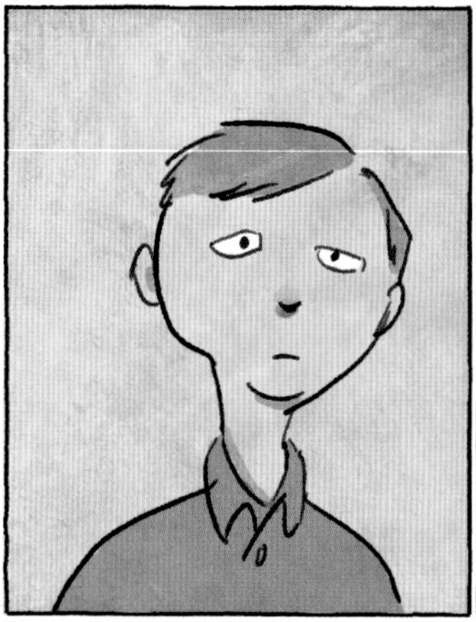

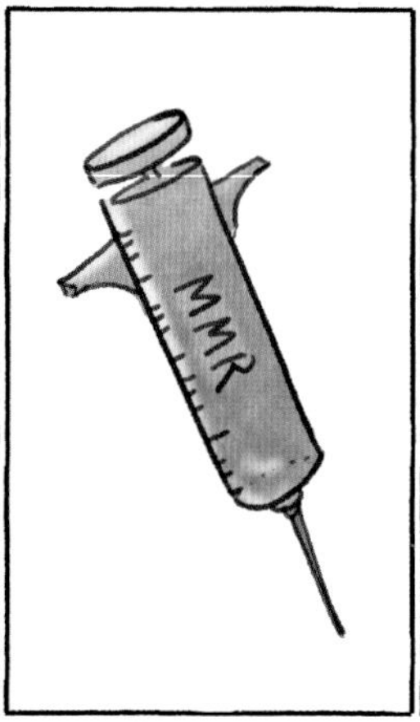
MMR

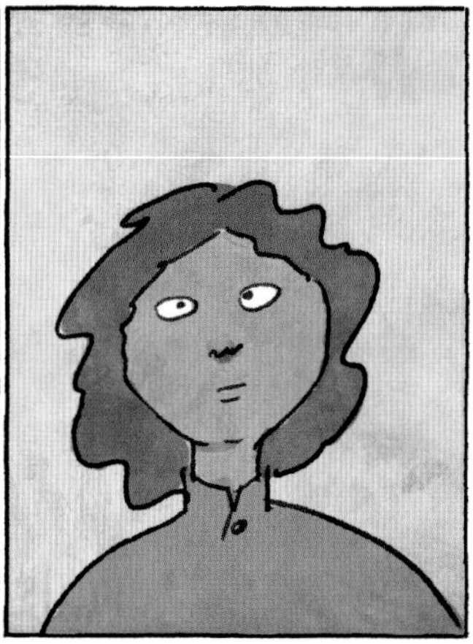

Many frightened parents stopped submitting their small children to the essential vaccine. As a result, measles broke out in Europe, Australia, and the United States.

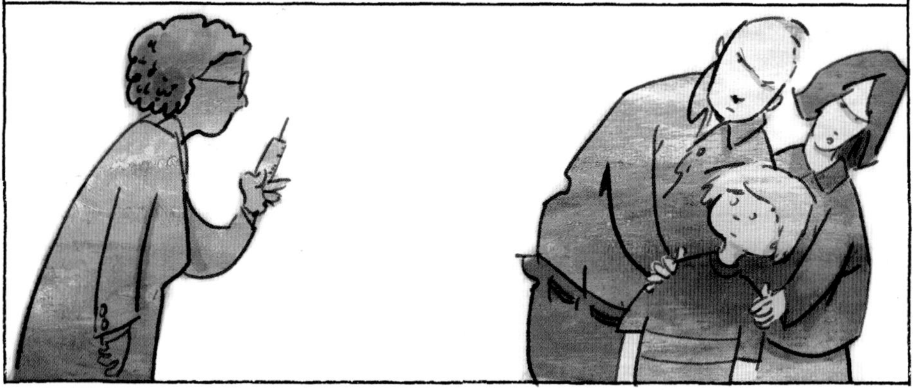

But there was a problem with Wakefield's big idea: It was a lie.

Wakefield had misreported his information in hopes of making money by offering a "safer" vaccine. In short, his report was a fraud.

Research has proven the MMR vaccine is safe and has no connection to autism. In one study in Denmark, where more than four hundred forty thousand children were vaccinated . . .

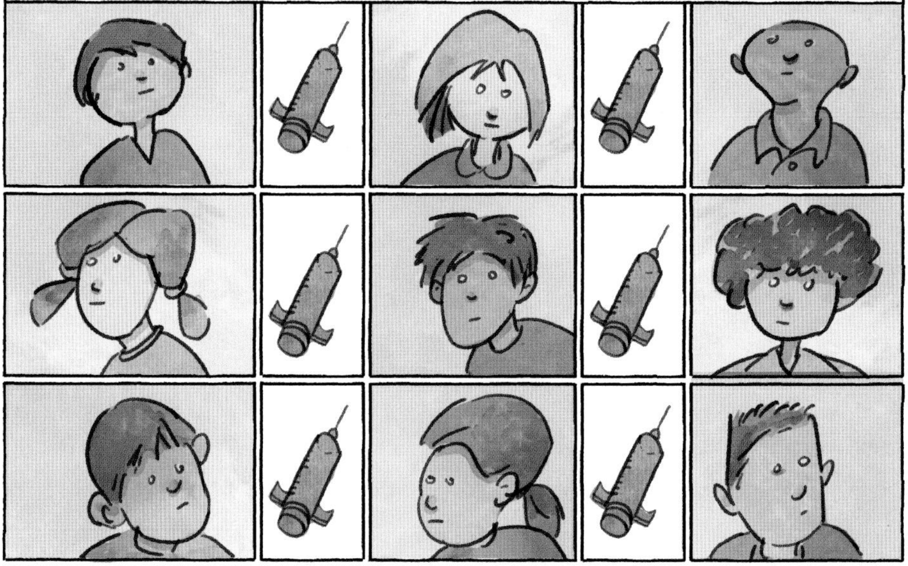

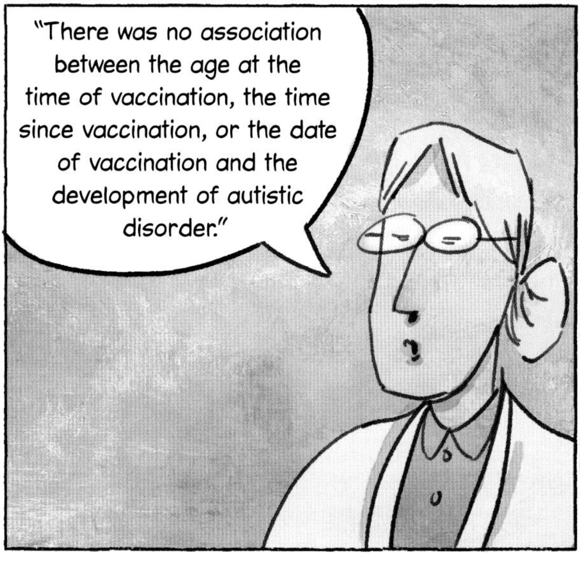
"There was no association between the age at the time of vaccination, the time since vaccination, or the date of vaccination and the development of autistic disorder."

Yet despite the evidence, some people cling to the belief that the vaccine is harmful and refuse to have their children vaccinated.

In the end, Wakefield was stripped of his medical license, proving that not all big ideas are correct and good.

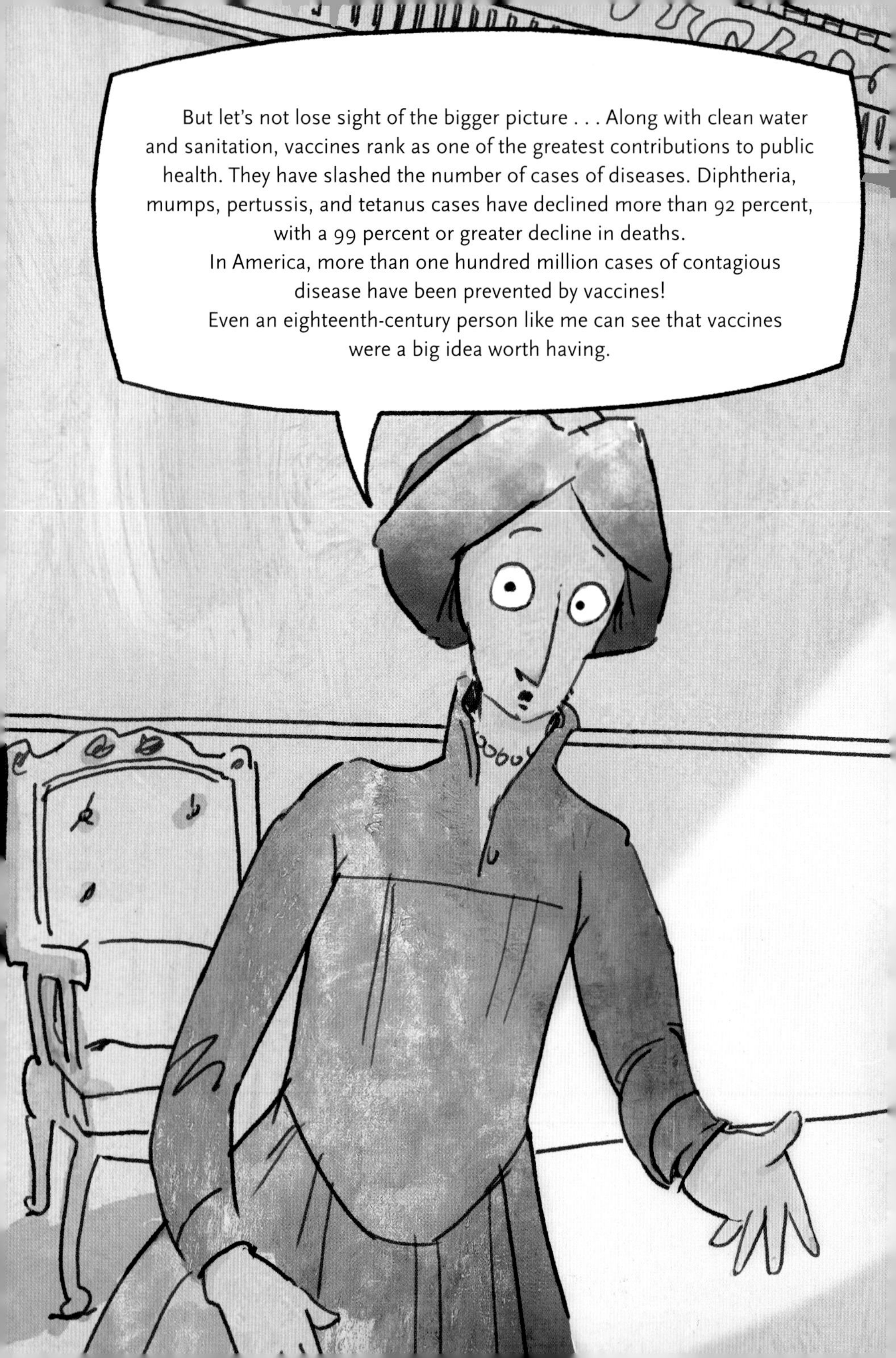
But let's not lose sight of the bigger picture . . . Along with clean water and sanitation, vaccines rank as one of the greatest contributions to public health. They have slashed the number of cases of diseases. Diphtheria, mumps, pertussis, and tetanus cases have declined more than 92 percent, with a 99 percent or greater decline in deaths.
In America, more than one hundred million cases of contagious disease have been prevented by vaccines!
Even an eighteenth-century person like me can see that vaccines were a big idea worth having.

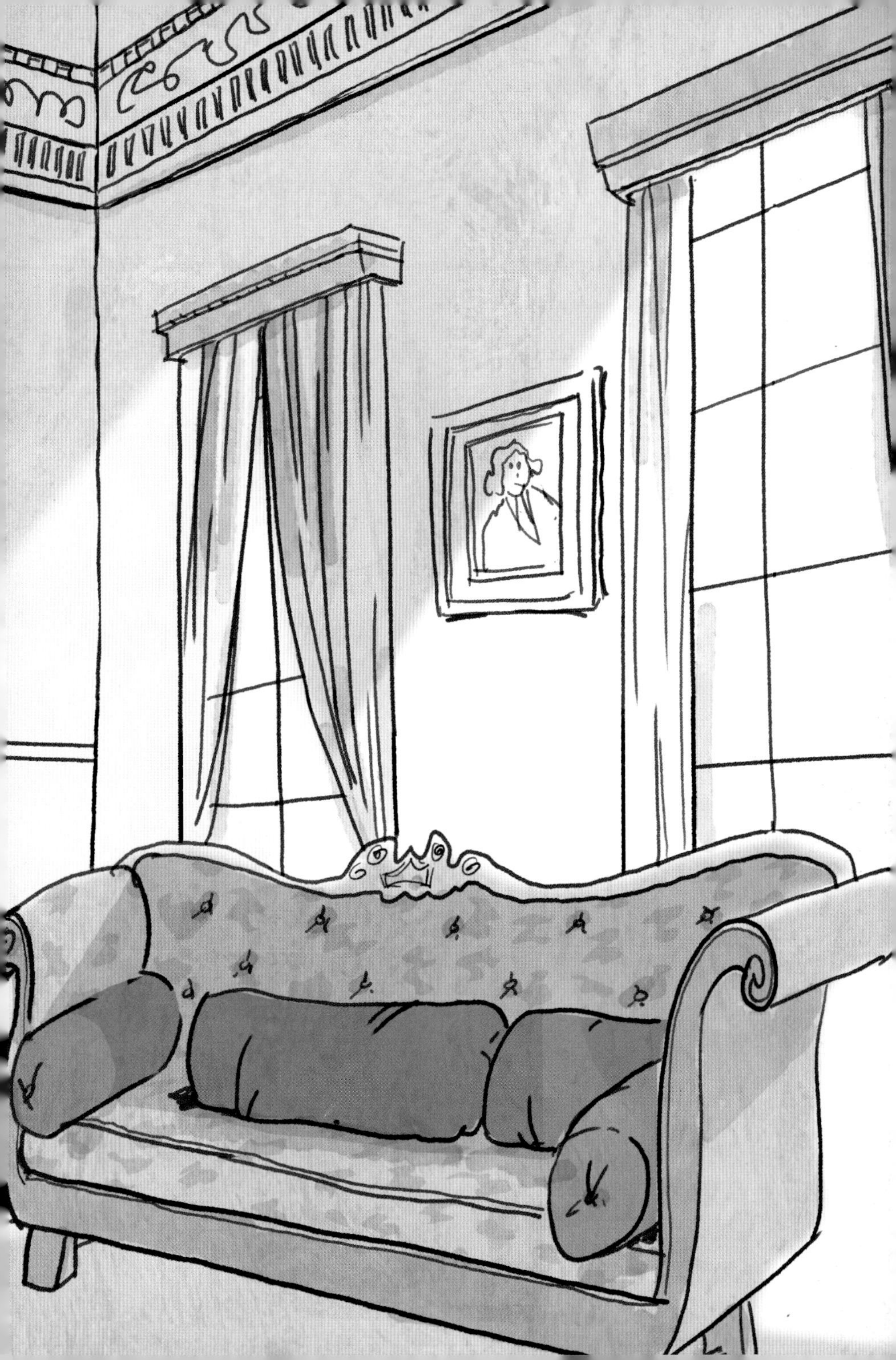

COVID-19

In the fall of 2019, a few people in Wuhan, China, suffered fever, coughing, and muscle aches . . .

And then vaccines became world news again . . .

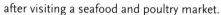
after visiting a seafood and poultry market.

They passed the pneumonia-like sickness to others, and by the end of December at least sixty people had fallen ill. In January 2020, Chinese authorities announced the first death from the disease.

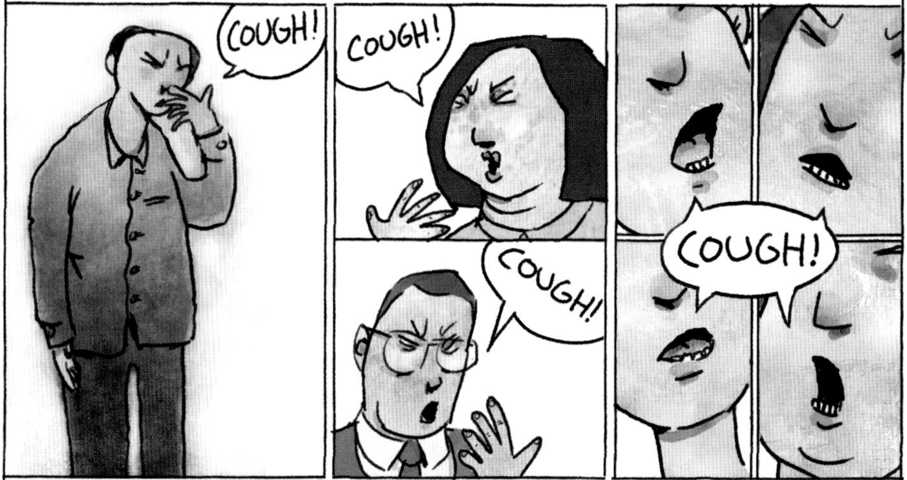
COUGH!
COUGH!
COUGH!
COUGH!

Seven months later, the disease had sickened about fifteen million people around the world and killed about six hundred thousand of them.

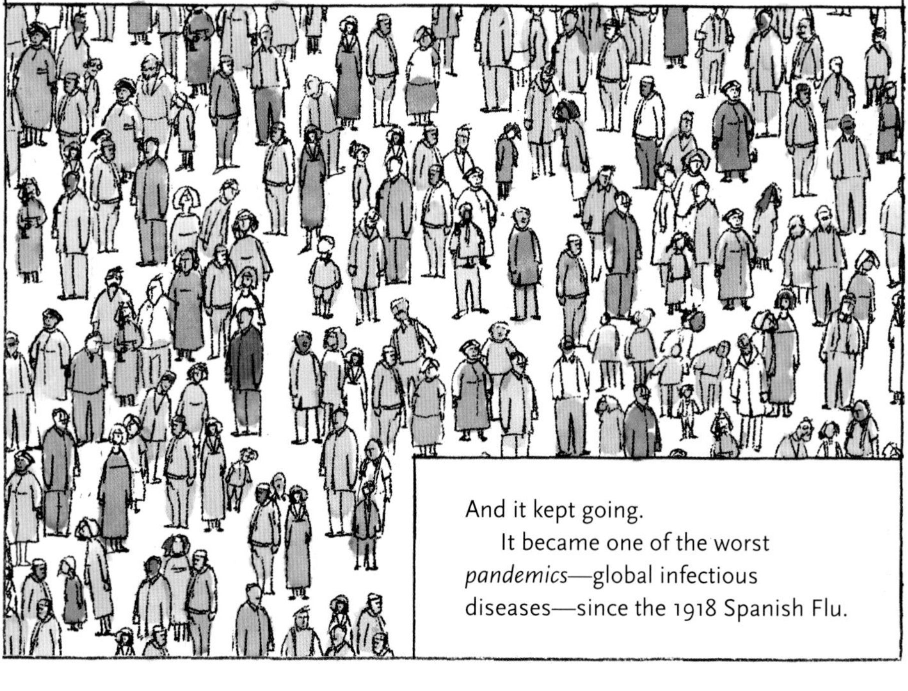

And it kept going.

It became one of the worst *pandemics*—global infectious diseases—since the 1918 Spanish Flu.

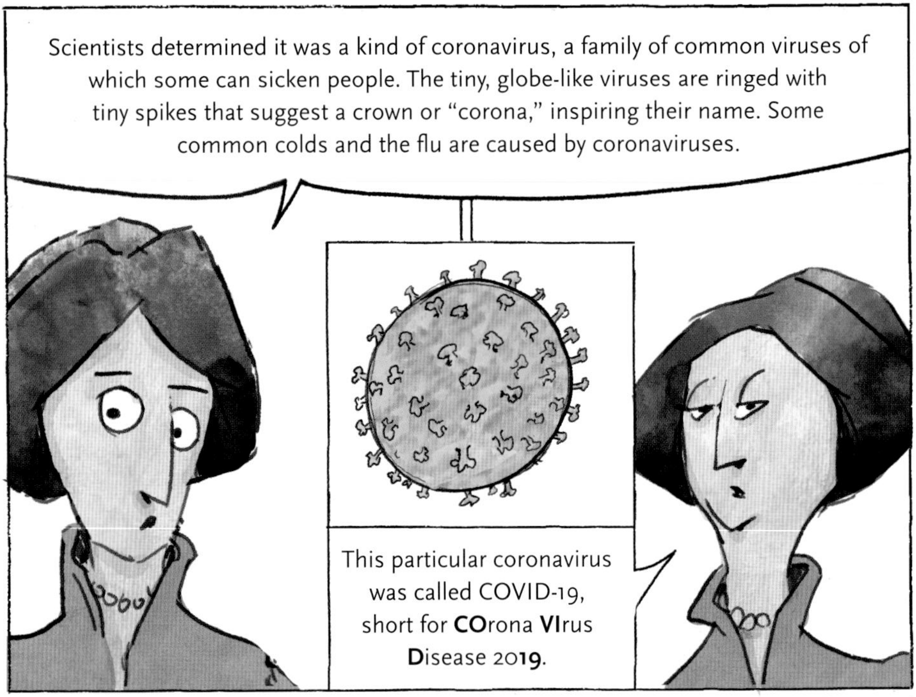
Scientists determined it was a kind of coronavirus, a family of common viruses of which some can sicken people. The tiny, globe-like viruses are ringed with tiny spikes that suggest a crown or "corona," inspiring their name. Some common colds and the flu are caused by coronaviruses.
This particular coronavirus was called COVID-19, short for **CO**rona **VI**rus **D**isease 20**19**.

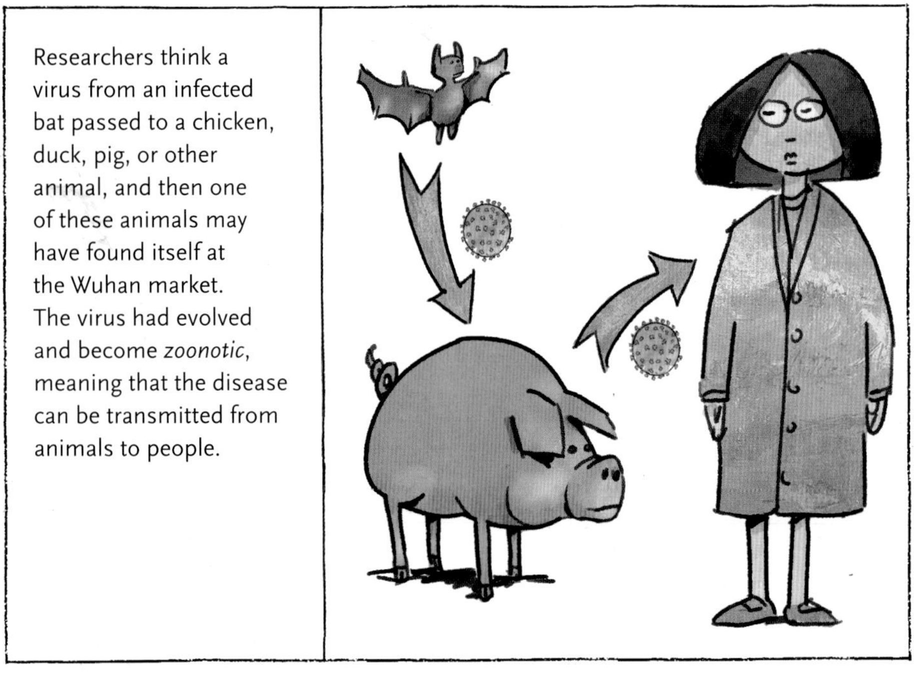
Researchers think a virus from an infected bat passed to a chicken, duck, pig, or other animal, and then one of these animals may have found itself at the Wuhan market. The virus had evolved and become *zoonotic*, meaning that the disease can be transmitted from animals to people.

This particular virus mostly targets cells in people's lungs, using those cells to reproduce, which damages the lungs. With each breath, the victim sprayed the virus into the air, where it could be drawn into another person's lungs and make another victim.

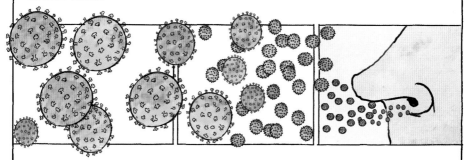

Medicine or therapy to help the afflicted was limited. Hospitals were swamped with sick people. Beds and supplies fell short. The risk of death varied from country to country. Older people proved more vulnerable than younger ones. The memory of the fifty million dead from the Spanish Flu frightened people.

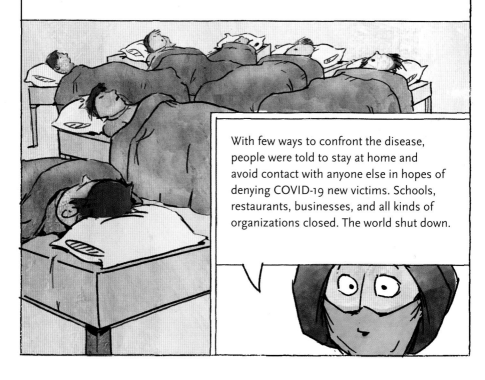

With few ways to confront the disease, people were told to stay at home and avoid contact with anyone else in hopes of denying COVID-19 new victims. Schools, restaurants, businesses, and all kinds of organizations closed. The world shut down.

The sick were isolated from the healthy, and rates of infection dropped where people kept strict seclusion. But it came at an extraordinary cost. People were shut off from their jobs and income, so some couldn't pay rent or buy groceries. Governments helped, but lives were greatly disrupted.

Life will stay disrupted until there are medicines to treat the disease or scientists have developed a vaccine to prevent it.

Like smallpox, measles, and polio vaccines, the idea is to promote the body's natural defense system, in which immune cells are thrown into action against an intruding virus or bacteria and are then available to fight it if it returns.

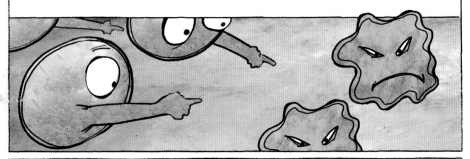

Scientists from all over the world are racing to make a COVID-19 vaccine. Some are following the path used by traditional vaccines like smallpox, in which harmless or dead versions of the disease are introduced into the body to fire up the immune system.

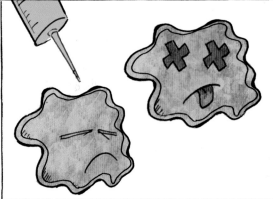

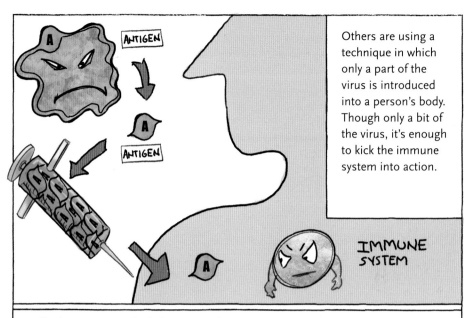

Others are using a technique in which only a part of the virus is introduced into a person's body. Though only a bit of the virus, it's enough to kick the immune system into action.

IMMUNE SYSTEM

Still other scientists think they can trick a person's own body into manufacturing an immune response.

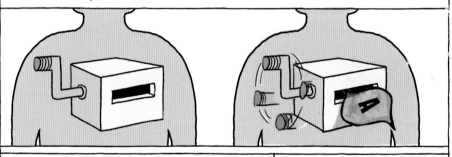

By November 2020 scientists were reporting positive results for several possible vaccines. If one or more are approved, then within months disease-preventing doses can begin to be administered to people around the world. Billions of dollars are being spent to make this happen. Still, no vaccine has ever been created as quickly or in that quantity. The world holds its breath . . . and hopes.

SELECT TIMELINE

Third century BCE
Evidence of smallpox in Egypt.

166 CE
Smallpox likely killer of 10 percent of the Roman Empire.

Fourth through seventh centuries
Smallpox afflicts China, India, and the Middle East.

c. 1000
Chinese inoculate against smallpox using the dust of dried smallpox scabs.

Eleventh century
Crusaders spread smallpox through Europe.

Fifteenth century
Europeans spread smallpox to western Africa.

1715
Lady Mary Wortley Montagu contracts smallpox.

1717
Montagu lives in the Ottoman Empire with her diplomat husband. There she learns about inoculation and has her son inoculated.

1721
Back in England, Montagu has her daughter inoculated in the face of a smallpox epidemic. Princess Caroline of Wales is convinced to do the same for her two daughters. Inoculation spreads.

In Boston, Cotton Mather promotes inoculation in the face of a smallpox epidemic.

300 BCE   1500   1825

Sixteenth and seventeenth centuries
Europeans spread smallpox to the Western Hemisphere.

Eighteenth century
With the knowledge that smallpox can attack a person only once, the practice of infecting otherwise healthy people with a mild form of smallpox to protect them from a more dangerous and lethal version is used in Asia and the Middle East. It is called *inoculation* or *variolation*.

The British introduce smallpox to Australia.

1768
Dr. John Fewster of England, among others, observes that his patients who have had cowpox seem to be protected from smallpox.

1777
George Washington orders mandatory inoculation of Continental Army.

1796
Dr. Edward Jenner, former assistant to Fewster, inserts material from Sarah Nelmes's cowpox scabs into James Phipps, which inoculates him from smallpox. Jenner called the treatment a *vaccine*, inspired by the Latin word *vaccinia*, "cowpox."

1840
Britain bans variolation, the transfer of smallpox from person to person, and promotes vaccination through cowpox.

1855
Massachusetts passes the first law mandating vaccinations for schoolchildren.

1874
Compulsory vaccination becomes the law in Germany. Deaths from smallpox plummet.

1876
Dr. Robert Koch of Germany reveals the life cycle of anthrax.

1885
First vaccine for cholera.

Pasteur creates a vaccine for rabies. He calls his treatment a *vaccine* in honor of Edward Jenner, separating the word from its specific cowpox/smallpox origin and making it a generic term referring to any kind of weakened microorganism administered to promote immunity from a disease.

1896
First vaccine for typhoid fever.

1897
First vaccine for bubonic plague.

1850   1875   1900

1879
By chance, scientist Louis Pasteur discovers that employing an attenuated—weakened—strain of chicken cholera makes an effective vaccine against the disease. Some point to this discovery as the birth of immunology.

1885
One hundred thousand anti-vaccination protestors gather in Leicester, England, to argue against British mandatory vaccination laws.

1890
Koch publishes his postulates, the steps to follow in microbiological research.

1901
Tainted smallpox vaccine kills nine children in Camden, NJ.

1902
The United States government passes the Biologics Control Act to regulate the sale of viruses, serums, and vaccines.

1905
In *Jacobson v. Massachusetts*, the United States Supreme Court rules that the state has the right to order mandatory vaccination in pursuit of the public health.

1914
First vaccine for pertussis (whooping cough).

1916
Measles kills nearly twelve thousand. Most of its victims are under five years old.

1918
The Spanish influenza kills tens of millions of people around the world. Various vaccinations are employed against it to little or no effect.

1921
First vaccine for tuberculosis.

New York politician Franklin Delano Roosevelt is stricken with polio. His legs are paralyzed for the remainder of his life.

1939
First vaccine for tick-borne encephalitis.

1945
First vaccine for influenza.

1952
Jonas Salk begins testing a polio vaccine.

1954
More than 1.3 million American children participate in a test of the Salk polio vaccine.

1955
The results of the Salk polio test show the vaccine is 80 percent to 90 percent effective. It goes into immediate widespread use across America.

1900 | 1925 | 1950 |

1923
First vaccine for diphtheria.

1924
First vaccine for scarlet fever.

First tetanus toxoid vaccine.

1930
First vaccine for typhus.

1937
First vaccine for yellow fever.

1938
The March of Dimes is born to raise money for a polio cure.

1955
The Cutter Incident. Flawed polio vaccine from Cutter Laboratories results in seventy thousand cases of polio. One hundred sixty-four are left paralyzed and ten people die.

1954
First vaccine for anthrax.

1960
Albert Sabin's polio vaccine is licensed. It contains a live, weakened polio virus in place of Salk's dead virus. Sabin's vaccine can be taken orally. It comes to be the preferred vaccine in the United States.

1963
First vaccine for measles.

1967
First vaccine for mumps.

World Health Organization launches the Smallpox Eradication Program.

1969
First vaccine for rubella.

1974
First vaccine for chickenpox.

1977
Ali Maow Maalin of Somalia becomes the last person to have naturally acquired smallpox.

1978
First vaccine for meningitis.

1975

1978
In England, Janet Parker becomes the last person to die of smallpox, the apparent victim of a biological laboratory accident.

1980
The world is declared free of smallpox. Its eradication has been hailed as the greatest victory for international public health.

1981
First vaccine for hepatitis B.

1991
First vaccine for hepatitis A.

1998
First vaccine for Lyme disease.

First vaccine for rotavirus.

British doctor Andrew Wakefield publishes an article suggesting that the measles, mumps, rubella (MMR) vaccine triggers autism in children.

2006
First vaccine to prevent cervical cancer.

2010
In the wake of scientific studies and investigative journalism, Andrew Wakefield has his medical license revoked for "dishonestly and irresponsibly" making an "utterly false" assertion that the MMR vaccine triggers autism.

2000

2015
First vaccine for malaria.

First vaccine for dengue.

2019
First vaccine for Ebola approved.

In spite of Wakefield's discrediting, America has its worst measles outbreak since 1992, the consequence of some parents clinging to Wakefield's discredited paper linking the MMR vaccine to autism.

COVID-19 detected in Wuhan, China, in December.

2025

2020
COVID-19 infects more than ten million people around the worl. and more than a half million have died at the time this book went to press.

125

WHO WAS
MARY WORTLEY
MONTAGU?

Mary Wortley Montagu with her son, Edward—who was
inoculated against measles. Detail of oil on canvas, circa 1717,
by Jean Baptiste Vanmour.

Born **Mary Pierrepont** (May 26, 1689–August 21, 1762), she was the eldest child of a wealthy English duke. Mary displayed a knack for writing and authored two volumes of poetry and a novel as a teenager. Along with her precocious talent, she possessed an independent streak: She rejected a marriage arranged by her father and eloped with politician Edward Wortley Montagu in 1712.

A year later, tragedy struck when her twenty-year-old brother died of smallpox. Mary contracted the disease in 1715. She escaped death but not disfigurement. It seems the loss of Mary's beauty brought on the loss of her husband's affections and their marriage sank into one of appearance only. In 1716, Mary accompanied Edward Montagu to the Ottoman Empire, where he had been appointed ambassador at its capital, Constantinople, known today as Istanbul, a cultural and economic center of Turkey.

There, Mary witnessed the practice of transferring a mild case of smallpox from one person to another. The Ottomans were using the common knowledge that smallpox could be suffered only once, so infecting a secondary person with a "softened" version of the disease prevented death or disfigurement. With her own unhappy experience with smallpox in mind, Mary had her four-year-old son Edward inoculated. The smallpox pus of a lightly afflicted victim was inserted into a scratch on the boy's skin.

The Montagus returned to England. When a smallpox epidemic arose there in 1721, Mary had her daughter inoculated. The practice was taken up by Princess Caroline of Wales, who had her daughters inoculated. Having received something of a royal seal of approval, the practice became widespread in England.

Mary made observations of life in the Ottoman Empire in a series of fifty-two letters that became known as the Turkish Embassy Letters. Along with a description of smallpox inoculation were sympathetic notes on Ottoman life including law and religion, although her descriptions of a benevolent slave culture were opinions probably not shared by the enslaved. She revealed the private life of Ottoman women—observations denied to male writers. The Embassy Letters became an inspiration to subsequent female travel writers.

Mary lived much of her life in Italy and France apart from her husband. She became ill and died in 1762, leaving a legacy of intelligence, independence, and wit.

NOTES

Page 10—"Could it not be contrived to Send the *Small Pox* . . . to Reduce them." Gill, Harold B. Jr. "Colonial Germ Warfare."

Page 25—"A face is too slight a foundation for happiness." Lord Wharncliffe, p. 175.

Page 29—"The good Woman went to work . . . with my own instrument and with so little pain to him." Halsband, p. 81.

Page 62—"What renders the Cow Pox . . . so extremely singular is that the person who has been affected is for ever [*sic*] after secure from the infection of the Small Pox." Jenner, p. 7.

Page 64—"I selected a healthy boy . . . each about half an inch long." Jenner, pp. 29–32.

Page 73—"has the right to protect itself against an epidemic of disease which threatens the safety of its members." Biss & Biss, *The Atlantic*.

Page 76—"I took up a little of it in a glass phial . . . a thousand times smaller than the smallest ones I have ever seen." Carey, pp. 28–29.

Page 94—"I have been very much concerned . . . which must continue unless this disease can be brought under control." Franklin D. Roosevelt Presidential Library and Museum.

Page 95—"The March of Dimes will enable all persons, even the children . . . if a million people send only one dime, the total will be $100,000." *Origin of our name*. March of Dimes Organization.

Page 97—"During the past few days bags of mail have been coming . . . Literally, by the countless thousands, they are pouring in." March of Dimes Organization.

Page 99—"This is one of the most important projects in medical history." "The Polio Crusade," 37:40.

Page 113—"There was no association between the age at the time of vaccination, the time since vaccination, or the date of vaccination and the development of autistic disorder." Madsen, *The New England Journal of Medicine*.

SELECTED BIBLIOGRAPHY

A Shot in the Arm! is a work of cartoon art and representations of people, places, and dress are drawn within those parameters. However, I used a variety of publicly available online sources, including those in the bibliography, to ensure accuracy as needed to convey the situation.

Books

Carey, John, ed. *Eyewitness to Science*. Cambridge: Harvard University Press, 1995.

Halsband, Robert. *The Life of Lady Mary Wortley Montagu*. New York: Oxford University Press, 1960.

Irwin, Richard S., and James M. Rippe. *Intensive Care Medicine: Sixth Edition*. Philadelphia: Walters Kluwer, 2008.

Jenner, Edward. *An Inquiry into the Causes and Effects of the Variolae Vaccinae*. London: D. N. Shury, 1802. ia800404.us.archive.org/15/items/b28521730/b28521730.pdf

Kinch, Michael. *Between Hope and Fear: A History of Vaccines and Human Immunity*. New York: Pegasus Books, 2018.

Plotkin, Stanley A., ed. *History of Vaccine Development*. New York: Springer, 2011. books.google.com/books?id=Wf2jS_4lCOAC&printsec=frontcover

Wharncliffe, Lord Archibald. *The Letters and Works of Lady Mary Wortley Montagu*. London: Henry G. Bohn, 1863. archive.org/details/lettersworksofla01inmont/page/n5

Articles

Belluz, Julia. "Research Fraud Catalyzed the Anti-vaccination Movement. Let's Not Repeat History." *Vox*, March 5, 2019. www.vox.com/2018/2/27/17057990/andrew-wakefield -vaccines-autism-study

Belongia, Edward A. and Allison L. Naleway. "Smallpox Vaccine: The Good, the Bad, and the Ugly." *Clinical Medical Research*, April 2003. www.ncbi.nlm.nih.gov/pmc/articles /PMC1069029/

Berche, P. "Louis Pasteur, from Crystals of Life to Vaccination." *Clinical Microbiology and Infection*, October 2012. www.clinicalmicrobiologyandinfection.com/article/S1198 -743X(14)61355-0/fulltext

Biss, Eula and Mavis Biss. "Are Anti-vaxxers Conscientious Objectors?" *The Atlantic*, July 29, 2019. www.theatlantic.com/family/archive/2019/07/anti-vaxxers-measles -conscience-morals/594646/

Blakeslee, Sandra. "No Evidence of Autism Link Is Seen in Vaccine, Study Says." *New York Times*, April 24, 2001. www.nytimes.com/2001/04/24/us/no-evidence-of-autism-link -is-seen-in-vaccine-study-says.html

Boylston, Arthur. "The Origins of Inoculation." *Journal of the Royal Society of Medicine*, July 2012; 105: 309–313. www.ncbi.nlm.nih.gov/pmc/articles/PMC3407399/

Brennan, Zachary and Sarah Owermohle. "Why One Breakthrough Drug Won't End the Pandemic." Politico, April 30, 2020. www.politico.com/news/2020/04/30/remdesivir -drug-coronavirus-227208

Davidson, Helen. "First Covid-19 Case Happened in November, China Government Records Show—Report." *The Guardian*. March 13, 2020. www.theguardian.com /world/2020/mar/13/first-covid-19-case-happened-in-november-china-government -records-show-report

Deer, Brian. "How the Case Against the MMR Vaccine Was Fixed." *BMJ*, January 6, 2011. www.bmj.com/content/342/bmj.c5347

Engel, Leonard. "Climax of a Stirring Medical Drama." *New York Times*, January 10, 1954. www.nyti.ms/31X3Jmn

Eyler, John M. "Smallpox in History: The Birth, Death, and Impact of a Dread Disease." *The Journal of Laboratory and Clinical Medicine*, October 2003. www.translationalres.com /article/S0022-2143(03)00102-1/abstract

Farmer, Laurence. "When Cotton Mather Fought the Smallpox." *American Heritage*, August 1957. www.americanheritage.com/when-cotton-mather-fought-smallpox

Fitzpatrick, Michael. "The Cutter Incident: How America's First Polio Vaccine Led to a Growing Vaccine Crisis." *Journal of the Royal Society of Medicine*, March 2006. www.ncbi .nlm.nih.gov/pmc/articles/PMC1383764/

Gearon, Eamonn. "Who Was Lady Mary Wortley Montagu?" National Trust Organization. www.nationaltrust.org.uk/features/who-was-lady-mary-wortley-montagu

Gill, Harold B. Jr. "Colonial Germ Warfare." Colonial Williamsburg Foundation, 2004. www.history.org/Foundation/journal/Spring04/warfare.cfm

Greenwood, Brian. "The Contribution of Vaccination to Global Health: Past, Present and Future." *Philosophical Transactions of the Royal Society G: Biological Sciences*, June 19, 2014. www.ncbi.nlm.nih.gov/pmc/articles/PMC4024226/

"Infantile Paralysis Is Spreading Up State." *New York Times*, August 23, 1921. www.nyti.ms/2HkSAE2

Kluger, Jeffrey. "FDR's Polio: The Steel in His Soul." *Time*, September 12, 2014. www.time.com/3340831/polio-fdr-roosevelt-burns/

Kupper, Thomas S. "Old and New: Recent Innovations in Vaccine Biology and Skin T Cells." *Journal of Investigative Dermatology*, March 2012. www.ncbi.nlm.nih.gov/pmc/articles/PMC3644944/

Madsen, Kreesten Meldgaard, et al. "A Population-Based Study of Measles, Mumps, and Rubella Vaccination and Autism." *The New England Journal of Medicine*, November 7, 2002. www.nejm.org/doi/full/10.1056/NEJMoa021134

Miller, Elaine R., et al. "Deaths Following Vaccination: What Does the Evidence Show?" *Vaccine*, June 26, 2015. www.ncbi.nlm.nih.gov/pmc/articles/PMC4599698/

Reidel, Stefan. "Edward Jenner and the History of Smallpox and Vaccination." Baylor Medical Center Proceedings, January 2005. www.ncbi.nlm.nih.gov/pmc/articles/PMC1200696/

Robinson, Leonard Wallace. "Now the Sabin Vaccine for Polio." *New York Times*, September 6, 1959. www.nyti.ms/2PpX7f5

Roush, S. W. and T. V. Murphy. "Historical Comparisons of Morbidity and Mortality for Vaccine-Preventable Diseases in the United States." *Journal of the American Medical Association*, November 14, 2007. www.ncbi.nlm.nih.gov/pubmed/18000199

Rusnock, Andrea A. "Historical Context and the Roots of Jenner's Discovery." *Human Vaccines & Immunotherapeutics*, March 22, 2016. www.ncbi.nlm.nih.gov/pmc/articles/PMC4994746/

Sathyanaravana, T. S. Rao and Chittaranjan Andrade. "The MMR Vaccine and Autism: Sensation, Refutation, Retraction, and Fraud." *Indian Journal of Psychiatry*, April–June 2011. www.ncbi.nlm.nih.gov/pmc/articles/PMC3136032/

Schmeck, Harold M. Jr. "Dr. Jonas Salk, Whose Vaccine Turned Tide on Polio, Dies at 80." *New York Times*, June 24, 1995. www.nyti.ms/2HhKoWr

Smith, Kendall A. "Louis Pasteur, the Father of Immunology?" *Frontiers of Immunology*, April 10, 2012. www.ncbi.nlm.nih.gov/pmc/articles/PMC3342039/

Sternberg, Steve. "Which Polio Vaccine Is Really Better?" *Washington Post*, July 25, 1995. www.washingtonpost.com/archive/lifestyle/wellness/1995/07/25/which-polio-vaccine-is-really-better/92b13aba-b5dc-4e13-8730-102831af287e/?noredirect=on

Tabrah, Frank L. "Koch's Postulates, Carnivorous Cows, and Tuberculosis Today." *Hawaii Medical Journal*, July 2011. www.ncbi.nlm.nih.gov/pmc/articles/PMC3158372/

Theves, C., P. Biagini, and E. Crubezy. "The Rediscovery of Smallpox." *Clinical Microbiology and Infection*, March 2014. www.clinicalmicrobiologyandinfection.com/article/S1198 -743X(14)60860-0/fulltext

Van Panhuis, William G., et. al. "Contagious Diseases in the United States from 1888 to the Present." *The New England Journal of Medicine*, November 28, 2013. www.ncbi.nlm .nih.gov/pmc/articles/PMC4175560/

"Wakefield's Article Linking MMR Vaccine and Autism Was Fraudulent." *BMJ*, January 6, 2011. www.bmj.com/content/342/bmj.c7452

Worral, Simon. "The Strange History of Vaccines—and Why People Fear Them." *National Geographic*, February 26, 2017. www.nationalgeographic.com/news/2017/02 /vaccine-race-history-science-politics-meredith-wadman/

———. "History of Vaccination." *Proceedings of the National Academy of Science of the United States of America*, August 26, 2015. www.ncbi.nlm.nih.gov/pmc/articles/ PMC4151719/

Radio

Brink, Susan. "What's the Real Story About the Milkmaid and the Smallpox Vaccine?" NPR, February 1, 2018. www.npr.org/sections/goatsandsoda/2018/02/01/582370199 /whats-the-real-story-about-the-milkmaid-and-the-smallpox-vaccine

Television

"Immunity and Vaccines Explained." *NOVA*, PBS, September 9, 2014. www.pbs.org/video /nova-immunity-and-vaccines-explained/

"The Polio Crusade." *The American Experience*. PBS, 2009. vimeo.com/29504165

"U.S. Polio Vaccines: Then and Now." *NOVA*, PBS, September 9, 2014. www.pbs.org /wgbh/nova/video/us-polio-vaccines-then-and-now

Websites

Centers for Disease Control and Prevention. "Diagnosis & Evaluation." www.cdc.gov /smallpox/clinicians/diagnosis-evaluation.html

Centers for Disease Control and Prevention. "Origins of Smallpox." www.cdc.gov /smallpox/history/history.html

Centers for Disease Control and Prevention. "Polio VIS." www.cdc.gov/vaccines/hcp/vis /vis-statements/ipv.html#reaction

Centers for Disease Control and Prevention. "Smallpox: Signs and Symptoms." www.cdc .gov/smallpox/symptoms/index.html

Centers for Disease Control and Prevention. "Spread and Eradication of Smallpox." www .cdc.gov/smallpox/symptoms/index.html

Centers for Disease Control and Prevention. "What is polio?" www.cdc.gov/polio/about /index.htm

The College of Physicians of Philadelphia. "The History of Vaccines." www.historyof vaccines.org/content/protection-cowpox-infection

Franklin D. Roosevelt Presidential Library and Museum. "I have been very much concerned . . ." www.fdrlibrary.org/documents/356632/390886/polio_nfipcreation.pdf /e0c36fdc-5a79-4d7c-a57c-c8b43637e019

Franklin D. Roosevelt Presidential Library and Museum. "FDR and Polio." www.fdrlibrary .org/polio

Healthfully. "Body Systems Affected by Smallpox." Frank Whittemore. July 27, 2017. healthfully.com/body-systems-affected-smallpox-5368472.html

History Channel. "The Rise and Fall of Smallpox." Jesse Greenspan. www.history.com /news/the-rise-and-fall-of-smallpox

Howard Hughes Medical Institute. "Seeing the Invisible: Van Leeuwenhoek's First Glimpses of the Microbial World." October 21, 2014. www.youtube.com/watch?v =ePnbkNVdPio

Immunization Action Coalition. "Vaccine Timeline." www.immunize.org/timeline/

Labroots. "From Variation to Vaccination." Kerry Evans. January 1, 2017. www.labroots .com/trending/microbiology/4928/variolation-vaccination

March of Dimes. "Origin of our name." https://www.marchofdimes.org/mission /eddie-cantor-and-the-origin-of-the-march-of-dimes.aspx

Mayo Clinic. "Rabies." www.mayoclinic.org/diseases-conditions/rabies/symptoms -causes/syc-20351821

Mayo Clinic. "Smallpox: Symptoms and Causes." www.mayoclinic.org/diseases -conditions/smallpox/symptoms-causes/syc-20353027

National Institutes of Health. "Biologics: A Short History of the National Institutes of Health." www.history.nih.gov/exhibits/history/docs/page_03.htm

The Nobel Prize. "Robert Koch." www.nobelprize.org/prizes/medicine/1905/koch /biographical/

Oxford Vaccine Group. "How Do Vaccines Work?" May 25, 2018. www.ovg.ox.ac.uk/news /how-do-vaccines-work

PBS. A Science Odyssey: People and Discoveries. "World Health Organization Declares Smallpox Eradicated 1980." www.pbs.org/wgbh/aso/databank/entries/dm79sp.html

University of California Berkeley Museum of Paleontology. "Antony van Leeuwenhoek." ucmp.berkeley.edu/history/leeuwenhoek.htm

YouTube. "Micro-Biology: Crash Course History of Science #24." October 15, 2018. www .youtube.com/watch?v=2JdBH2tys6M

AUTHOR'S NOTE

I'm not the first to say Big Ideas stands on the shoulders of earlier, lesser-known big ideas. But repeating it doesn't make it any less true. Or less exciting! The Big Ideas That Changed the World series celebrates the hard-won succession of ideas that ultimately remade the world.

The arrival of vaccines was a very Big Idea. It, along with sanitation and clean water, have ushered in profound advances in public health. The trio have rescued the lives of hundreds of millions of people. They have helped extend human life-spans and are central pillars of our complicated modern cultures.

The marriage of folk knowledge and reasoned intuition brought us the first vaccine, for smallpox. Thoughtful observers knew that smallpox attacks a person only once, and deduced that a mild case of the disease might allow a person to escape a more lethal version, a practice called *inoculation*, or *variolation*. It was a terrific solution . . . except when it wasn't. Infecting a person with a mild version of smallpox sometimes resulted in the full-blown, deadly, disfiguring version; inoculation was kind of like playing Russian roulette with your health. Then Edward Jenner noted that former sufferers of cowpox, a much more benign disease, attained the same protection against smallpox that one acquired after having the actual disease. And it protected without the risk of death or disfigurement. On that observation, the BIG IDEA of the smallpox vaccine was born.

Jenner could boast that the vaccine worked, but he would have been hard pressed to explain *how* it worked. No, let's be more frank: Jenner had as much understanding of how it worked as a hamster's understanding of how a can opener works.

That is, none.

The explanation of how vaccines work required the contribution of scientific dilettante, Dutchman Antony van Leeuwenhoek and his microscopic examination of lake water. I've wondered what prompted him to examine lake water in the first place. There seems to be no reason to. It's clearly . . . *clear*. Oh, there might be fish in it, but why did he have the BIG IDEA that there are things in lake water that were so tiny that they required the use of a microscope to be seen?

Yet Van Leeuwenhoek wondered as much and revealed the heretofore unknown world of bacteria. From his vaulted curiosity a direct line can be drawn to the discoveries of Koch and Pasteur, the birth of microbiology, virus research, and the rollout of one vaccine after another, all to incalculable health benefits for us all.

But . . .

In 1998, British doctor Andrew Wakefield asserted that the measles, mumps, and rubella (MMR) vaccine can cause autism. Subsequent scientific data has proven Wakefield a fraud and a hoax. Yet, some people ignore the evidence, refuse to vaccinate, and put other people's health at risk. It is evidence of an unfortunate rise in hostility toward science and scientific inquiry. Whether scientific evidence is mocked when it doesn't square with pre-existing beliefs or disparaged by unsupported claims of faked data in the service of nefarious political-cultural conspiracies, it is a dismal and frightening turn of events for a world that relies more and more on accurate science.

I, on the other hand, come down firmly on the side of science and scientific inquiry. I'm thrilled by scientific BIG IDEAS, and by BIG IDEAS of all kinds that have changed our world. And it's good to remember that BIG IDEAS are not an end point but just one stop on a continuum of ideas, big and small, that stretch across time. Whether an inspired success or a tragic failure, the ideas are a trail I'll follow in this series. And, like other trips, the pleasure will not be in the destination but in the journey.

INDEX

Phipps, James, 64–65
Pierrepont, William, 22
plague vaccine, 90
Plett, Peter, 54–56, 58
polio
    children and, 91–92, 94–95, 97–99
    infantile paralysis, 91, 94–95
    March of Dimes and, 95–99
    Roosevelt and, 92–95, 97
polio vaccine
    immunity and, 102–3
    March of Dimes and, 98–99
    mismanufactured, 102
    of Sabin, 102–3
    Salk and, 98–99, 101–2
    success of test, 100–101
Pontiac, 10
Pure Food and Drug Act, 90

Q

quarantine, 37, 120

R

rabies, 86–88
rabies vaccine, 88–89
Ramses V (pharaoh), 3
Roman Empire, smallpox in, 4
Roosevelt, Franklin Delano (FDR), 92–95, 97

S

Sabin, Albert, 102–3
Salk, Jonas, 98–99, 101–3
slavery. *See* enslavement
smallpox, 2. *See also* Montagu, Mary Wortley
    in Africa, 7
    in Asia, 5
    in Boston, 42–43, 46–47
    British Army and, 10–11
    in China, 5, 14–19
    coughing and sneezing in spread of, 3
    cowpox and, 50–51, 54, 57–58, 60, 62–63

    defining, 3
    enslaved people and, 11
    in India, 5, 20
    in London, 30, 68–69
    Native Americans and, 8–10
    in the "New World," 8
    in Ottoman Empire, 21
    in Roman Empire, 4
    scars, 3
    variolation for, 49
smallpox, death from, 3
    Boston epidemic, 46
    in 18th century Europe, 12
    in 20th century, worldwide, 13
Smallpox Eradication Program, of World Health Organization, 110
smallpox-infected blankets, 10
smallpox inoculation
    in Africa, 40–41
    in American colonies, 38
    Caroline of Wales and experiments with, 32–35
    cowpox inoculation and, 65
    evidence for, 47
    Maitland and, 28–29, 31
    Mather and, 38, 40–43, 45
    Montagu and, 28–29, 31, 36
    Montagu in popularization of, 36
    of Montagu's children, 28–29, 31–32
    Onesimus on, 40–41
    quarantine and, 37
smallpox vaccination
    government enforcement of, 67
    in London, 68–69
    opponents of, 67–72
    spread of, early 1800s, 66
smallpox vaccines, 74, 110
Spanish Flu, 1918, 117
Supreme Court, U.S., 73